SITUATED STORIES

SITUATED STORIES

VALUING

DIVERSITY

IN COMPOSITION

RESEARCH

EDITED BY

EMILY DECKER

KATHLEEN GEISSLER

BOYNTON/COOK PUBLISHERS
HEINEMANN
PORTSMOUTH, NH

Boynton/Cook Publishers, Inc.
A subsidiary of Reed Elsevier Inc.
361 Hanover Street
Portsmouth, NH 03801–3912

Offices and agents throughout the world

Library of Congress Cataloging-in-Publication Data
Situated stories : valuing diversity in composition research / edited
  by Emily Decker, Kathleen Geissler.
     p.   cm.
  Includes bibliographical references.
  ISBN 0-86709-440-0
  1. English language—Rhetoric—Study and teaching—Research.
2. Minority college students—Social conditions—Research.
3. College students—Social conditions—Research.   4. Education—
Demographic aspects—Research.   5. Pluralism (Social sciences)—
Research.   I. Decker, Emily.   II. Geissler, Kathleen Mary.
PE1404.S566   1998
808'.04207—dc21   97-42257
                                                  CIP

Editor: Peter R. Stillman
Production: Elizabeth Valway
Cover design: Jenny Jensen Greenleaf
Manufacturing: Courtney Ordway

Printed in the United States of America on acid-free paper
02 01 00 99 98 DA 1 2 3 4 5

To Moira, and Sam and Becky and Eliza,
who are likely to be students one day in classes like these.

Contents

Introduction

This book was conceived at a meeting of the Committee on the Status of Women, sponsored by the Conference on College Composition and Communication. We had organized the first preconvention workshop focusing on feminist issues; we had lobbied for a special interest group at the convention specifically for women; we had worked to have gender listed in the index of the program. Those efforts had been very successful, and the next step seemed to be the creation of a book that would enlarge our research community, expanding on both the questions we ask and the ways we go about answering those questions. We make no bones about our political commitments—we believe that writing classrooms are sites of personal and political change, places where writers can begin to see the ways in which personal and political issues are intertwined. We also believe that writing programs are equally imbued with political and personal issues, existing as they do within a range of institutions. We do not subscribe to the notion that writing courses are merely service courses, intended to help students learn the ropes of academic writing. Instead, we believe that writing courses are sites for mutual negotiation, where people from all kinds of backgrounds meet head-on the dominant institutional values. Ideally, both parties are affected—students learn how to create places for themselves within the institution, and the institution changes so as to enfranchise the diverse students who enter its door.

Our commitment to feminist practice is manifest not in an exclusive focus on gender issues, but in the approach to research that we advocate. While no research method is inherently feminist, in the introduction to *Feminism and Methodology*, Sandra Harding (1987) argues that powerful feminist analyses share three features. First, feminist research generates its problematics from the perspectives of women's experiences (with an emphasis on the plural). Hypotheses must be tested against these experiences, and, says Harding, women themselves need to reveal what these experiences are. Second, Harding argues that feminist research is designed *for* women; it is not simply research *on* women. Finally, Harding argues that in powerful feminist research, the researcher places herself on the same critical plane as the overt subject matter—the researcher appears as a "real historical individual with concrete, specific desires and wishes" (9). The chapters in this book follow similar guidelines, in that the motive for doing the research comes directly from the writer's questions about how to be more effective in the

classroom, more responsive to students. The research is not "on" students—
it is "on behalf of" and often "with" students. And finally, we have encouraged the writers in this book to be explicit about who they are and what their
investment in the topic is.

The stories in this book are important because they remind us, in many
different ways, how complicated and how critical is the teaching of writing.
Our students come to us from diverse backgrounds and situations, and their
relationships to "academic" writing are anything but simple. When we ask
students to write, we are asking them to present a version of themselves, to
negotiate the fit between who they are and what the institutional expectations
are. Ideally, both our classrooms and our institutions are guided by a commitment to constant negotiation. Often, however, and historically, the institution resists change, and the students are expected to conform. Such conformity exacts a price from both the student and the institution. The institution
loses because it never learns to hear; students lose because they either learn
to talk like the "other" or they leave. Writing classes can be powerful per-
petuators of conformity, but they do not have to be. We can encourage students to engage in the process that we ourselves are engaged in, a process of
reflection, which includes examining who we are as writers. By listening to
stories such as those in this book, and by listening to the students we meet
each term, we can learn to teach in ways that enfranchise diverse students.

Our goal in this book is to expand our research community. We want to
enlarge the scope of the questions we ask; we want to expand upon the
methods we use for answering them. In *The Practice of Theory*, Ruth Ray
(1993) argues that "compositionists in the 1990's will have to broaden their
concept of 'research' and 'researchers,' opening up the field to practitioners
in a multitude of settings, listening to what they say, learning from their
observations, and acknowledging the importance and credibility of what they
know" (23). The writers in this book help broaden our concept of research
by introducing us to some new dimensions of composition studies. They
describe the issues, challenges, and aspirations of a variety of writers; they
share their struggles to define what it means to teach composition; they
reflect on what it means to do research. Led by a commitment to help students grow, to claim a place in the academy, to develop strong effective
voices, writers in this book have struggled to find the right names for things.
The chapters offer new definitions of meaningful questions, and of legitimate
answers, all the time helping to define what it means to truly value diversity.

We are also committed to promoting a style of writing about research
that is accessible to all members of our profession. We want the language of
these chapters to be inclusive, not exclusive. The same jargon that indicates
specialized knowledge and researcher status can also cut us off from each
other, from our students, and from people outside our institutions. As feminists, we take to heart bell hooks' caution in *Talking Back* (1989):

> Feminist theory is rapidly becoming another sphere of academic elitism,
> wherein work that is linguistically convoluted, which draws on other such
> works, is deemed more intellectually sophisticated, in fact is deemed more
> theoretical (since the stereotype of theory is that it is synonymous with what
> is difficult to comprehend, linguistically convoluted) than work which is
> more accessible. Each time this happens, the radical, subversive potential of
> feminist scholarship and feminist theory in particular is undermined. (36)

In our view, the aim of feminist research is to address questions that affect
women, and men, with the hope of changing oppressive social systems and
helping excluded people gain access to more powerful positions. Writing can
be one of the most powerful tools for gaining access to positions of power, for
influencing decision making, for changing the status quo, for shaping critical
awareness about the forms oppression takes, for imagining alternative futures.
Writing can also be done "harmlessly," "properly," without changing either
the writer or the institutions or the communities of which they are a part. If this
book is successful, it will be because it supports change. We hope that the
chapters in it challenge teachers to rethink their approaches to students in their
classrooms, to recognize the differences among them, to strive to create classrooms that support all of them. We hope this book also inspires teachers to
reconsider their goals as teachers of writing—what are we about, anyway? In
the face of shrinking institutional resources, national testing, and flooded job
markets, it is easy to forget that writing is like fire, capable of having a
tremendous impact as long as it gets fed, as long as the spark doesn't go out.
We hope this book prompts others to think about the kinds of questions they
need to ask, the kinds of stories they need to hear, and the kinds of directions
research in composition needs to take.

Composing Research/Valuing Diversity

The three chapters in the first section of the book create a frame for reading
the remaining chapters. Each of these chapters talks about the doing of
research—raising questions about the kinds of questions we ask, the size of
the claims we make, the sources of our information, and the ways we need
to learn to listen differently. Taken as a whole, the chapters remind us that,
ultimately, research grows out of our very personal and situated experiences,
and that the "goodness" of our research depends on our ability to be open to
what we don't expect.

In "Indiscretions: A Story of Investigating Gender and Literacy," Shirley Rose tells a story about a piece of research. Her reflections on the twists
and turns of a project—which began with a belief that she could find general
claims—offer a parable of the journey taken by our profession in our collective search for credibility and clout within the realm of higher education,

where the size of your claim is often directly proportional to your clout. Rose writes that while she began her study with plans to describe "the cultural myths of literacy," she ended up with "a description of three teachers' ways of reading thirteen student narratives." Through the telling of her tale, Rose argues for a new equation, in which credibility is linked not to the size of the claim, but rather to the self-reflectiveness, and the honesty, of researchers in sharing with the reader their process of "composing."

In "Portfolio Assessment and the Social Construction of High School Writing Instruction," Roberta Herter argues that valuing diversity in research begins with the creation of reading and writing classes that value diversity among student writers: "The rich store of commonsense knowledge that students bring to the classroom, coupled with their individual expectations, provides a rich source for a variety of texts and contexts for language activity." The key issues for Herter as teacher and researcher are these: to "connect [writing] to the lives of students" and to provide experience with writing that "lead students to expanding literacies." Her work demonstrates that only by learning to listen to students will we ever come close to finding answers.

Helen Fox also talks about the importance of listening to students in "'Getting It': When What Is *Not* Said Is the Most Important Data." Learning to listen is the basis of valuing diversity in our teaching and in our research, and when we are trying to listen to students who come from countries outside the United States, our task is even more challenging. According to Fox, a speakers and writers may "in fact just have a *feeling* about the way they want to present themselves, a voice that holds back, or talks around, or strives for a kind of relationship between the audience, the text, and the self that is markedly different from what is expected in the U.S. context." If we want to value diversity among our students, we have to learn to listen with full awareness that our own culture's channels for communication may interfere with our ability to hear. The first part of the research process is learning to hear; the second, equally difficult, is learning to translate what we have heard into a form that other researchers will recognize.

Dimensions of Diversity

One of the easiest observations to make about teaching writing today is that the students in our classrooms are very diverse. It is no longer useful to divide the world of writers up into two categories of expert and novice, or student and professional. Our students vary in terms of their language backgrounds, ethnicity, class, race, gender, sexual orientation, and nationality. If we are to teach them, if we hope to create classrooms that embrace them, we need to recognize that each writer we work with has her or his own set of challenges and goals. The chapters in this section all address dimensions of diversity in our classes, helping us see more clearly who our students are or might be.

In "'They've Got the Power—They're Hearing': Case Studies of Deaf Student Writers at Gallaudet University," Brenda Jo Brueggemann recaps the 1988 uprising at Gallaudet against the appointment of a president who could not use American Sign Language (ASL). Brueggemann argues that we need more research into the relationship between literacy and freedom. She writes that our students want to be freed, not ensnared, not "trapped by our way of reading, writing, and interpreting—a way that is as foreign to them as their ways are to us. We composition teachers and researchers are generally 'hearing' (or white, or male, or upper middle class, or college educated, or straight, or whatever; whatever we are, we generally have power." At Gallaudet, ASL-speaking students rejected a hearing president because she could not speak their language—they rejected the argument that they should mimic hearing students. As composition teachers, are we in danger of being rejected by our students on similar grounds?

Meditating on why English teachers are failing Hispanic students, Renee Moreno begins "Going for Broke: Valuing Differences in the Classroom" by telling a story about her nephew, Ramon. Moreno argues that even though many teachers now recognize that there are often "language mismatches" and "cultural incongruities" between home and school, simply knowing that differences exist is not enough. As teachers, we need to reflect on our theories, and in particular, we need to question the apolitical assumptions of the process paradigm. In examining her own teaching, Moreno writes that she became aware of "how easily blindness happens." If we want to keep our classrooms alive, we need to make connections between the writing we ask students to do and the writers themselves—connections between discursive practices and material reality—and we need to stay mindful of the power inherent in our classrooms, our institutions, and our society.

Anne Aronson's "Danger Zones: Risk and Resistance in the Writing Histories of Returning Adult Women" argues that writing is hazardous, because what is at stake is "participants' basic sense of self-worth, and more specifically their sense of competence and authority as knowers, thinkers, and language users." In her chapter, Aronson presents case studies of two returning adult women who traversed the danger zones by developing strategies to protect themselves, to use writing for their own purposes. In both of the stories, Aronson traces relationships among contextual factors, paying attention to the ways race, class, sexual orientation, and ethnicity mutually construct one another. Aronson looks at the strategies these women developed in order to claim their identities and control their degree of vulnerability, including choosing the level of self-disclosure, choosing identities to create in writing, and learning other discourses of possibilities in which personal and political issues are connected.

Pamela Olano challenges the easy expressivist assumption that students can write from experience in "The Unclaimed Self: Valuing Lesbian and Gay Diversity in the Writing Environment." Gay and lesbian students and gay and lesbian teachers who choose to come out in the classroom have to reckon with the silencing effect of hostile comments from other students or from teachers. This chapter is based on a survey Olano did of gay and lesbian students, graduate and undergraduate. She writes that her "decision to conduct this project grew from the writer's block I often experienced as I sat down to compose. If I was stymied by the privileging of heterosexual themes and assumptions, what might be happening to undergraduates and other graduate students as they tried to write papers, articulate theories, brainstorm ideas, plan classes?"

In "The Role of Response," Sally Barr Ebest describes an experimental writing course she designed in order to test a way of reading and responding to students' writing that is fully informed by an awareness of power issues in the classroom. Ebest explains how her class varied from common practices in focusing neither on process, nor on shaping a product for an academic audience, nor on providing workshops on grammar or style. Instead, students attended to the language features they and their peers used in writing about personal and political beliefs, focusing on the specific ways their language choices revealed those beliefs. Traditional ways of responding to students' writing, particularly grades, frequently lead students to abandon writing as a way of making meaning out of and in the context of their own experiences, in favor of sounding like the teacher, of doing the "right" thing. In order to create a classroom where students can question their assumptions, teachers have to find ways of responding that increase students' awareness about the assumptions and beliefs that are revealed in their use of language.

Following up on the work of Shirley Brice Heath, Constance Chapman lived with a family in order to look at the fit between literacy tasks at school and literacy needs at home. "The Morrises: A Study of One Family's Writing" reports on this research. Chapman's conclusions that schools have to reach out to parents with weak literacy skills—that teachers need to help students connect school and home—echo those of other researchers, but the power of her work, and of ethnographic studies in general, is that the claims are grounded in particular settings. Chapman's method suggests that if the purpose of school, of teaching writing, is to help everyone gain control of the powerful tools of reading and writing, then we all need to become ethnographers because we all have individual students we need to reach.

Through an examination of the transcript of a computer conference in a course for prospective secondary teachers, Ted Lardner shows that the question of dialect diversity requires a response more complicated than the one traditionally offered. "Item 50: Dialect Diversity and Teacher Preparation" demonstrates that it is not enough simply to acknowledge that teachers need to help students become politically savvy in various rhetorical contexts, making appropriate choices about language use. In Lardner's discussion of the transcript, we see prospective teachers grappling with the issue of dialect diversity. As Lardner writes, language differences are bigger than conventional wisdom would like us to believe, and perhaps the best thing we can do is invite students into the conversation about this problem that remains unresolved.

In "English—Yours, Mine, or Ours: Language Teaching and the Needs of 'Nonnative' Speakers of English," Yuet-Sim Darrell Chiang addresses the overt and covert marginalizing of 'nonnative speakers' by reflecting on her own experience as a writer and teacher. Chiang begins by telling a story about writing a letter in English for her Chinese aunt. Should she write it in proper English, or should she make the English sound Chinese? Because of her Chinese features, colleagues of European descent react to her as though her relationship to English is not as strong as theirs. Like Moreno, Chiang reflects on the contradictions of her own experience, as she realizes that she has been teaching her class of ESL students "the basics" rather than "the real thing." As part of her reflection, Chiang writes, "Ultimately, I believe, it is the embracing of our duality, or plurality, that will give us, language learners and users, the power to claim, rather than be claimed by, and the power to shape, rather than be shaped by, the postcolonial English-speaking world."

Valuing Diversity: Next Steps

The three chapters that make up the closing section of the book begin to imagine what we might do as we learn to value diversity. All start with the assumption that writing is more than a means of achieving academic success—if we choose to see it and use it that way. All three also assume that students are in college, and in writing classes, for a variety of reasons, and that as teachers we need to know who our students are and what they hope to learn before we can figure out how to "teach." We cannot value diversity and maintain the status quo: our classes have to change; our institutions have to change; the ways we think about writing need to change. Most important, the way we listen to students, and the way we read their writing has to change so that we are changed, just as our students change.

In "Multiple Languages, Multiple Literacies," Alice Roy looks at the fit between the curriculum of a large public university and the needs and strengths of an undergraduate whose family has recently immigrated to the United States. In her conclusion, Roy argues that the university is failing this student: "[Linh] fails in one class because she is not acculturated enough to handle the material that is used to teach the more abstract concepts. She succeeds in classes where the demands are, mainly, to reproduce the concepts and material presented. Where she fails, she is not asked to draw on her own cultural material to substantiate conceptual learning; where she succeeds, she is not asked or guided to develop those strategies that would allow her to 'problematize,' as Freire (1982) has it, her learning or her experience." While the composition courses can be an oasis of active learning, they aren't enough. Linh will be able to graduate with a degree certifying her ability to reproduce, not create.

Deborah Davies argues in "Facts, Artifacts, Counterfacts, and Differences" that writing teachers, especially basic writing teachers, desperately need to reclaim the role of affect. She writes that "attempts to limit affect in student writing . . . limit ways in which students can explore differences between their lives and representations of the dominant culture." Davies argues for a richer paradigm for intellectual development that includes affect as a critical element. Davies argues that in contrast to helping students "invent the university," assuming a voice of academic authority from which overt traces of situated knowledge and personal experience are typically removed, writing classes should be places where students, particularly working-class students, work with each other to name their experiences, gain some perspective, and see the experiences in a larger framework. In collaborative settings, Davies writes, stories "reclaim areas of reality for academic discourse." The point of personal writing is not simply to express, but also to transform.

In "Women Students' Autobiographical Writing: The Rhetoric of Discovery and Defiance," Joy Ritchie, Manjit Kaur, and Bee Tin Choo Meyer write about their experiences working together in a composition class, in which Kaur and Meyer were students and Ritchie was the teacher. Both Kaur and Meyer were engaged in the process of writing autobiographical material, and in this chapter they write about that process—about the ways they learned to work with their writing, to name their experiences, to claim an identity, to reclaim and connect contradictory parts of themselves. Especially for Meyer, the process of claiming a strong effective writing voice was both powerful and painful. In turn, Ritchie describes how she had to learn not to romanticize the struggles Kaur and Meyer were engaged in, nor to take over their texts or to impose her notions of appropriate form. These challenges of her work with Kaur and Meyer led Ritchie to reexamine her response to the writing of all her students and to recognize the ongoing risk we as teachers run of "colonizing" students as we read and interpret based on our own personal and cultural assumptions. Only by learning to read differently can we hope to create classrooms in which students can harness the power of autobiography and in which we can help students "see their writing as a interpersonal, rhetorical *action* rather than merely as an academic activity.

When we began this book, we did not know what an emphasis on valuing diversity in composition research would lead to. The writers in this anthology have shown that the process of doing effective research begins with stepping out of a situation, and reflecting on it. When we stop to do this, we realize how multidimensional the work of writing and of teaching writing is. Furthermore, we need to be reflective about how we compose the stories of our research and of our teaching because our research is also always composing us—the community of composition teachers, our classes, our students. The stories we make up frame our way of seeing, and they frame what happens in our classes. For us, good research in composition tells stories that help us see more clearly and act more effectively in our classrooms and professional situations. The chapters in this anthology offer insight into particular situations, but each is also a carefully told story, designed to show how a commitment to diversity might be expressed.

We want to keep alive the idea that writing classes are places of mutual negotiation, rather than inculcation, particularly when there are pressures within the educational community and the society at large to document achievement, to measure results. The kinds of results we hope for may well be measurable in some form, but above all, we are talking about changes in the way we think, as well as changes in the way we imagine our relationships with each other and with our local communities. Our vision of all writers being heard is not one of cacophony. Rather, we believe that democracy only works when every citizen feels empowered to speak the truth from his or her perspective. Writing classes play an important role because in them, students can experience the power of speaking up; they also can get experience with the discipline of listening to other people's ideas. Only when we all are able to speak and to listen, can we hope to achieve a vital society.

1

Indiscretions
A Story of Investigating Gender and Literacy

Shirley K. Rose

In this chapter I present a "life history" of a research project on gender and composing. Because I conducted the project, it is also a story about me. In writing this autobiographical narrative, I am *composing* myself; but constructing a coherent autobiographical narrative also involves a series of decisions about *exposing* oneself. I've coded this exposure as "indiscretion" because it is so closely tied to my understanding of the research process as a series of decisions guided by the researcher's discretion.

Walter Fisher (1987) suggests that "all forms of symbolic action . . . may be seen as stories, interpretations of things in sequences" (24). If Fisher's suggestion is useful, perhaps my readers will accept my narrative as a version of an argument about research methods in composition studies. Though this narrative will focus on the project's process rather than on its "conclusions," readers will recognize that I've used my findings to construct the narrative itself.

In the summer of 1983, as a graduate student, I began an investigation of students' attitudes toward literacy. This project had grown out of my increasing doubts about some of the claims made for the uses of literacy. Few of the literacy theorists and researchers I was reading at that time questioned the premise that literacy universally brought good—advanced technology, increased cognitive functioning, etc., etc. But my students—at least as I saw them—were less than eager to develop their literacy. That summer I was teaching a class of freshman composition students during a six-week term. For my research project, I first thought of using a questionnaire to discover their attitudes toward literacy. But I wasn't sure what questions to ask—how to frame the questions to be generative and understandable without overdetermining the answers I would get. I had been doing reading for the dissertation I planned on literary autobiography, so I was immersed in autobiography theory and had read many autobiographical texts, from Augustine to Maxine Hong Kingston. I decided my first step would be to ask my composition students to write an autobiographical narrative about their literacy experience. These narratives might suggest some questions for me to use in my questionnaire.

My class included very capable writers about to graduate as well as underprepared students who were beginning their freshman year a little early by taking a summer class. I began to read their narratives, looking for the similarities, the clues to attitudes toward literacy, or what I had begun to call "literacy values."As I read the narratives, I tried to identify the conventions for an autobiographical literacy narrative, the formal constraints, and the recurrent themes. It seemed obvious that the best narratives were very specific, rich in concrete and specific detail. In considering themes, I was more impressed with the narratives that described incidents that took place outside school. But was this a thematic preference of mine? Was it a coincidence that the students who had written the better essays on other class assignments were writing about experiences apart from school?

How could I distinguish between the "good" narrative and the "poor" narrative? How did my value judgments reflect my own beliefs about the uses and usefulness of literacy? Was I investigating my students' literacy values or my own? How important was the quality of the narrative to the information it could give me? Was the well-written narrative more informative? Was it a better reflection of the writer's experience and attitudes? Was the narrative that was more satisfying to read the narrative that best expressed the writer's intentions? How could I know how well the narrative reflected experience and attitudes? And there was always that perpetual problem of autobiography: was it factual? Did it matter if it wasn't? Readers read autobiography as presentation of fact, whether they believe or not. If autobiography is presentation or representation of self, then it is subject to all the deceits and doubts presentation of self is subject to in everyday life.

No, I could not go looking for fact in autobiography. I could only look for what writers wanted to present as facts. And if I could not find facts in the rich autobiographical narrative, I would certainly never find them in the responses to a questionnaire. I decided to forget the questionnaire and change my question from "What are students' attitudes toward literacy?" to "What attitudes toward literacy do student writers choose to represent in narratives of their experiences of becoming literate?"

Making this choice, exercising this discretion, was a big step. Research is supposed to discover something, so I had to find a way to see the potential for knowledge—the information—in the "lies" as much as in the "truths" the student writers chose to tell. One way to do this was to adopt the notion of "myth," defining a "literacy myth" as a shared story about the value of literacy in a culture. Writers could expect readers to recognize, understand, and respond favorably to a retelling, or representation, of this myth. The myth of the literacy theory I had been reading was that literacy brought individual autonomy, higher cognitive functioning, advanced civilization. Was this same myth then reflected in the student narratives? My project would be to discover my students' cultural myth for literacy.

As I began my analysis of the "myths" represented in the student narratives, I realized that I was looking for values embedded in a narrative structure, for myths are essentially story outlines. I posed the question *"What was the outline for the literacy story?"*

Here, my reading of published literary autobiographies came into play. I would examine an autobiography by an established, recognized writer who had explicitly discussed his or her acquisition of literacy and identify the basic narrative elements, the "macroplot" suggested by the barest outlines of the account of the acquisition of literacy. I chose John Stuart Mill's *Autobiography* because I could expect my readers to be familiar with this work. Presumably, the same macroplot I described for Mill's *Autobiography* could be used to analyze the students' literacy narratives. It seemed I could identify a pattern for the generic literacy autobiography narrative—at least the plot shared by Western-educated writers: *skills acquisition* led to use of the skills, *skills practice*; this practice led to an *awareness of oneself as literate*; and this awareness was followed by an *awareness of the utility of literacy*, which motivated further *skills acquisition*.

Both the "good" student narratives and the "poor" student narratives used this macroplot to structure their stories. There were similarities, but could I identify any differences between the "good" narratives and the "bad"? Again, I faced that problem: the "good" narratives were good only because I thought so as a reader. I decided to use my students' overall course grades, which were based on their performance on a variety of writing assignments, to distinguish between the good writers and the poor writers. Still, these value judgments were my own, and had not been "verified" or seconded by any other readers. Even so, since I was engaged in a self-reflexive investigation of my teaching/reading practices, what significance would another teacher/reader's evaluation of the students' work have? It would only tell me that one or more other teachers did or did not share my values. It would not confirm the validity of our shared standards; it would only confirm that the standards were shared.

Whether or not we shared standards was not my question, nor was it my assumption. I settled the problem by choosing to distinguish between "successful" and "unsuccessful" college writers ("success" determined by overall course grade) rather than between "good" and "poor" writers, because "success" implies conformity to cultural values—which was what I was trying to get at. Since I could assume that in the actual rhetorical situation of the classroom all of the students were attempting to pass the class with as high a grade as they could earn, whether or not their writing performance allowed them to achieve that goal seemed a valid basis on which to distinguish between the essays and group them.

After grouping the essays on this basis, I was able to identify differences in the way the writers had employed the generic literacy autobiography macroplot: *successful writers constructed themselves as independent learners; unsuccessful writers constructed themselves as obedient students.* I looked for confirmation of my analysis in the narratives I continued to collect from my students over the next two semesters. The more narratives I read, the more I found repetitions of particular themes and motifs in the narratives. I was especially eager to know whether cultural differences would be reflected in the narratives as differences in attitudes toward literacy because I was very uncomfortable with making what would seem to be universal claims about literacy myths when my analysis had been so narrowly defined. But I was finding "cultural differences" to be an elusive term.

I was focusing on what I called "academic" culture, but perhaps that term was too vague, more general than my actual analysis. The only "culture" I was certain was shared by these students was the culture of our particular classroom. Yet they were not a homogeneous group. The "cultural" differences that seemed to be most obvious and easy to identify were ethnic differences. My students that year seemed to be an unusually diverse group. But looking back, I wonder whether I was simply more aware of their diversity than I had been before with other groups of students. At the time, the prospect of accounting for this diversity seemed overwhelming.

I decided to look closely at several published autobiographical narratives that explicitly discussed learning to read and write and the authors' literacy practices. I chose three autobiographies with "cross-cultural" themes—those by Malcolm X, Richard Rodriguez, and Maxine Hong Kingston—because each of these writers had explicitly used autobiography to write a cultural identity. That each had created a different cross-cultural identity seemed to add to the richness of the comparison, but certainly I wouldn't claim any was representative of a particular multiethnic perspective on literacy nor that they were typical autobiographies.

In making my analysis of the published autobiographies and writing them up, I was on familiar ground. I was writing literary criticism, which I was practiced at, and the concerns about how generalizable my claims were didn't plague me as they had with the student narratives. I noticed this, couldn't explain it to my satisfaction, but went ahead. The analysis of the published autobiographies allowed me to advance claims about how writers construct cultural identities in the act of autobiography. If ethnicity, an aspect of cultural identity, could be a linguistic construct, so could literacy. If literacy practices were culturally differentiated, a literate self could be constructed in a literate act—autobiography.

In time, my dissertation was neatly finished and I was credentialed. Like many other new Ph.D.s, I spent the first few months of my assistant professorship revising my dissertation and submitting it for publication. While I was waiting for favorable reviews from editors (which never came), I learned of our university's special grant fund for research by and about women. How could I qualify? What could I do that would make use of the groundwork I had already laid? I outlined a project for examining the differences between female students' literacy practices and those of male students. I would use the same method and methodology I had used for the earlier research—I would analyze literacy autobiographies. I didn't assume that I would find differences and I certainly didn't predict what those differences would be, but I didn't question whether I could find the differences if they existed and I didn't question male/female dichotomy itself. I was, in Kenneth Burke's (1945/1969) terms, "selecting a circumference" by choosing these terms (84–90).

I received a grant for the project I had proposed. For this new project, I added to my collection of literacy narratives contributions from students in each of the freshman composition classes I had taught since my original project began. I proceeded to look for the differences between the narratives of my female students and those of my male students. One advantage of having collected so many narratives was that I was able to see patterns emerging from the repetition of themes. I began to suspect, for example, that the fifth grade was an important time in reading development because so many students wrote about undertaking large self-directed reading projects then. Other themes emerged; for example, stories about "playing school" with siblings constituted a subgenre, with recognizable conventions for the portrayal of the playschool teacher. These suggested interesting possibilities for further exploration.

But I already had a basic framework for my analysis of gender-based differences. I used the four-stage recursive model I had developed from my earlier comparison of successful and unsuccessful students. I imposed this model upon several narratives and looked for gender-correlated differentiations at each of the stages. It was neat. It was systematic. That helped to ease my uncomfortable feeling that I was going to find whatever I went looking for. I modified my recursive model of literacy acquisition to reflect the differences in the themes for males and for females (see Figure 1–1).

Still uncomfortable about the extent to which I might be reading what I wanted to read in the narratives, I applied for and received the aid of a graduate research assistant, Joyce Kincaid. I had removed the authors' names and assigned code numbers to each of two hundred students' literacy narratives. On a separate list, I recorded authors' names, composition section numbers, and the new code number for each essay. I erased the "male" and "female" headings from the model and provided a copy to Joyce to use with her reading report sheet. Joyce's job was to read each of the narratives and assign it to either the "left" side or the "right" side of the model, marking her

Figure 1–1

Differences Between Myths Explaining Acquisition of Literacy

Myth of Participation (Metaphorical Female)	Myth of Autonomy (Metaphorical Male)
Acquisition of Skills	
Focus on process and cooperative effort	Focus on measurable results; individual achievement
Practice of Literacy	
Participation with others; shared experience	Solitary activity; comparison of achievement against others
Awareness of Literacy	
Own or others' expression of surprise, praise	Achievement of goal set by self or others
Awareness of Uses of Literacy	
A way to please; hopes for gaining an audience	A way to satisfy expectations; hopes for gaining control over self and others

identifications on a report sheet. Joyce did her job cheerfully, conscientiously, and thoroughly; and as she returned the narratives and report sheets she remarked that she would have had an easier job of it if she could have identified the narratives along a continuum from left to right instead of one or the other. Of course.

A colleague who was interested in my project suggested we introduce another variation. He asked his freshman composition students to write literacy autobiographies, using the assignment I had developed. We removed names and assigned code numbers to the narratives, and then the two groups of students exchanged narratives. A class period was devoted to quick "read-arounds" of the narratives, each student attempting to read all of the narratives in the batch (twenty-four in one batch, twenty in the other). As they read, they were to mark redesigned report sheets on which they guessed the gender of the author and placed each narrative along a continuum from "autonomy" to "participation." We also asked them to note if the narratives contained explicit statements about their authors' gender and to identify any other obvious "clues."

There was no remarkable degree of agreement among the students' decisions about the thematic content, but their gender guesses were about 80 percent accurate. We were impressed. We decided not to explore the nagging little question of how we could be so certain about the "gender" of the student authors ourselves. At the time, *sex* and *gender* were interchangeable terms for us, and we were confident that we could tell the male from the female students. As the project matured, however, I realized that our identification of the student authors' "actual sex" was a product of a series of assumptions about names, outward appearances, and behaviors and was as "constructed" as our readers' "gender guesses" about the authors of the narratives. I doubt that biological tests would have proved our identifications wrong, but they too were only guesses—our constructions of the student writers' gendered identities.

That same semester, I was teaching a class called "Introduction to Teaching College Composition." The students in this class were first-semester graduate teaching assistants, each of whom was currently teaching two sections of first-year composition. I asked the eleven women and two men in the class to do the same exercise the freshmen had done, with some variations. It would, of course, have been more convenient if the enrollment in the class had been better balanced between males and females—it would have made for a better "design," but the makeup of the class that semester was not unusual.

In addition to identifying narrative theme and guessing author's gender, the teacher/readers were to guess the ethnic background of the author, guess the income level of the author's background, and then evaluate the "quality" of each narrative on a scale of one to ten and predict the author's likelihood of successfully finishing college. The group of thirteen read thirteen narratives chosen at random from the group the first-year students had read earlier, after narratives with explicit statements about or "obvious" clues to gender were eliminated from the batch. Because the sample included narratives by eight women and five men, I explained to the readers that there was not an even distribution between sexes and they understood that their gender guesses could not be informed by the process of elimination.

At that point, I was not particularly interested in the guesses about income and ethnicity—I had included these to draw attention away from my primary interest in the gender guesses these teachers-in-training would make about the student authors of the narratives. Though I understood that, like "gender," "ethnicity" and "class" were cultural fictions constructed by discursive practices, at the time I thought these cultural fictions could be examined discretely.

As a group, these readers did not read consistently with one another. And their readings were not consistent with my own. The project was beginning to look like a series of challenges to interpretive authority. However, there were some interesting correlations between gender guesses and narrative quality ratings or between gender guesses and predictions for successfully completing college for individual readers.

I was stymied. I could identify gender-based differences in the literacy narratives I read, but I couldn't get enough other readers to read the way I did. I could identify individual readers' gender biases, but I couldn't identify group biases. The significance of the project was shrinking. It seemed that all I had to report was my own gender-differentiated readings or the readings of a few inexperienced teachers. Neither could claim to be particularly compelling for others. I believed I needed research findings that could be generalized—or at least they had to be about someone other than myself.

A year later I repeated the narrative reading/ identification exercise with another group of "Introduction to Teaching College Composition" students in the hope that the larger "data base" could generate more significant correlations among the readings. It did, but twenty-eight readers wasn't a very much larger number than thirteen. I wanted the confidence a statistically significant sample size would provide. Definitions of statistical significance tormented me. I read and reread introductory statistics textbooks, following their logic, working through their formulas for r and t by hand instead of using a computer program just so I could understand where the answers had come from. I learned how to operate NWASTATPAK, a statistical program that would run on my Kaypro computer. I entered my data and ran it through the statistical program. I generated stacks of statistical reports. A colleague in psychology looked at what I'd done and said that my sample was so small that the high correlations were either meaningless or incredibly significant and he would have designed the project entirely differently and maybe we could collaborate if I would start over. I went on to other projects.

In the spring of 1988, I was ready to return to the project. Perhaps I could make an examination of a few teachers' biases in reading interesting. From among the thirteen members of the first group of teacher readers, I found three women who were willing to help me continue with the project. By that time, these three were finishing their fourth semester as graduate teaching assistants. When they had first read the student narratives they had been in their first semesters as teachers of writing.

Each of them repeated the exercise of reading the narratives and guessing the authors' gender, evaluating the quality of the narratives, and predicting the authors' likelihood of completing college successfully. I had two conversations with each of them. The first was on the occasion of their second readings, when we talked about their perceptions of how this second experience of doing the readings differed from the first. I suspected that their memories of identifying the narratives the first time might influence their second readings, but each of them said that though they could remember some of the narratives, they could not remember how they had identified or evaluated them.

In the second conversation with each, I explained statistical descriptions of the differences between their readings, and we discussed whether these descriptions "rang true" with them. Then we went on to discuss their own experiences as teachers and writers. For each of the three, I thought I could identify a different "stance" toward the question of differences between male and female writing: "gender blindness," "gender adherence," and "gender suppression." But as I proceeded to reread the transcripts of the conversations more closely, I had to admit that all three teachers had, instead, moved from one stance to another, then another.

In 1991, I sent transcripts of the conversations to these three women, asking them to comment on the conversations from the perspective of several years' passing. I asked them whether they were still teaching, writing, and/or teaching writing. I also invited them to edit out any part of the conversations they would not want published and to tell me whether they wanted their real names or fictional names used. In the process of "writing up" their readings, I understood that I was reading/writing them, just as they had read/ written the authors of the student narratives, and I was uncomfortable with the authority I was assuming in doing so. The project had demonstrated to me that readers of texts compose the writers of those texts—or, to turn Walter Ong's (1975) phrase, the reader's author is always a fiction. I wanted these three women to have an opportunity at least to counter my readings of them with readings of their own. Two of them answered my letter: both used a very "light hand" in editing the transcripts of the conversations, and both commented on the ways they felt they had changed in their attitudes about male and female writing.

With each stage of the project, the claims became more qualified, more conservative, more particular. I had begun with plans to describe "the cultural myths of literacy." I ended with a description of three teachers' ways of reading thirteen student narratives. My narrative ends here, but the research process itself is never-ending. I continue to generate questions. Did we develop any "knowledge"? What is the status of the knowledge? Does anyone want to know this particular bit of knowledge?

I have chosen not to include an account of the series of rejections and negative reviews my attempts to publish my "findings" received at various stages of the project. The fact that reports on early stages of the work weren't published is one reason for my continuing on to successive stages.[1] I've also chosen not to include a narrative of my reading of theory and research on literacy, on gender, and on feminist methodology. I've dramatized my inquiry as an interior monologue rather than as a dialogue with other researchers and scholars. I have two reasons for this: first, I've found it impossible to reconstruct what I read when, what I read again, whose work advanced my own, whose work gave me writer's block; and second, to invoke these others' authority would undermine my attempt to take responsibility for my discretions and indiscretions, the right and wrong decisions I have made along the way. As I review my story now, I see that I have not made a clear distinction between the failures of my "theses," failures of my methods, and my own failures of heart. I also recognize that my story is only one of many that could be told by literacy researchers.

My final indiscretion is the act of composing this narrative. Thanks to my own research project, I am conscious of the gendered nature of this narrative even as I write it. I pretend to maintain silence about my reviewers' verbal battering because naming it would be indiscreet. Troubled by the egotism of telling my own story, I claim the story is one of many. I try to compose myself as likable and credible. I expose myself and worry whether readers will like what they see. These are choices I have made. Gendering my narrative has suited my own purposes as well as it has suited the expectations of my audience. Even the limited insights I've gained from the project have been enough to teach me that there is discretion even in being indiscreet.

Note

1. As of November 1997, the book-length discussion of the project was under consideration by an academic press.

2

Portfolio Assessment and the Social Construction of High School Writing Instruction

Roberta J. Herter

I am a classroom English teacher. For the past twenty-seven years I have taught secondary students in Detroit Public Schools, the last seventeen at Henry Ford High School, a comprehensive neighborhood school with an enrollment of 2,600 students in a predominantly African American working-class community. Observing the processes of students constructing new knowledge as they critically reflect on and evaluate their own writing has led me to question long-held assumptions about the connections between writing instruction and writing assessment. As both a classroom teacher and graduate student, I have had the advantage of incorporating conversations with researchers into my daily planning and teaching of writing. While relating some of the changes in my teaching practices enabled by research, this narrative also fits into the growing genre of "fundamentally social and constructive" texts written by teachers (Cochran-Smith and Lytle 1993, 98). In brief, what I propose is to describe instructional changes in one classroom that drew on the combined observations and reflections of students, researchers, and teachers.

The past twenty-five years have produced significant changes in writing instruction. Although much of the research literature addresses college composition and early language and literacy acquisition, shifts in assessment practices as well have illustrated how teachers might "help themselves become more successful with students and more accountable for learning" (Darling-Hammond, Ancess, and Falk 1995, 252). Overlapping research in assessment, literacy, composition, and cultural studies has created openings for writing workshops and whole language approaches to writing that are increasingly familiar practices in secondary English instruction. However, a broader application of research in the social construction of knowledge and its impact on school learning is still relatively absent from classrooms where order, back-to-basics, and teacher-centered instruction take priority over more interactive student-centered instruction.

Fifteen years before Lisa Delpit's (1995) work, my colleague and neighbor Doris Cook reminded me more sternly than gently that I was teaching "other people's children," words of caution I took with appreciation and seriousness. I have learned to depend on students for confirmation of the effectiveness of instructional practices, it has been collaboration with school and university colleagues that has helped me link theory and practice in order to justify the changes I've made in teaching writing.

Redefining Research and Practice

Reflective teaching and the situated knowledge that grows out of practice have enabled me to replace some of the teaching myths and lore that dominated my early career. As a beginning teacher I believed that writing was a solo performance, done best in isolation and, when possible, in silence. Although the classroom provided few opportunities for quiet or privacy, I followed the lead of experienced colleagues and persisted in a pedagogy that discouraged sharing or other forms of social interaction among students while composing. In this practice, there was an implicit assumption that those who knew how to write would, and that those who didn't would pick up what they could from their corrected papers, direct instruction, and the grammar text. I knew there were superficial tricks I had picked up from friends who were writers that made any piece of writing more readable, but it hadn't occurred to me that it was only in conversation and in reviewing my writing with them that I had begun to improve as a writer. I rarely "interfered" with my students' writing while they were composing, and saw their work only after it had been turned in for checking. Though it doesn't feel like many years ago, these practices now seem not only outdated but self-defeating.

In the late sixties, when I began teaching, the cultural deficit view of students dictated that drills in standard English and practice with oral language would mediate dialect differences. Writing meant copying and grammar drill. The seventies opened the door to some new possibilities, including Labov's (1972) pioneering distinction between dialectical differences and the judgments of teachers. Things were beginning to get interesting. The language that students used at home, in all of its vibrancy and richness, no longer stayed at home. Throughout the seventies I recall my own conflicted practice of defining the differences between school language, oral language, and written language until a more enlightened pedagogy began to emerge. For me it wasn't until reading Heath's *Ways with Words* (1983) in the early eighties that I took seriously the possibility of recreating a classroom that accommodated the differences in students' voices and experience. And, through the elegant prose of Vivian Paley, I saw that a teacher had much to learn by listening to her students.[1] With the publication of Stock and Robinson's "Literacy as Conversation: Classroom Talk as Text Building" in 1990 and Lave and Wenger's *Situated Learning* in 1991, I had theoretical frames to support rethinking the ways students were using their time in class. The more conscious I became of the interactions of students with one another, and my interactions with them, the more clearly I chose instructional practices ensuring more student-talk and less teacher-talk, thus shaping a more dynamic, productive, and engaging learning environment.

Writing Lives, Writing Worlds

The transition from a reading-based curriculum to a writing-based curriculum, in which the primary texts were student generated, meant some major instructional, social, and curricular changes. I recognized that students were taking valuable steps toward improving not only their writing but also their commitment to learning in a different kind of writing instruction. The students and I were questioning how pieces were put together and whether their appeal was genuine, and together we set criteria for evaluating pieces of writing.

I began to see students as collaborators, working with me to share in the process of reading and writing with one another. We spent more time talking about writing and reading student writing in conferences than marking and checking red-penciled errors in the vain hope that students might learn from my correction, one of the many assessment myths that Pat Belanoff (1991) has described (65). In addition to the changing tenor of the class, I began to see significant changes not only in the students' engagement but also in their sense of responsibility to one another. We had not spontaneously become a community of writers, but we were working openly toward that end. I expected students to increase their range of topics and incorporate new ideas into their writing, to try new forms of writing and to take chances in their thinking. They expected me to support the risk taking, challenge their ideas, and guide them toward appropriate resources. Teaching and learning were becoming a more reciprocal and systematic process of discovery. As we wrote about our lives in and out of school, the students and I began to see the classroom as a productive rather than a prohibitive space, as a space, that is, where students share responsibility for the outcomes.

Teachers can enable students to make judgments about their writing by showing them how to recognize growth and to respond to other students' writing in ways that promote growth. Portfolios offer broad possibilities for curricular innovation and instructional change. These changes result primarily from two features common to portfolios used in writing/reading assessment. First, portfolios collect student writing, self-assessments, and critical reflections. These texts form the basis of a student-centered curriculum, replacing conventional anthologies and skill-based writing texts with the students' own writings, which form the core of readings for the class. Second, the critical reflections generated by these texts inform the students' developing writing processes by documenting the changes, growth, and uses of literacy student writers experience over time.[2]

The final exam essay has become an opportunity for students to present their case for growth as writers by using evidence in their writing portfolio. This is a sophisticated task to require of students—one in which their judgment is based on criteria that they and I have developed over the year through our reading and writing together: what makes a good essay; what do we expect business letters to look like; what do convincing scholarship essays look like? Each class undertakes this process of developing criteria for judging the quality of their work in order to understand that the conventions of writing, spelling, and formatting a paper, for example, haven't developed arbitrarily out of the netherworld of textbooks, but out of real readers' needs and demands on writers. This eventually gets students to think more critically about the presentation of their work and their expectations of themselves as writers. In the course of reading and writing, students are encouraged to think about what makes a piece of writing effective. What draws attention, holds interest, informs, describes, or satisfies a particular reader, and why? Developing the criteria for assessing writing is not only a difficult task, it is also one that depends on specific contexts with all the complexities of audience variables, writing purposes and intentions, and even taste. I am not the sole arbiter of quality in the classroom—the standards are set by readers of their writing, and students learn to expect others to live up to the standards they themselves set. While we may agree on effectiveness, we may disagree on aesthetics, but students and teachers are learning to generate questions from these issues and to understand the contingencies contributing to readers' responses.

Our classroom curriculum takes into account the complexity of thinking reflected by the writing of thirty-five urban adolescents who use portfolios to represent learning in their English class and beyond. Because the curriculum is localized, it is responsive to the expressed needs and interests of the students defining it. Bethany, for example, is a student who has worked at defining herself as a future businesswoman, while at the same time laboring over her writing. She also works at refining her social consciousness by writing short stories and by doing research on black businesses and the community support necessary to make them viable. For her, writing has been a means of exploring values within her community and classroom, as well as a means of increasing self-awareness. Reading through her portfolio together, Bethany and I agree that she is beginning to write with more authority now that she has supported her writing with background reading, which is reflected in a recognizable voice in her later work. These insights help her focus on a specific audience and gain control over her use of language. Through discussions and disagreements with others in the class, she has begun to use writing purposefully in order to make herself heard.

Bethany's story illustrates my concern as a teacher and researcher that writing not only should connect to the lives of students, but that it may also lead students to expanding literacies. In "Forming an Interactive Literacy in the Writing Classroom," Cathy Fleischer (1992) argues that providing students with opportunities to read and write from their lives and in their own language contributes to their understanding an interactive literacy in service of their own needs and purposes. My classroom experience bears out her conclusions. When the writing represents the writer and her world, it possesses both an explicit and an implicit value. It makes sense to have students ascribe meaning to the work they produce by making it the content of the course and the basis for our interaction.

Since students have come to view one another as audience and correspondent, there is new regard for their shared expertise. James Boyd White (1984) identifies community formation and its consequences in the reciprocal process of reconstitution as "it addresses, and seeks to educate, the reader as one who will engage in that activity on his own, as a fellow author" (284). With class-generated texts acting as threads that tie our school activity to the broader world, students and teacher attempt to use the language as we speak it, read it, and hear it, to record our place in the world. My roles as teacher and researcher have been shaped by the students' portfolios as an inevitable extension of their influence on what I know and need to know in order to respond appropriately to a written product very different from that which a less socially constructed pedagogy produces. As students begin to take themselves seriously as writers, they more fully participate in and shape the classroom community. They begin to see connections between the kinds of thinking that writing requires and what reading contributes to our understanding of ourselves and the world around us. This spirit of inquiry has generated an enthusiasm for questioning.

My students and I continue to raise questions about writing such as, Why is it that some revised papers are occasionally lifeless, voiceless reductions of lively first drafts? Is this the result of overt instruction? What features of a student's writing are sound indicators of growth? How can we honor students' idiosyncratic habits as writers and accommodate their less conventional needs and still create meaningful classroom time and space? Some students report that they only write at home, or can only write alone, or have to have music playing in order to write. What difference does it make that we often have two or three adults in the classroom reading and writing with us? How do the social interactions in the classroom affect the students' writing growth? These are questions that inevitably affect teaching and learning and also reveal the disruptions of an authentic pedagogy that invites interrogation in order to meet students' ever-changing needs, as Timothy Lensmire (1994) describes in his third-grade writing classroom.

Struggling with Grades

Grading has emerged as one of the most intransigent disrupters of an evolving classroom practice. It prevented me from being one more reader and writer in the class because grades create unnatural boundaries in classrooms, marking territory and inhibiting access to one another. It was apparent that as *A* students moved more easily than others—were free to question and gain attention within typical classroom conventions—they were also being constructed as more powerful agents within the classroom. *D* and *F* students experienced the isolation of failure. As grades were constructing them, they had less access to the rest of us because of their reluctance to participate in the way other students did. Grades had separated and divided us in familiar and offensive ways. I was powerless to do anything about the larger bureaucratic structure of schooling, which demanded grades, but I could change the grading culture of our classroom, if students were willing to work at this with me.

Grading as I knew it could reward but just as often punish and even silence students. As a fairly straightforward terminal act, grading contrasts with evaluation, which seems a little more slippery. After all, I am evaluated by supervisors, and the process suggests a context, some negotiation, and a complexity that grading doesn't necessarily take into account. From the Latin, *assess* means to sit beside. Like evaluation, assessment suggests a context and implies a social interaction. The differences between grading and assessment sharpen when I reflect on students' comments such as, "This grade doesn't prove anything. I still learned something." Grades don't necessarily reflect learning, but represent something that may or may not be articulated in the teaching/learning process. For some, grades mean more than learning, yet for others who find intrinsic value in what they learn, grades may hold little meaning. Grades divide process and product, emphasizing one over the other in a way that conflicts not only with common sense but with our goal of extending what students can do with words. Sports analogies were useful here. If we thought of drafting as practice, then writing a draft could be a safe space to err without the necessity of grading. Practice counts. In the end, everything counts, but does everything have to be graded? Students got the point.

Grading student papers coincided with writing as a solo activity. Assigning grades after reading for error fit into the old picture. As we moved to a more interactive construction of teaching and learning, grading became a more collaborative activity. With the additional readers in class, students could get more responses to their writing and learned how to evaluate their own work. Assessment offers another possibility, one that assists or expands instruction by opening the process to the judgments of others—those who sit side by side—including and especially students.

Talking Writing

Developing writers learn more effectively through their social interactions. Multiple fields of research support this claim and contribute to instruction in reading and writing, teaching and learning. When there are so many complex facets of knowing at work in the instructional process, the temptation is to attach to the familiar. I was content at first to look only at what the writing students were doing and to ignore other areas of inquiry because of their inherent complexity. However, students contributed to the reshaping of my questions as they wrote and read and responded to one another with an increasing frequency about the influence their readers had on their writing when they could talk about it. What had begun as the stickiest part of implementing the portfolio process, the need for students to interact freely around their writing, had now taken over and reshaped the questions I was asking myself about the effectiveness of portfolios. The quality of the interactions has improved to a point where a trust and openness among students is visible. Together we have learned that time spent writing and talking about writing affects the development of our processes and cuts across content to communicate socially constructed goals.

What students "know" in their everyday lives, their commonsense "knowledge," is what "constitutes the fabric of meanings" (Berger and Luckmann 1966, 15). The rich store of commonsense knowledge that students bring to the classroom, coupled with their individual expectations, provides a rich source for a variety of texts and contexts for language activity. Students generate written pieces that demonstrate an awareness of audience and a sense of purpose ranging from entertainment to problem solving to exposition, depending on the specific nature of the writing task students set for themselves. Students take a major step toward independence when they learn that purpose and audience determine the form of their writing. They come to understand genre inductively by choosing what form of writing is appropriate for the message they are attempting to communicate. They learn to say, "This is what I want to say, and how I want to say it," knowing that they must depend on readers for their measure of success in meeting their writing goals. Additionally, they research the conventions of the genre they select in order to honor their readers' needs.

All of these steps toward writing invite a variety of conversations. The effects of these outside conversations are recorded by students in self-reflections that document how readings affect their revisions and how suggestions for revision affect their writing. The students' texts provide them with evidence of the importance of written language and its uses. An equally important outcome is the increasing confidence writers gain in their peer readers. The overall effect displaces the teacher from the center of assessment and focuses on the classwork. No longer is assessment a separate, terminal act that generates no new knowledge for students, but as the portfolio develops over the year, students acquire and generate a critical and reflective awareness of their reading and writing. As Vito Perrone (1994) observes in a cautionary note on reflection, "If students are not regularly writing across a variety of topics and in a variety of styles for diverse purposes, then promoting self-evaluation has limited value" (13).

Valuing the Writer and the Writing

I have learned to value student writing as I've come to see it as expressions of young writers who are struggling to make sense of their enormously complex lives. Collecting the writing inevitably enhances its value. Like the appreciation in value of collections of artifacts—studying their origins, development, and changes—writing, too, grows in value. Over the years our classroom has become a gathering place, bringing together students of diverse interests and experiences with readers who are eager and hospitable to reading. The writing embodies growth and development over time, and the portfolios document student learning in whatever shape it finally takes.

Each class takes on a character of its own and evolves in an individual way, at its own pace, moving in its own direction. It is difficult to describe this process at any given point for a given class because of the fluid nature of the ongoing changes. Life in our classroom is happily less predictable than it once was. Many more students experience success and find themselves called upon by others for their expertise. In a final reflection, students were asked, What do you know about yourself as a writer that you didn't know before? Charles responded, "That's a hard question! I guess I could only say that now I am more honest with myself and my readers. I don't feel as if my first draft is the best piece ever composed on paper. Also I know it's better to share the spotlight and be together than to own the spotlight and be alone."

Students see themselves and their writing in relation to their lives and their audience. Their social roles within the class largely determine how they come to view and value their own literacy. Writing portfolios have worked to form a community of readers and writers in and beyond the classroom and to nurture students' confidence in their writing, in order that more and more of them will be able to use their writing in service of their own needs and in response to the more complex demands that the future will make on them.

Notes

1. Paley makes keen observations of her students in a complex teaching environment and provides a model of one way to look at classroom interaction for teachers at all levels. See particularly *White Teacher* (1979) and *Wally's Stories* (1981).

2. Key issues are elaborated in Camp (1993, 1992); Moss (1994, 1992); Moss and Herter (1993); and Moss et al. (1992).

3

"Getting It"
When What Is Not *Said Is the Most Important Data*

Helen Fox

Until I started doing composition research, I never figured I had any serious difficulty communicating across cultures. I had lived and worked most of my adult life outside my own country—first in India, then for a long period in a farming community in francophone Quebec, and later, briefly, in West Africa and the South Pacific—and I had always found it interesting to talk with people who understood the world differently than I did. But when the kinds of conversations I so enjoyed in the classroom and in the homes of friends had to be turned into research data, I became stymied by a cultural difference I had been only vaguely aware of before.

My research concerned the problems that many international graduate students, especially those from "non-Western" countries, have when they try to write for the U.S. university. I had asked sixteen graduate students from twelve countries—Korea, Japan, the People's Republic of China, Indonesia, Nepal, India, Sri Lanka, Cote d'Ivoire, Somalia, Cape Verde, Brazil, and Chile—to talk with me about their frustrations with their instructors' feedback on their writing and to speculate about the causes of their difficulties with assignments that expected them to "analyze" something, whether it was a social problem, an educational system, or their own research data. Most of my informants had been students in my classes in graduate-level writing at the School of Education at the University of Massachusetts at Amherst, and many had been good friends for years and had often asked me to work informally with them on their class papers and on drafts of their master's and doctoral theses. Almost all were colleagues at the Center for International Education, which, besides being a graduate department, is a close-knit community with a shared commitment to international development, empowerment, and social justice. Thus I had been intensely involved in my informants' lives and they in mine even before my research questions became crystallized or my topic became clear.

My difficulties in understanding and interpreting my informants' answers did not have so much to do with the struggles some of them were having with English, although at times the idiosyncrasies of their pronunciation and vocabulary combined with the poor quality of my tape recorder made transcribing a challenge. But when it came to the level of meaning, to getting the point of what they were trying to tell me, I began to notice a subtle difficulty. I say "subtle" because at the time I was unaware of the extent to which culture influences communication style; I only understood the full significance of this influence after I had looked carefully at my data and noticed how my informants were speaking in interviews and trying to express themselves in writing as well as what they were saying about their backgrounds and cultures. What I learned both surprised me and gave me some insight into why I was having so much trouble "getting straight answers" in my interviews, or even finding nice, concise quotes in the transcripts that would function as the kind of evidence expected by the U.S. university.

Most of my informants came from cultures that value indirect styles of communication. Thus, they tended to pay more attention to the context of an idea than the idea itself, perhaps giving the historical background or discussing events that occurred when the idea was in vogue without ever really connecting them to the idea in question. They might find it more elegant or intellectually sophisticated to avoid precise definitions, or to subtly suggest a point through allusion or metaphor, or by telling a story or giving an example of something similar but not *exactly* pertinent. They might make grand generalizations or exaggerated claims, not intending for the audience to take them literally, but rather to create an effect, a feeling of solidarity within the audience that would give authority to the idea they were trying to get across.

All this, of course, was a large part of the reason why my informants were having trouble writing analytical papers for the U.S. university—as I came to realize only much later. If a student has been taught from childhood to value group harmony and to keep individual opinions to herself, she may have great difficulty meeting her U.S. professor's expectations that she make her point clear or give straightforward reasons for her opinions, or even that she make explicit transitions between paragraphs, all of which may seem aggressive, or uncultured, or terribly impolite. "In my country, you don't say, 'Listen, I want to talk to you about *this!*' " an exasperated student from Cote d'Ivoire finally told me. "If you want to talk to me about something and you already said it, why should I listen any further? I'm going," he said, getting up abruptly and walking toward the door to emphasize his point. "You try to make a sort of suspense," he added, "and as we say, 'It brings appetite to the conversation,' you know? The person is thinking, 'What is he or she going to tell me?' And you really pull him to listen to you, you see? And finally you say it. And by the time you say it, you are also at the end of what you are going to say."

But U.S. "mainstream" culture teaches its members to speak directly to the point and to be relatively quick about it. "What are you driving at?" we ask, when children digress. "Oh god, not another shaggy dog story." "I don't get it." "Can you give me an example?" "So basically, what you're saying is . . ." These cultural habits of direct and explicit communication underlie almost all of the features of what the U.S. university counts as "effective speaking," "good writing," or "good analysis": coming to the point quickly and directly, valuing literal meanings and explicit statements of cause and effect, elaborating ideas by giving directly relevant examples, reining in digressions, and summing up ideas and linking them at various points in the discussion. And most important, if perhaps obvious, it is seen as the responsibility of the writer or speaker to do the analysis for the audience, to let them know exactly where the argument is going and why.

Of course, even within the U.S. university there are styles of writing that are not as direct or explicit as this. Literary critics, for example, are allowed more liberties than those in political science or psychology. Journal articles in social anthropology or women's studies are generally more abstract and ornamental than the straightforward prose of biology or chemistry, which strives for correctness, simplicity, and dispassionate reporting of concrete detail even at the expense of reader interest. But even in less strictly scientific disciplines at the U.S. university, there is an underlying *tendency* to directness, to precise relationships between verbs and subjects, to clear and relatively obvious transitions, to announcements of intent and summary statements.

But many cultures around the world consider this explicitness a kind of spoon-feeding; a sophisticated, "mature" audience should be able to make their own meaning, to fill in their own cause-and-effect connections if they feel the need. This is a problem for the U.S. university, which tends to react to this assumption about communication not by acknowledging it as an interesting difference in outlook or communicative style but as "undeveloped" thinking or "informal" or "colloquial" speech or inadequate writing ability.

And so when it came time for me to do what the university expected, that is, to get from informants some concrete "data"—the explicit, literal, concise statements of what they *meant*—I was often in trouble. For as I listened to what the students were saying in answer to my questions about their educational backgrounds and their understanding of cultural differences in writing and speaking, I often felt both excited and vaguely frustrated, as if I were close to understanding something terribly meaningful, but couldn't pin down exactly what it was. And even when I was beginning to "get it"—to make the meaning myself as I was expected to do—I knew I would have even more trouble speaking to the university about my results. You will see the difficulty in the following example, much condensed and paraphrased from my interview notes.

Carla, a master's student from Chile, was telling me that her strategies for writing a class paper had not been understood, either by the U.S. students who were supposed to be giving her feedback, or by her instructor. She was telling me how she had resisted blurting out her main point, even though she had learned how to do so in my writing class, because her culture valued a more contextual approach, what she called "looking at the subject from far away."

"If I don't get far away and look at it from another dimension, people in my country wouldn't be happy with it," she told me. "They would treat it like it's nothing." But when I asked her to explain how, in her style, she would look at the subject from far away, she said it had more to do with politics than anything, "because when you go to university, everything is politics." Carla then went on to talk about how people divide themselves into "left, right, and center" and critique the subject from a political point of view, using the vocabulary of their political persuasion to let people know where they stand, though it had been difficult to take a stand under a dictatorship, and how students in the eighties, when she went to school, were different from those in the seventies or sixties, and that her generation of students began to criticize "teachers who were very technical in terms of what they teach and what they talk." These teachers were just taking things apart, "discomposing" them, never looking at the surroundings. She gave as an example the psychology department at her university, which at the time was emphasizing behavioral science.

"I think that is very, very American," she told me. "Behavioral science is like, I feel it is typically American. The behavioral sciences were very important in the seventies there. And what happened was that in my school, with the dictatorship, behaviorism became more important because they gave out solutions about behaviors of human beings without questioning the context."

I must have looked confused.

"It was like, all the teachers were behaviorists."

"And why was that?"

"Because it was a theory that could explain all the behaviors without looking at the context. Just like, you know, if your kid is not doing well in school maybe we have to look at the reinforcement and the environment and maybe the teacher. But they never question why the teacher might have been aggressive with the kid. What was happening with the teacher? Was she underpaid? Was she afraid? Was she what? It doesn't matter, it's 'We have to change the teacher's attitude.'"

I was struggling to understand, wondering vaguely what connection all this had with Carla's difficulties with analytical writing. If the two of us had been talking at a party or having lunch I would have gone with the flow, just listened, having faith that I would get the point eventually, or not even being so concerned with the point, just listening to the story because I was interested in Carla's personal history and her life at the university under Pinochet. I would have relaxed and let pictures come into my mind of Carla sitting at a crowded lunch table with other young intellectuals voicing their concerns about the pernicious influence of the United States on their school. And I might even have guessed, or have gradually come to understand from her rapid, scattered dialogue, that insisting that writers look at a subject scientifically might suggest that they could—or perhaps should—avoid considering the political context, just the thing to play into the hands of a dictator such as Pinochet and allow him to maintain his stranglehold on the country.

But because this was an interview for "research," it was hard to allow myself the luxury of bathing in the conversation, letting the stories she was telling me seep in slowly and begin to form a cohesive, interwoven context on their own. For I knew that even if I could "get it" the way Carla expected me to, doing my own guesswork would never pass for research data. I needed a more direct, precise explanation.

"OK, so how is behaviorism better for a dictatorship?" I pressed her.

"How? It was better in the sense that you were learning things that did not . . . It was a theory that was perfect, um, how do you say it?" There were language issues here, too.

"I'm going to explain it another way," said Carla, seeing my discomfort. "And I'm talking now in a very simplistic way," she warned, looking at me sternly so that I wouldn't find fault with her for being so direct and obvious. "Because at that time the theory got more complex and they started to bring in some cognitive stuff. But they never explained the behavior in terms of what was happening in Chile. That means that people were afraid? That means that people disappeared? So if this kid had problems in school because his father was not at home anymore . . ." Carla trailed off, letting me finish her thought.

By this time I had given up my attempts at forcing her to make the connections I needed and had begun to concentrate on the stories themselves, paraphrasing parts of them to be sure of her meaning, encouraging her with "uh huhs" and "OKs" and supplying a word in English now and then when she asked for one. And so Carla continued her explanation in the way she felt comfortable, returning to the students who were dissatisfied with the U.S.-educated instructor and how they refused to take her classes, and how eight teachers even had to change their careers because nobody would listen to them. And that all this was consistent with the movement they had started to have at the university, and that it was now more political and there were a lot of strikes, not real dangers, but protests and all that, so Pinochet would have to leave.

Suddenly it struck me that Carla was doing in her answer to my question the same thing she had done in her class papers and that she had been describing to me earlier, "looking at the subject from far away."

I said, "You know, I've noticed that you're doing in talking the same thing you do when you write."

"Yeah?" Carla asked in surprise.

"And I find it really interesting. Because I'm here to interview you about writing, right? And so I'm looking at the subject, which I expect to be, let's see, 'What are the problems you are having with writing?' But what you're doing is, you're taking writing and you're looking at it in this whole context. Now you're telling me about behaviorism and the dictatorship and all this stuff. It's interesting, it really makes your point."

It is difficult to describe the expression on Carla's face at that moment: apologetic, embarrassed, disgusted, but also seeing the difference between us a little more clearly.

"It really makes my point," she repeated, laughing ironically. "I'm sorry . . ."

"No, not to say that!" I said quickly, trying to let her know by my tone and expression that I understood and was sympathetic to the context she had been speaking about: the political collusion between the United States and the Chilean dictatorship and the way that mirrors, or is an example—in a long string of historical examples—of U.S. dominance in Latin America, including even the dominance in thinking and writing styles and thus the implied inferiority of other ways of understanding the world. All this was embedded in that quick moment of my apology and in the millisecond of silence that followed.

"I can tell you things that would be useful for me in a writing course," said Carla, laughing a little to break the tension.

"Yeah," I agreed.

Carla paused a moment and seemed to gather her thoughts together. "OK, I'm talking this way because I think that it is the only way I can make my point. And I think I have certain assumptions about writing. I've been thinking that maybe one of my assumptions is that you always have to give the context to make the point. So if I was taking my first writing course again, it would be helpful for a teacher to show me these assumptions I am working with."

Later, as I looked over transcripts from interviews with students from Africa, Asia, Latin America, and other countries, I found statements like this one— direct, concise, and to the point—interspersed with longer conversational passages using indirect strategies, each a little different according to the communication style of the culture or area the informant came from, but all subtle and contextual, all requiring much more of the audience than is reasonable or "logical" in the U.S. "mainstream" context. At the same time, my own questions and comments, while mostly direct and straightforward, are likewise interspersed with occasional indirect strategies like the unstated allusion to the political context that I mentioned above. Noticing this helped me remember an important point: that directness and indirectness are really not so foreign to each other, that communicative styles are tendencies, sometimes strong tendencies, to use particular abilities among many in the human repertoire, to value them, to find them logical, elegant, and sophisticated, and to devote considerable attention and care to using them well.

But the U.S. university is not particularly knowledgeable about other communicative traditions and has, in fact, been skeptical of indirection for a long time—ever since the use of subtlety went out of fashion during the Protestant Reformation, when any prose that was "unclear, contextual, symbolic or not strictly grammatical was judged as . . . an offense to God's natural law" (Scollon and Scollon 1981, 44). Even today, instruction in our cultural habit of directness and precision is tinged with judgments of worth and character—as many of us can recall from comments made on our writing by teachers who seemed personally offended by our gropings toward clarity, perhaps because our lack of skill suggested to them that we weren't properly brought up or were lazy or didn't care. And because of this confusion of what is different with what is morally suspect, the problem of understanding informants from indirect cultures can get especially complicated when we sense that we might be dealing with both cultural difference in communication style and lack of preparation or practice at the same time. Sometimes informants really *haven't* thought much about the topic and therefore don't quite know what they mean to imply. Or sometimes, when they digress, they might simply get sidetracked instead of deftly encircling the issue ("so it can't escape," says Paulo Freire, commenting on his own digressive, contextual style in a mischievous moment [Horton and Freire 1990, 156]). Because perfection of any communicative style takes practice and care, our informants' attempts at a meaningful metaphor, or an illustrative story without explicit commentary, or a comparison without direct contrasts between the things being compared, may not be crafted well enough to convey meaning even in cultures with a high tolerance for the contextual or symbolic. These speakers or writers may in fact just have a *feeling* about the way they want to present themselves, a voice that holds back, or talks around, or strives for a kind of relationship between the audience, the text, and the self that is markedly different from what is expected in the U.S. context.

All of these complications make it difficult for "mainstream" researchers—even culturally sensitive ones—to do what we are expected to do in research: pin down hard data. How are we to be sure that our informants have something valuable to tell us, given the tendency for skill in one culture to mirror deficiency or lack of preparation in another? How can we be sure we are grasping our informants' intended meaning, given *our* lack of skill and preparation in listening to extended and varied forms of subtle implication? How do we encourage our informants to open themselves up to us despite our inadequacies: our direct, rapid-fire questions that can seem rude and insensitive, our impatience with the time it might take our informants to get to the heart of what they want to say, our frustration with answers that tell us only what we want to hear or that don't seem to respond to our questions at all? How can we train ourselves to read between the lines, or, if this becomes too difficult, how can we help our informants speak to us more often in ways we are familiar with? And finally, how do we put what we may only have inferred, or partially inferred, from our data into a form that seems valid to a U.S. university audience?

I cannot hope to answer these questions satisfactorily, for this problem of communicating across very different traditions has only just begun to engage our thinking as writing teachers and researchers.[1] What I can offer is some of my trial-and-error learning over the years that has helped me both to recognize that these questions are important and to attempt, within my own practice, to bring the two traditions a little closer to mutual understanding.

The main thing I have come to realize is perhaps obvious: if we want to "get it," if we want to learn to decipher what our interview informants only imply, we need to spend time learning how they experience the world. This means becoming familiar with many different traditions, both by learning *about* them—through books, films, travelers' stories—and by soaking them up through direct experience, the way we might immerse ourselves in a second language. And like language learning, the amount of time it takes to learn to appreciate another worldview can be formidable. Looking back at the five years I spent as a graduate student at the Center, I can see that perhaps four of those years were spent getting to know people who would later become my informants or who came from the cultures of those informants. My progress, of course, was not linear, not without setbacks. At first I tried to get information that seemed relevant to my research much too quickly, without first building personal relationships—crucial to people coming from cultures that base their communication on shared knowledge and value group harmony and solidarity.[2] My cheerful, self-confident manner gave some of my informants the impression I was approaching a complex situation too simplistically, treating a serious problem much too lightly. I vastly underestimated the emotional impact my initial, "objective" research question— "What difficulties do graduate students from non-Western countries have with analytical writing?"—would have on the people I needed to trust me. But at the same time, partly by chance, partly because I was learning from my mistakes, I was doing other things that eventually gave me the skills and credibility that would convince my informants to open up to me. I was spending time talking with them in personal settings—at their homes, at parties, over coffee or a glass of wine on my back porch. It was at such times and places that I began hearing stories that didn't seem to have anything to do with my research questions—memories of war and the scattering of extended families, incidents involving friends and relatives back home, family histories. But these stories helped fill me in on the necessary context, the "givens" of my informants' remarks in later, formal interviews and, at the same, time, had the effect of drawing us closer.

As we became more comfortable with each other, the conversation, too, grew closer to the heart of the matter. I began to hear of the difficulties they were suffering in their new environment: their homesickness for spouses and children, the pain of being misjudged and devalued when they wrote and spoke in ways that in their home countries had made them highly successful students and professionals. All of this was crucial to my understanding of their resistance—sometimes quite stubborn and angry resistance—to the changes in their thinking and communication style that were being forced upon them. They had naively assumed they could come to the U.S. university "for the knowledge alone," they told me, but soon it had become evident that the content was impossible to separate from the form, and the act of trying to express themselves differently—directly, precisely, individualistically—was changing them at their core. As Carla wrote in one of her first papers in my writing class after a great struggle to force herself to adopt the style I was telling her was "just another technique":

> Learning to write in an American style, it is much more than learning a new technique. It is a way this culture "normalizes" me to the system, shaping on me new values and new ways of looking at the world. Therefore the writing style is not value free; it has ethical consequences depending if it is empowering or disempowering for me in this new culture or in the culture of my home country.

As I gradually became aware of these political and emotional issues—issues that were rarely explained to me this directly—I began to appreciate the magnitude and importance of the stylistic differences. Carla was right; communication is not objective, not value free. I would not get the insight I was looking for if I simply prodded my informants to speak more to the point or if I imagined that the brief, direct answers they sometimes gave to my straightforward questions told anything close to the whole story. Communication styles—seemingly so innocuous—are touchy and political. Not only are they deeply ingrained habits of speech, thought, cultural sophistication, and politeness, they also have ethical consequences.

Once I realized these implications, I took even more seriously my task of learning to read between the lines. I began to listen more carefully for tones of voice, and to watch for facial expressions, for the body language that gives significance to what is being said or implied. I began to paraphrase less as I learned to wait for the conversation to develop slowly, creating a life of its own. I developed an unexpected patience—unexpected because I had been told by students for years that I was a patient teacher, and so I thought I understood what patience was: waiting, poised, for long minutes while a student struggled for vocabulary, counting slowly to five after I asked a question in class before rephrasing it or asking a different one. But what I was learning now was patience of a different magnitude. Maybe it should not even be called "patience" at all, because the word implies an ability to wait for the point to be made, the expected outcome to occur. What I was beginning to learn was to slow down.

Slowing down implies a number of things for "mainstream" U.S. re-searchers. It means getting to know our informants first, establishing personal ties and learning the context of their cultures. It means interacting with them longer and with more personal investment, feeling and showing more genuine interest and delight each time we meet. It means meeting more often to talk about the same subjects again and again, perhaps coming at them from different angles. It might mean giving up using surveys and questionnaires, even to get basic, straightforward information ("How many years have you studied English?" "How much writing did you do in high school?" "What kinds of writing did you do in your English classes?"). In cultures that value the contextual, informants will need to tell us a good deal more than they might be able to write because of language limitations, or that they will want to write because the context is so complicated, or that they will be able to explain clearly and concisely as we expect them to. Thus, the tendency of our informants will often be to give short, very general answers ("We mostly did grammar exercises") that leave out the most important information, or say what they think we want to hear, or express only what is polite or expected in their cultural context. Slowing down means coming to an interview with questions that are focused enough for the informant to understand what we want to know, but that at the same time allow for stories, for seemingly random factual details, for excursions into philosophy, for enjoyment of the moment.

But even after we have put aside our own cultural expectations and learned to understand our informants in a different way, we are still left with the problem of communicating this knowledge in academic form, back-translating, as it were, across traditions. It has taken me a year to figure out how to write this chapter, and still I am not satisfied that I have been convincing. Because in order to communicate some of the things my friends have told me, I need to tell not only what I have learned, but how I have learned it. And I cannot really tell how I have learned it without telling stories, without recreating the mood, the feeling, the intensity and closeness of the space between speaker and listener. I cannot explain, in the academic style that I teach and in fact value, how it could be that Mohammed, in speaking about how as a child he first came to know war, was also giving me some insight into why he has so much difficulty understanding "how this culture thinks"—and how that makes his life almost unbearably frustrating when he tries to write his course papers. And what makes it even harder for me as researcher, writer, and interpreter across traditions is that Mohammed may never express that unbearable frustration in words, but communicate it instead in the tension in his voice and in the way he stubs out his cigarette as we sit in the dark on my back porch, the tape recorder long since retired. It is not quotable, but it is there.

Communication across cultures takes time and space and imagination. It takes making the audience feel as well as think, feel what it is like to experience the world differently. It requires us to listen differently, too, and even to *be* different, if only for a little while. *Spend time with people. Stop asking them what they mean all the time. Stop filling up the silence with words. Laugh harder and longer. Relax. Absorb. Slow down.*

Notes

1. See, for example, Fox (1994); Lu (1987); Matalene (1985); Maphahlele (1993); and Shen (1989). Much of my study of what is written on the subject has come from other fields. In communications, see, for example, Asante and Gudykunst (1989); Ting-Toomey and Korzenny (1991). In anthropology, see, for example, Hall (1976); Shweder (1991). In linguistics, see, for example, Kachru (1988); Kaplan (1986). In psychology, see, for example, Bond (1986); Triandis et al. (1988).

2. Anthropologist Edward T. Hall (1976) makes a useful distinction between what he calls high- and low-context cultures. High-context cultures rely on much shared, unspoken knowledge—like communication between twins that have grown up together—while low-context cultures like the United States require extremely explicit verbal information (91). Many high-context cultures are also collectivist, that is, they value the group over the individual, which has interesting implications for communication as well. Personal opinions are more likely to be kept veiled in the interests of group harmony or solidarity. See Triandis et al. (1988).

4

"They've Got the Power—They're Hearing"
Case Studies of Deaf Student Writers at Gallaudet University

Brenda Jo Brueggemann

The study of the deaf shows us that much of what is distinctively human in us—our capacities for language, for thought, for communication, and culture—do not develop automatically in us, are not just biological functions, but are the most wonderful gifts—from one generation to another. We see that Culture is as crucial as Nature.

Oliver Sacks, *Seeing Voices: A Journey into the World of the Deaf*

In March 1988, some 2,000 deaf students at Gallaudet University formed a single voice that was seen (and yes, even heard) by the world; they formed a community with a cause in an uprising now historically recorded as "Deaf President Now" ("DPN") (Gannon 1989).[1] For 124 years Gallaudet's president had been a hearing person elected by a principally hearing board; for 124 years deaf persons, then, had held no power, had had no representation at the very place they should most have had power and representation—their exclusive deaf university. So, when in March 1988 their hearing board elected yet another hearing president over two fully qualified deaf candidates, Gallaudet's students closed the gates to their university, formed a powerful community, and increased deaf awareness worldwide. One Gallaudet student, Shane Marsh, conveyed strongly but simply how much their language, American

Sign Language (ASL), meant in this issue as he signed to the crowd during one rally the title quotation of this chapter: "They've got the power—they're hearing."

By the time the week was up, their new hearing president, Elisabeth Ann Zinser, had resigned; their board chair, Jane Spilman, had resigned; the students had a new deaf president, Irving King Jordan, himself a graduate of Gallaudet; they had promises of a restructured board to be at least 50 percent deaf; and the world had not only heard these deaf people but had also, for the most part, supported their cause. "Deaf Awareness," "Deaf Power," and "Deaf Pride" had come of age.

Before this, deaf education in American schools had gone principally by the hearing world's agenda. Oral communication was strongly insisted upon and manual communication (the use of the hands and body to express oneself) was discouraged, if it was allowed at all. The reasoning behind such an agenda? If deaf people are to function and communicate at all, the argument goes, they must do so *as if they can hear*; if they can't get along in the hearing world, they can't get along at all. And knowing the dominant (that is, hearing) culture's language is the key to "getting along." End of argument.

By now, we should recognize this argument. It is an argument based on "literacy" standards and rhetoric—on the power, politics, and pedagogy of a dominant, empowered culture. It is meant to keep that culture in power primarily through its language and rhetoric—through its "social grammar," as Henry Giroux (1988a) would have it (158). The dominating social grammars in the case I'll be most concerned with here are oral and written standard English; the language of the less dominant deaf subculture is gestural ASL.

In large part what has kept American deaf people a subculture (if a culture at all) is the status of ASL. Until recently, ASL was not recognized as a "real" language by the hearing world.[2] Now, however, it is; and now, consequently, Deaf culture, Deaf communities, and deaf individuals everywhere[3] share a new sense of worth as the hearing world grows increasingly aware of the not-so-silent deaf minority.[4] It is my belief that this growing awareness will provide fertile ground for studies in rhetoric, literacy, and composition since it is an awareness advanced and marked by issues we pay particular attention to—issues of power, politics, pedagogy, persuasion, literacy, linguistics, and the social and cognitive construction of knowledge.

It will be my first argument that the linguistic awareness and redefinition of literacy that have accompanied the acceptance of ASL as a real language constituted the primary ingredient for an uprising such as DPN: that because ASL finally gained acceptance linguistically and, therefore, was being used more openly and proudly as part of the Deaf culture's identity, the students at Gallaudet could use it to form their own power, to establish their own political and pedagogical agenda.

By extension, in the second part of this chapter, I want to continue arguing that this linguistic redefinition has made a significant difference in the way many Gallaudet students view the acquisition of English literacy. To illustrate this thesis I first need to lay out the social, literate, and linguistic history of major issues in American deaf education and ASL. From those foundations I will then outline the social significance of the DPN uprising in more general terms of power, politics, and pedagogy—in terms of literacy and rhetoric. Finally, I will end my discussion by focusing on my own research, presenting some results and telling some stories from case studies I conducted of deaf student writers at Gallaudet University in the fall of 1991.

The Dominance of Oral Methods in American Deaf Education

Persons with hearing losses (whether Deaf or deaf) have always been deaf (audiologically), but they have been defined and educated by the more dominant hearing culture in various ways throughout American history.[5] As Henry Giroux (1988a) reminds us, schools are immensely significant in the social construction of our society and selves, and for almost two hundred years now the orally based traditions of deaf education have contained a number of what Giroux calls "implicit visions about the role of the citizen and the purpose of community" (158). In the implicit visions of hearing people usually in charge of deaf curriculums (as they mainly are, even today, at Gallaudet), the deaf citizen is a fully functional, literate member of society, "saved" from deaf and dumb existence by the dominant hearing culture.[6] Little matter that deaf citizens often do not fit that picture—our tradition of literacy keeps on demanding that they should, that they can, that they will. Our literate tradition has tended to devalue sign language as a language in and of itself, and it has done so in various ways. First, we have kept alive the "methods" debate—should oral language or sign language be the focus and medium of a deaf child's education? Traditionally, oral languages are almost always the method of choice by hearing educators in charge of deaf education curricula. And second, we have kept alive negative attitudes about the linguistic and conceptual capabilities of sign languages: the perception that ASL isn't a real language, that it is incapable of representing either abstract thought or formal register. This argument, fostered by Helmer Myklebust in *The Psychology of Deafness* (1964) and by Hans Furth's work in the 1960s and early 1970s, is still popular. But deaf people themselves, as well as many new linguists studying sign languages, now have a very different view of their language.

ASL: The Power of a Real Language

Deaf author Carol Padden (1990) writes that the "all-important value of the [Deaf] culture is respect for one of its major identifying features: American Sign Language" (95). In fact, she goes on to explain, ASL forms such a major identifying feature of Deaf culture that the culture deliberately disassociates itself from speech.[7] The beginning of the legitimization and resurrection of both sign languages and Deaf culture (particularly in the United States) is credited, for the most part, to William C. Stokoe and his 1960 study, *Sign Language Structure*, "the first-ever serious and scientific attention paid to the 'visual communication system of the American deaf'" (Sacks 1989, 140). Since Stokoe's work, Ursula Bellugi (1980) has also done much to advance the linguistic validity of ASL. After ten years of ASL research at the Salk Institute for Biological Studies, Bellugi discussed (and diagrammed) in great detail various morphological features of ASL: referential indexing, reciprocity, grammatical number, distributional aspect, temporal aspect and focus, manner and degree, derivational features such as nouns created from verbs, predicates created from nouns, extended meanings, and compounding. In other words, Bellugi's research illustrated that ASL contains many of the same features we attribute to spoken (and written) languages. She concluded, however, that ASL contains rules and features that make it unique among languages, that "the visual-gestural communication system of deaf people has been shaped into an independent language with its own grammatical rules" (72). Furthermore, she argued, such similar yet unique features of ASL illustrate something powerful about humans and language in general: "the human capacity for building complex linguistic systems is the same—whether we speak or sign" (72).

Because it is real and natural, sign language has, as do spoken languages, a wide range of forms: SEE (Signed Exact English) I and II; MCE (Manual Coded English); PSE (Pidgin Signed English); SimCom (Simultaneous Communication); and the true language of the American deaf, ASL (American Sign Language)—to name but a few. Like speech, Sign is not the same in different languages—there is French Sign Language, Spanish Sign Language, Chinese Sign Language, and so on. Finally, like speech, Sign comes in a wide variety of ethnic and regional dialects—blacks sign differently than whites, males often sign differently than females, midwesterners sign differently than southerners (Woodward 1976, 1980). Additionally, there is a continuum between speech and Sign, and because of this continuum, ASL is inherently "diglossic." Its more "literary" variety (approaching Signed English, essentially a one-on-one signed translation for each word spoken) is used in formal conversations, in places such as churches and classroom lectures, while its more "colloquial" variety is used in smaller, less formal situations, for intimate conversations (Woodward 1980, 120).

This diglossia illustrates how much ASL is community- and culture-oriented; as Woodward explains, "When a Hearing person enters a conversation where Deaf people are using ASL, the Deaf people will automatically switch from ASL to a more English-like signing. This code-switching prevents the Hearing person from seeing and learning to use ASL and thus, from being able to participate in intimate interactions with Deaf people" (121).[8]

Thus, diglossia serves ASL as both an inclusive and exclusive gate into the culture and community of the Deaf. There is even a social etiquette to signed conversations that differs substantially from the etiquette for spoken conversations, and because of these differences, it is often easy for native signers to tell who is a relatively new signer in a conversation; aside from their personal signing skills, their etiquette gives them away (Hall 1989).

In his book about Deaf culture and sign language, *Seeing Voices*, Oliver Sacks (1989) offers verification for the reality of sign languages from virtually every angle. He lauds sign languages as the only languages that incorporate the unique dimension of space, making them a "four-dimensional channel of expression" (three unique spatial dimensions plus the dimension of time) (87–89), and he places them above and beyond speech in their capacity to "simultaneously evoke a concreteness, a vividness, a realness, an aliveness, that spoken languages, if they ever had, have long since abandoned" (120–21). Likewise, he marvels over the personal power of sign languages, for whereas "one can have or imagine disembodied speech, one cannot have disembodied Sign" (119). More scientifically, drawing on Ursula Bellugi's work (1980), he points to evidence for the biological (innate) grammar of sign languages (46, 118), and their cerebral hemisphere verification as a language, since they, like spoken languages, are processed in the left hemisphere (despite their strong use of spatial figurations, typically a right hemisphere function) (89).[9]

Finally, and most important for my argument, Sacks maintains that, for the Deaf, sign language is "an embodiment of their personal and cultural identity" (123). In agreement with writers such as Kannapell (1980, 1989), Padden (1990), and Trybus (1980), Sacks sees sign language as the admission ticket into Deaf culture. If sign language forms the basis for and entry into Deaf culture, it's little wonder that its validation should lead to the increased strength of Deaf culture, to the growing awareness of Deaf culture (by both the Deaf and hearing populations), and eventually to the empowerment of deaf persons at places such as Gallaudet University.[10]

I believe that the students at Gallaudet had come of age through language, because of language. Having a language to call their own, one supported by the linguistic research of scholars such as Stokoe and Bellugi, those students had something to stand on, something to "speak" with. Before the linguistic acceptance of a language they called their own, deaf people had no weapon or wedge against the dominant "social grammar," nor any way to persuade and empower. Persuasion and power, definition and acceptance of both self and society, begin with language—in every and all cultures. And such socially and individually constructed beginnings among the Deaf, such issues of literate and linguistic (re)definition with the use of ASL, such successful display of power and persuasion as occurred at Gallaudet in 1988, form the core of studies in rhetoric, literacy, and composition. So it is that I think we would be wise to listen to the deaf; they have much to tell us—about themselves, their culture, and their language as well as about ourselves, our culture(s), and our language(s). Some case studies I recently completed of deaf student writers at Gallaudet University set out to do some of this listening.

Deaf Student Writers at Gallaudet University

As I've hinted before, the cultural and social context of Gallaudet University presents a rather unique literacy situation. First, it is the only liberal arts university for the deaf. Deaf and hearing-impaired students from all over the world come here to study, and regardless of their skills in any signed or spoken language, they are generally expected to become skilled users of Gallaudet's two predominant languages—American Sign Language (ASL) and standard written English (SWE). ASL, a visuospatial language, is the "dominant" language used in daily interactions by most students and faculty. And yet students are not only expected but are required to demonstrate proficiency in reading and writing the English language.[11] Thus, within the same institution, two very strong—but opposing—literacy agendas are set forth. These agendas are particularly opposing since ASL and English (particularly SWE) differ radically—syntactically, conceptually, modally—in almost every way.

To further compound these problems, some students (and even some faculty) come to Gallaudet having almost no skills in any sign language (having been taught primarily by "oral" methods), while just as many arrive having almost no skills in any oral (or written) language (having lived and been educated primarily in a sign language). And as if the language oppositions weren't enough, Gallaudet is also "occupied territory" in terms of cultural conflict (Treesberg 1991): relations between "hearing" and "Deaf" culture are always tense and are often volatile.

While on Gallaudet's campus for one semester in 1991, I keenly felt the tensions of such past and present cultural conflicts. The 1988 DPN rally still resonated as a key event in the lives of most of the deaf students I met. The campus also remained tense over the recent death of a disgruntled English 50 student, Carl Dupree, at the hands of five Gallaudet security personnel who did not understand him as they "restrained" him outside the student center following his angry protest of his failing English 50 grade. Born profoundly and prelingually deaf, Dupree did not speak English coherently; the guards did not know ASL.[12] A year later, the English 50 students I was working with took up the death of Dupree in a computer network discussion I was leading. They had been revealing their own fears over the upcoming English Placement Test when one student warned the others, "Beware the English 50 Monster. . . . English 50 monster love staff not students. . . . English 50 monster kill Carl Dupree."

Suffice it to say that English 50—or any English class—was not highly regarded by most Gallaudet students. Even within the overall university structure, I sensed that the English department was often "under fire" and little esteemed by other departments. Furthermore, the election of a new English department chair the semester I was on campus had the department itself split between language and cultural affiliations; the largest debate over the competency of the two candidates centered on their opinions of language use in the classroom—ASL or (oral) English—and their own cultural emphasis, whether they were "Deaf" or "hearing."

Finally, as but one last example of the unique literacy oppositions and cultural border tensions that characterized Gallaudet, I myself often felt split between these language and cultural affiliations. Any time I was introduced to someone new, either faculty or student, he or she usually first wanted to know whether I was "Deaf" or "hearing." In short, the person wanted to be able to draw quick linguistic and cultural borders around me, to name me as either one of *them* or *us*.

My central research question grew out of all these linguistic and cultural tensions: How well can deaf students write "in English" at the same time that their cultural and linguistic ties to a very different culture and language are also being used and emphasized?

The Language Choice Issue

Aside from and in addition to the fact that most of Gallaudet's students are asked to be (or become) "bicultural"—to proudly maintain Deaf culture at the same time they learn how to function better in the hearing world—they are, of course, being asked to become bilingual. Thus, I wondered more specifically how central the issues about language choices (ASL or English?) are to these students, how those language issues show up in the students' written products, and how the issues also affect the students' literacy process. One of the most pressing problems at Gallaudet is the issue of language— how much and what kind of sign language should be used in classrooms, for example. The students I worked with brought this issue up at every turn in their writing; they all seemed to be angry and frustrated at the preposterously poor signing skills of many of their teachers, although they took widely varying individual stances on exactly what kind of language should be used in the classroom, from strict ASL to the voice-supported system now called "SimCom." Anna, one of the students I interviewed at length, chose to write one of her papers in answer to the question "What is good about mainstreaming for deaf students?" And while she seemed to advocate the mainstreaming experience (it was, after all, the one she had), she couldn't help but throw in a line, smack in the middle of her sales pitch for mainstreaming, that "Sometimes you'll find frustrated at the mainstream school" [sic]. Later, in my interview with Anna, she explained that "interpreters" (or the lack of good ones) were her main frustration as a mainstreamed student.

Anna, you see, has trouble interpreting either language—English or ASL. She became confused and frustrated—even angry—when her English teacher at Gallaudet suggested that she try translating her English into ASL or vice versa. She told me in an interview how she tried to limit her own ASL so that it wouldn't transfer much to her writing. "ASL," she concluded, "makes your writing messed up."[13] Because ASL "messes up" her writing, Anna became adamant about keeping ASL out of her English classroom. One of her chief complaints about her English 50 class was that the teacher would often ask them to sign (in ASL) an English sentence so they could discuss the differences (and similarities) between the two sentences. "Why?" she asked me. "This is not sign language class. That's confusing. I don't want to know how to write an ASL paper." I tried for a moment to explain that perhaps such a comparison helps some students to know more clearly the differences between the two languages—so that they do *not* confuse them. But she did not buy my argument. "That's the problem," she responded emphatically, "ASL and English don't combine. It's confusing."

Because of her belief that the two languages are only in conflict and confusion with each other, she became quite upset at the end of the semester when her English 50 teacher suggested to her, as a strategy for helping her on the English Placement Test, that she "try [to] sign ASL in English" as she writes. "I told him," she said, "I don't know any ASL deep—it's *sign language* [as she told me the story she emphasized those two words]. All I know is talking English. That's the only way I pick up my English—writing and reading. If I do that I'm not going to use sign language much." Here Anna is clearly confused and frustrated by the indistinct boundaries between the two languages and the unclear "rules" about how, when, where, and which of them she must use. Most of the students I worked with and observed that semester at Gallaudet seemed to feel much as Anna did; I have only offered her as a detailed example.

ASL Skills and Writing "in English"

In addition to having an interest in the issues about which language, ASL or English, should be central in any one communicative situation, I was interested in how students' ASL skill levels directly affected their writing skills in English. Most of the deaf students I worked with at Gallaudet didn't seem to care or to believe much that writing was a mode of learning. To them, writing was necessary, and it certainly served important social and career purposes, but it didn't seem to matter much on a more personal level. Anna once told me that if writing was assigned by a teacher, it might help students summarize a book or answer specific questions about it, but it doesn't necessarily help students learn anything. When I asked Gallaudet students this question directly—"How is writing connected to your learning? How does writing help you learn?"—they usually looked puzzled and couldn't answer beyond the fact that writing helped them learn English (since they had to write in English, after all—not in ASL). Given the fact that many of these students rely on a visual language that has no written form (and is therefore, by Walter Ong's [1982] terms, a highly "oral" language), the relatively insignificant role of writing in a Deaf student's personal life and learning isn't all that surprising.

Also, given the fact that these students do most of their expressive and receptive interacting in a visual, real-time language, it isn't surprising to find that they have some remarkably different cognitive processes for composing. First, I did not see much recursiveness in their process: they tend to start writing and they don't stop to look or read back until the end of a paragraph, and sometimes not until the end of the paper.[14] Second, related to this first feature, they do what I call "whole-concept composing." If you give them a topic to write on, they tend to look up for usually less than a minute, and then they just start writing, as if they were recording a whole picture at once, devoid of the subordination and lexical cohesion most hearing writers use. In other words, they don't seem to have much of a feel for the linear, time-controlled narrative structure of English prose. And yet, they do use narrative; in fact, it's the most frequent way of structuring their writing. (Deaf culture thrives on the sharing of stories.)

But they tell stories in different ways than we do: they tend to paint whole pictures at once, while we tend to proceed from point to point through time. Here is but one small example from a student who was asked on the first day of class to describe her "history with reading and writing":

> I learned how to writing when I was young girl. Later, I learn how to read. When I went to NWC [Gallaudet's Northwest Campus, the prepatory school], I really know some rules but I tend to forget them while I writing. When I write essay and next day I found many mistake. I getting frustrate. I hate to think rules while I writing. When I writing I like to express it first then next day I found mistake. I wish that I could do that on test.

This writer's focal point is her frustration with the errors in her writing, and furthermore, her frustration with the way she must go about writing—having to focus too much on those errors while in the process of composing. She has chosen to write her "literacy narrative" by focusing not so much on a sequence of events (as the prompt clearly asks for with the word *history*), but more by centering on a feeling. She comes at that feeling from various directions and thus, gives us what I call more of a "whole picture" of frustration rather than a history, a progression through time. Certainly, the feelings of frustration progress temporally throughout her passage ("frustration" is, in essence, the resonance, the cohesion of the passage)—but it is a feeling, not a linear history, that she foregrounds here.

Such cognitive and conceptual differences, as in Anna's "whole-concept" composing, lap over into the already well-researched terrain of distinguishing stylistic and linguistic features used by deaf students in their writing. The general literature calls these features "deafisms." But I think these features are as much a result of students' ASL fluency as they are of hearing loss.[15] For example, deaf students often don't use articles when they write—*a*, *an*, and *the* don't exist in their visual language. If they try to guess where an article should be, they often get it wrong; however, if you underline a place in their text where they've left out an article they immediately know what the problem is and correct it. (Although, as Leonard Kelly [1988] has observed, they write with such "relative automaticity" that no matter how many times they commit article errors, they still infrequently pause in the act of writing to consider the possibility of such errors.)

They also often wrangle *have* and *be* and all the modal verb forms when they try to use them; again, ASL doesn't use these kinds of verbs. Their subjects and verbs almost never agree—they don't have to in ASL—and often at the end of a piece they will go back and "correct" this in their writing because they know it is a common problem, and because they know how central this concept is to correct English. But more often than not, they "correct" what was already right and turn it into something wrong. In short, they have no gut feeling (no "felt sense," as Sondra Perl [1983] might call it) about what is right when it comes to subjects and verbs. The same goes for using derivatives of root words. Thus, Anna uses "frustrated" when she means "frustrations"—because it is the one root word (in ASL) that works as either a noun, verb, or adjective.

As for idioms, deaf students sometimes get close to a correct idiomatic phrase, but they seldom get it right. One student who wrote about her attitudes as she was just entering her second semester of English 50 (having failed the English Placement Test the first time around) noted, "I think I'm ready and start to roll up and pass it." She really wanted to roll up her sleeves, of course, but instead she rolls all of herself up. And that's an adequate metaphor for what happens when these deaf students try to use English idioms. They want to use them, of course; they are aware that these idioms are an important key to true fluency in a language. But because the idiom is virtually untranslatable into ASL, they usually get rolled and wrangled up in the process.

Implications for Teaching and Research in Composition (Or, Who Has the Power)

We've probably all seen plenty of our own composition students get wrangled up in the process of creating academic discourse; we've seen them struggle to recreate the idioms, the tone, the organization of language that is still yet beyond them. Many of our students are now bilingual, bicultural, even bicognitive (in these ways they might certainly be similar to the deaf students I worked with at Gallaudet). Their various cultural, linguistic, cognitive backgrounds inform and reflect the various ways they think and write—all the way from affecting the topics they choose to write about, to the diction and stylistic nuances of their prose, to the ways they conceptualize and connect and organize their material.

Yet many of our students, like the deaf students at Gallaudet, are bright, inquisitive, motivated and willing to learn; they want to be freed, not coerced, entrapped, or colonized by the power of literacy. But because of all sorts of linguistic, cultural, contextual, and cognitive differences they may find themselves caught in what J. Elspeth Stuckey (1991) calls the "violence of literacy," trapped by *our* ways of reading, writing, and interpreting, ways as foreign to them as their ways are to us. We composition teachers and researchers are generally "hearing" (or white, or male, or upper middle class, or college educated, or straight, or whatever); whatever we are, we generally have power. And with that power comes a tendency, all too often, to lump sum our students—to categorize their "problems" as we seek to anatomize them and cure them. (The medical analogy is no coincidence here.) Our largest lump sum, of course, is "us" versus "them."

I think we might begin then to use our power to conduct more research that seeks to know their ways. And not just to know them, but to understand them as well. How might we best do that? The biggest move, I think, comes in substituting the conceptual framework behind "us/them" with that of "I/you." This means beginning to see, interact with, and teach not categories and generalized classes (in all senses of the word), but unique individuals. To be sure, the largest thing I have learned from working with deaf students at Gallaudet is how fruitless, even damaging, it is to lump sum their writing products or processes in search of some deaf student prototype (or, by extension, in search of any student prototype). I can't, even though I have often been asked to in my publications and talks about these students, make single unique individuals into a representative sample, a collective "other," a tidy package called "them." I've used "Anna" often as an example in this chapter—but "Anna" is not representative. And I've surely even tended toward some blanket statements—but I admit feeling a bit sweaty, if not suffocating, under those blankets.[16]

What Anna and all my other composition students—whether black, white, blind, deaf, whatever—have taught me is the necessity of making it my business in composition research and in the composition classroom to find out about the uniqueness of each person, to delve into the diversity that makes lump summing impossible. With such delving I believe that I might reinstate the close relational nature of "I/you" and shun the accusatory, distancing tone all too often echoed in "us/them." And I take this position because I believe there are untold of, unimaginable gifts and treasures to be had in such an understanding of "others" (particularly if I am teaching or mentoring them). Moreover, I believe there is immeasurable wealth to be had in what I might learn about myself along the way.

Notes

1. The research for this chapter was aided by a grant-in-aid from the National Council of Teachers of English; another version of the first half of this chapter appeared in *Rhetoric Review* 13.2 (1995): 409–20.

2. Research validating ASL began with Stokoe's *Sign Language Structure* (1960) and his first ASL dictionary. Bellugi (1980); Lucas (1990); and Woodward (1976, 1980, 1983) have since made major contributions to the linguistic study of ASL.

3. Within Deaf culture, "Deaf" (uppercase *D*) indicates cultural membership and "deaf" (lowercase *d*) denotes only audiological deafness. Hearing children of deaf parents may be "Deaf" but not "deaf," or one may be audiologically "deaf" but not a member of "Deaf" culture.

4. Edward Dolnick's provocative essay on "Deafness as Culture" (1993) illustrates well how visible "Deaf culture" is now.

5. On the thorny issues of deaf education's history, see works by Adler (1969); Brill (1984); VanCleve (1987); Dolnick (1993); Gallaudet (1988); Gannon (1981); Johnson, Liddell, and Erting (1989); Lane (1992); Maybery and Wodlinger-Cohen (1987); Moores and Meadow-Orlans (1990); Sacks (1989); Winefield (1987), and Woodward (1982).

6. Named the "pathological view of deafness" by scholars such as Reagan (1985, 1988a, 1988b, 1990) and Moores (1987a, 1987b) this view focuses clinically on deafness as a debilitating mental and physical handicap rather than attending to cultural aspects of being deaf and using sign languages. Lane's *The Mask of Benevolence* (1992) presents a comprehensive and powerful attack on this view.

7. Others who write on connections between American Deaf culture and ASL include Cohen (1994); Kannapell (1980, 1989); Lane (1992); Neisser (1983); Reagan (1986); and VanCleve and Crouch (1989).

8. Interestingly enough, many hearing children of deaf parents are also considered culturally "Deaf," and thus they too are included in "pure ASL" conversations.

9. Sacks' arguments about ASL, as some members of the Gallaudet community have made clear to me, sometimes approach idealism or romanticism, but many Deaf/deaf people consider them poignant. Readers of *Seeing Voices* should keep in mind that Sacks himself is a "hearie" and that his involvement in Deaf culture and ASL has been recent and marginal.

10. Sacks notes that artists heralded "the dawn of this new [deaf] consciousness" (145). He cites the founding of the National Theater for the Deaf in 1967; the development of Sign wit, song, dance, poetry; and, most noticeable, the development of a "bardic tradition" in Sign, with bards, orators, and storytellers who "transmit[ted] and disseminate[d] the history and culture of the deaf, and, in so doing, raised the cultural consciousness yet higher" (145).

11. Before students can enroll in "official" classes and complete a course of study at Gallaudet University, they are required to pass an "English Placement Test" (the "EPT"). This test has four parts: English vocabulary; reading/comprehension; English grammar/structure; and, most difficult of all, the 150-word writing sample. Students are asked to write 150 words on a topic (typically from a choice of four). The 150 words must, of course, be in "good" English grammar and structure. This causes Gallaudet students great difficulty. They may take the EPT four times, in four consecutive semesters, before they are no longer considered "college material" at Gallaudet and must disenroll. Well over 50 percent of Gallaudet's entering class each year does not pass their first attempt at the EPT. The English 50 class I worked with is a "voluntary" noncredit course in which students who have failed the EPT try to better their English literacy skills. Few students take the test four times—they usually fail the test once or twice and then disappear from campus.

12. Judith Treesberg, the (hearing) mother of one of Gallaudet's deaf students, wrote powerfully of Carl Dupree's death in a February 1991 article in *The Nation*. In September 1991, almost a year after the event, the five security guards were indicted for murder.

13. One feature of Anna's writing is her frequent reference to herself in the second person.

14. Leonard Kelly (1988), researcher at the Gallaudet Research Institute, suggests that this "relative automaticity" is a result of deaf students' lacking the "auditory loop feedback" that hearing writers depend upon.

15. Veda Charrow (1974) argues that these "deafisms" should be viewed as errors committed by nonnative speakers and writers.

16. Had I let categories matter too much, I might not have submitted this chapter for this collection, for "(dis)ability" is frequently left out of the difference triad of race, class, and gender.

5

Going for Broke
Valuing Differences in the Classroom

Renee Moreno

We are in a revolutionary situation, no matter how unpopular that word has become in this country. The society in which we live is desperately menaced . . . from within. So any citizen of this country who figures himself [and herself] as responsible—and particularly those of you who deal with the minds and hearts of young people—must be prepared to "go for broke." Or to put it another way, you must understand that in the attempt to correct so many generations of bad faith and cruelty, when it is operating not only in the classroom but in society, you will meet the most fantastic, the most brutal, and the most determined resistance. There is no point in pretending that this won't happen.

James Baldwin,
"A Talk to Teachers"

How Many More Victims?

I began to write this chapter sometime after my nephew Ramon began to hate school. At the time, he was in the fourth grade at a parochial school in Denver and was failing most of his subjects. My sister was called to school almost daily to deal with Ramon's "discipline problems"—not paying attention, "disruptive" behavior, "talking back."[1] Like others who believe that school systems care for our children, we put most of the blame on Ramon, saying, "You need to try harder in school." We did not understand why Ramon and his teachers conflicted so painfully (for him especially); we only knew that he hated school, did not do his work, and was failing. We only knew that the more he resisted, the more the teachers tried to control him, and the further he slipped away. As the scenario unfolded in meetings with Ramon and his teachers, my sister, and me, I discovered some disturbing issues centering on the pedagogy employed at Ramon's school, where surveillance and control of students' behavior were fundamental.

In these meetings, I also discovered that the teachers were speaking a language different from our family's talk with Ramon, that there was no genuine communication between Ramon and his teachers, and that their classroom language contrasted with the ways I framed language use. For I too had a difficult time communicating with the teachers—especially determining why little else seemed important to them than that Ramon be quiet, behave, and do his school work.[2] Pedagogical differences between my own teaching and theirs were issues as important as communicative differences. Because I had emerged from my graduate education valuing a process pedagogy that respected students' voices, management of Ramon's behavior and the linking of that behavior to his "teachable-ness" were at odds with my ideas of how best to teach. Further, in our family, children are conversational partners with adults, and in my sister's single-parent family, Ramon is certainly his mother's conversational partner. For Ramon, not "talking back" conflicted with tangible realities in his daily life—taking care of his younger sister and being an "adult" with her; *talking to* his mother, his aunts and uncles, his grandmother.

Ramon eventually transferred schools, and I began to wonder what was causing him, and other Chicano students like him, to fail. Ramon's experience reflected an even larger problem—Chicano students are dropping out of school in great numbers, in Denver school systems at least. Reports estimate that Chicano students account for "more than half of all [Denver public schools'] dropouts," and conservative estimates tally the Denver public schools' dropout rate at 45 percent (Cde Baca et al. 1990).

I believed initially that the questions emerging from my interaction with Ramon's teachers and their pedagogies and my research would lead to specific answers. I began this research by asking a very personal question: why was my nephew, Ramon, failing school? Then I revised it with another: why were his teachers failing him? That revised question led to even larger questions: why are so many young Chicanos failing, and why do school systems fail them?

In asking these larger questions I came to examine language issues: whose language *is* spoken in school, and what implications are there when one language, with its set of cultural values, is privileged over other languages—such as the languages of students of color and of working-class students?[3] What are the implications of "attempt[ing] to correct so many generations of bad faith and cruelty" (Baldwin 1988, 3)? These questions forced me to consider my own language for teaching writing, and I asked a question that began a process of unpacking my own pedagogy and its assumptions: What do process researchers/teachers assume about language competencies and language uses in classrooms, in writing, in speaking? How have I been taught to teach composition?

Research for some time has suggested that there is a "clash" between the language competencies that some students bring to classrooms and the expectations that teachers have about language competencies and usage.[4] This clash, though often subtle, leads to students' individual and collective failure. As early as kindergarten, students experience "language mismatches" and "cultural incongruities" that alienate them from their white, middle-class teachers and the system that those teachers represent (Heath 1982). When so many young people of color and young working-class people fail in an educational system, we, as researchers, must examine that system. And as teachers, we "must be prepared to 'go for broke,'" as James Baldwin suggests, by challenging that system before it claims more victims. We must "go for broke" by challenging the paradigms and pedagogies that serve to alienate and control students of color, shortchanging both students and their communities.

I remember a particularly telling example of how imperative it is to "go for broke." My sister, Ramon, and I had a meeting at school during which his teachers floated in and out of the room to complain about what a terrible student he was and, hence, a terrible child. At the end of this meeting—which functioned as a way for his teachers to prove their point about Ramon's being an undisciplined and unskilled student—his English teacher asked him to use the word *switchman* in a "good" sentence. After a deafening silence and through his tears and anger, he defined it in a sentence, which may or may not have been a good one. For his teacher to ask Ramon to perform academically after she and the other teachers had just hurt him (and his mother and me too) was outrageous. More than that, this teacher seemed unaware of all the competencies that she was gauging, all the ways that she was setting Ramon up for failure, and all the ways she had already failed him. Perhaps most important, she was unaware of all the power she was assuming and silencing. This teacher asked Ramon to define what *she* considered a good sentence. Thus, her pedagogy not only required that students fill in the blanks but also (and worse) required them to conform to her standards of language competencies.

At the same time Ramon was struggling in school, I became aware of an increase in violence in our communities when "Karen," a friend of mine, was viciously murdered by an unknown assailant who pumped her small, pregnant body with heroin and left her to die in the street in front of her house. Tragically, Karen's story is a familiar one in urban, working-class communities. At her funeral, the eulogist told of a boy of sixteen murdered the week before—a victim of gang violence—and she asked us to consider how we, as a community, could make sense of the loss of such young people. We *cannot* make sense of it, and we cannot ignore the violence and hope it will go away. "Failure" in school, a lack of education, and violence in our communities *are* related issues. The violence and the hurts may go away, I believe, if we start making more connections with young people and school, if we start validating young people by recognizing their experiences and moving further away from hegemonic classrooms.

Imagine, for a moment, that you are Karen. You go to a high school where the curriculum consists of typing and similar classes that get you through school but don't prepare you for what lies beyond. You are not encouraged. You don't hear your voice in anything you read. You don't hear that half-Spanish, half-English voice of your grandma—who always tells the most incredible stories. In short, you are not validated. You grow up thinking that you are less than those people who are validated. You manage to graduate—even though a few of your best friends drop out—and afterward you accept a menial job. A few of those menial jobs later, you are bored but accept your life as it is. After a while you try putting your life back on track by getting into school. Another typing job gets your bills paid and enrolls you in the local community college. This time you have a goal and can imagine better things for yourself and for your child. But just when you're about to achieve something, someone kills you. You are only twenty-five.

These are dangerous times if you are a person of color. Many young people of color and working-class young people die every day without anyone noticing: they end up in jail; run the risk of unwanted and unexpected pregnancies; drop out of school; or work low-paying, menial jobs. We will not bridge the distance from the classrooms to the streets (Gates 1990) unless we find ways to acknowledge and validate the students we teach—which is not always easy even when we have the best intentions, are most empathetic, and share the same backgrounds. We can begin by recognizing the diversity that makes up our classrooms and adapting to that diversity—along with changing the way we see our students. But in order to change and adapt, we have to examine closely the language used in our classrooms.

Whose Language Is Spoken Here?

In school, students are not merely taught certain language competencies. They are also taught culture, and along with the values of the dominant culture, they are being institutionally socialized. What students bring with them runs the risk of being ignored or undervalued. The consequence, in too many classrooms, is alienation, and the result of that alienation is high dropout rates, illiteracy in communities, victimization, perhaps even early death.

Imagine what it is like to be a Chicano child who has been a conversational partner with an adult and a responsible older sibling, only to be excluded as a conversational partner at school. But not only has the child been a conversational partner, he also has a language that reflects some material realities of life and he possesses coping strategies to deal with those realities (such as talking back, such as resistance). In school, however, teachers tell students to behave, be quiet, and do school work. In school these students become communicative outsiders and undergo an experience similar to the one that Alton Becker (1992) describes in "Silence Across Languages: An Essay," in which he narrates his experiences as a communicative outsider in Java. The silences he experiences are like the gaps in comprehension (those language mismatches and cultural incongruities) that students of color feel in a classroom structured around a culture that gauges competencies in different ways. Becker states that living in a "very different culture, speaking a very different language, feeling [his] identity eroding and reshaping" was a very painful experience (14). A linguist and a literate adult, Becker is aware of what he is experiencing; he is able to reflect on those "painful" experiences and find a language to articulate what is going on. If these are Becker's experiences, imagine what it must be like for students of color during a typical schooling experience, especially for students who may not have access to a language sophisticated enough to name the pain they feel.

In the spring of 1990, a young Chicano student, "Dennis," enrolled in my composition class. He moved hesitantly between his language and the academic language that he heard his teachers and white classmates speak. When I talked to Dennis, we had gaps in communicating with each other; we seemed to have language mismatches that led to our misunderstanding each other—even though I had expected to communicate well with Dennis. He had attended a local Catholic preparatory school and had had the same English teacher that I had had in high school. But these connections did not seem to give us any common ground.

Several times that semester we negotiated my accepting his late papers. Usually he told me in a very roundabout way that he had not finished them. He would say something like, "I attempted to do the paper this weekend. My writing is getting much stronger. I like you as a teacher, and I can really write for you. I practiced working on 'voice' this weekend, but I didn't get too far." When Dennis negotiated with me, I was forced "to read" him via his mannerisms or the tone of his voice because he would not or could not talk to me directly, although I also understood that he was coming from school and ethnic cultures that respect adults (especially teachers), where he did not "talk back."

In many ways, Dennis was caught between two languages—his own and the language of the academy that he heard people around him using—and he tried to negotiate his way through these languages not only in speaking but also in writing. In an informal journal entry written out of class in response to an article he read, he writes:

It is quite nice to have a reading assignment that had to do with child discipline. I have no children of my own but, I have seen my aunts and uncles raise their children. I am the second oldest of eighteen grandchildren in my family. I have changed diapers for probably twelve to fourteen of these kids. I have witnessed a lot of different methods of disciplining these children.

Child discipline is an essential part of the educational process for all children. I feel without discipline in a child[']s life he or she is missing out on learning an idea of what is acceptable behavior and not acceptable behavior. The children do not learn a sense of what is a right and wrong decision. In learning the process of making decisions I feel the children will learn to become independent thinkers and better individuals.

I see several things happening simultaneously in this journal entry, but mostly I get insights and knowledge, perhaps indicating what may be acceptable behavior for subordinates. Since one of the guidelines for the response was also to write about personal experiences, he understood that he needed to write about himself, yet he hesitates, shifting his voice from personal experience to a more objective-sounding voice: "Child discipline is an essential part of the educational process for all children." As I stated before, Dennis was caught between languages, and the result was silence, manifesting itself as undeveloped, late, or incomplete assignments, missed classwork, and potential failure. Dennis did not finish the class, and although I did not fail him, I gave him an incomplete, which he would have to complete with someone else.

In this composition class, I tailored my own practices around a process paradigm and "student-centered" approaches—I tried to put students "in the middle" of my class (Atwell 1987). I expected that students and I would work through our silences, that together we would negotiate our way around the language of the academy and their at-home, at times "private," language. I tried to value and nurture students' own voices by inserting personal experiences into writing tasks. But what sort of assumptions does a process teacher make when teaching students of color? What does a teacher have to do to validate and encourage students of color in a system that is already hostile to them? Is the process paradigm really "the fix" for these students?

On the surface the process paradigm—with its emphasis on empowering students and validating "other" (presumably "different") voices, with its "human-centered" definitions of writing as "somebody-talking-to-somebody-else-about-something"—would seem more accessible to students of color. But in many ways it is not. When I examined the theory of the process paradigm, I first questioned who articulates process theory and what assumptions process researchers make about language competency and language use. Many of the "canonical" researchers used in teacher training seminars have been white males—Elbow (1981), Murray (1982), Moffett (1983), Stafford (1978), Graves (1983), Britton et al. (1975)—and their theories make assumptions that may not be true for these students: namely, that classrooms are "free and easy spaces"[5] and that writing is a "level playing field" onto which students and teachers enter as "equals," where power is indeed open for negotiation.[6] How much power can students of color have in a classroom when their early language experiences have not been valued? Did Dennis really believe me when I said to him "find, use, and develop your own voice"? Why should he believe me, especially when he understands these power differentials? Dennis and students like him already hesitate and assume a position of subordination vis-à-vis teachers. They have been trained, as Ramon's teachers were so bent on training him, to behave, be quiet, and do school work, which too often consists of mimeographed work-sheets or typing classes. It is not reasonable to expect these students to embrace the "free and easy" structure of a process teacher.

In retrospect, I wonder how Dennis could have understood something such as Stafford's "A Way of Writing" (1978), which I used as part of an assignment: "Along with initial receptivity, then, there is another readiness: I must be willing to fail. If I am to keep on writing, I cannot bother to insist on high standards. I must get into action and not let anything stop me, or even slow me" (18). Failure to Dennis (just as it was to my sister, Ramon, and me) is very different from failure to Stafford. Students of color, whose language strategies adapt to someone else's ideas of "good," rarely cast fail-ing as a positive learning experience as Stafford does; failing is often humil-iating and reflects on students' self-esteem and sense of self-worth.

Like Becker learning a new language in Java, students of color learn to speak a different language in classrooms. This language can alienate and yet have very real meaning to them.[7] And it is through this learning of a new language that students, as did Becker, begin to have their identities eroded and reshaped—for better and for worse. It is through this "new language" that we give students the message that learning our academic language is imperative to their success (which it is), but we ought also to enlarge our discourse community to include their language. We don't want to render them "speechless," an effect of academic language that Michelle Cliff (1988) describes in her essay "A Journey into Speech," nor do we want them to fail by hiding power relations. We instead want to make power relations more visible because then writers can learn to mix forms, co-opt style, find ways to bridge and mix the languages of school and home. By teaching students to turn language to their own purpose, we are acknowledging and validating them, their voices, and the differences they bring to our classrooms.

I have had some success with "co-opting style" and with "mixing forms." In one Writing Workshop II course, for example, a Chicana student, Valerie, wrote an essay, "La Cultura Perdida" (The Lost Culture), that told the story of her grandmother:

Grandma was a big woman, not fat but tall and big-boned. Grandma was forever cooking and there was an eternal aroma of chilé verde that filled the air of her home. She miraculously always had enough food to feed anyone who happened to stop in. Closing my eyes, I can see her standing over her stove wearing her cotton apron that was a part of her everyday wardrobe and her white hair pulled neatly back into a bun. . . . She was a tough woman. It was her way or no way and I believe my grandfather, a quiet green-eyed Spaniard, knew this before he married her. How could he not? The whole San Luis Valley knew that she had almost killed a [white] man in her youth for trespassing on her land. . . .

[Her] stubbornness brings to mind a story about disagreement she and my father had for many years. My father, who was very proud of his culture and ancestry, overheard my grandmother telling somebody she was not of Indian descent.

So he confronted her by asking, "Grandma," he called her grandma out of respect and because that was what she liked to be called. "You look Indian. What tribe are you from?"

Furiously she answered, "Soy Española!"

"Grandma, how can you be Spanish? You're not from Spain," he would say.

"Sí, soy!" She would bark.

"Okay, if you are Spanish, how come you look Indian?"

"Este diablo Mexicano! Mis padres eran de España," she retaliated. Then she would proudly pull out her old photographs, and there stood my great-grandfather with two long black braids hanging on each side of his face and a black hat with a red band around it. One of my aunts said he was of Navajo descent.

After looking at the pictures, my father would laugh and teasingly say, "Yes, Grandma, maybe I am a Mexican devil but if your father was from Spain, he sure dresses and looks like an American Indian. . . ."

Writing this story allowed Val to express a side of her life that was absent from the public space of a classroom and allowed her to tell the story in a voice that combined both Spanish and English—something she in the past had to save for Spanish class (and only marginally was this mixing allowed there). Val was able to transgress the margins of this classroom and insert her own reality into a space not normally her own.

Resistance to Differences

Every time I read Baldwin's "A Talk to Teachers," I am surprised that he wrote it in 1963, for it describes in many ways what is happening now, when we seek to change a system that fails, by way of exclusive language and cultural practices, to recognize people of color. I came face-to-face with the resistance Baldwin alludes to when I taught ethnic literature and students asked why I was "distinguishing" literature written by people of color from literature written by white, canonical writers. In my attempt to correct "silence," the absence of texts and voices by people of color, I encountered resistance to accepting cultural differences and validating "different" experiences. "We are all the same," a white student said, "these are stories about the human condition." Such resistance initially surprised me, for I had expected them to accept that the texts we read were different, that the voices were something they had not heard before.

The resistance from my ethnic literature students, who were predominantly white, is the same resistance that I encountered from Dan, a white graduate student with whom I discussed the dropout problem. Dan stated that "Hispanic" parents often pay little more than lip service to supporting their children's pursuit of an education. He commented that at an alternative high school where he taught, Chicanas were encouraged by their parents to have children rather than to get an education. Chicano parents often get a bad rap regarding the importance of education; however, in the 1989 Hispanic Agenda Poll conducted by *LARASA,* a community research organization in Denver, Chicano parents identified education as a primary concern in their communities (Hero 1990). Chicano parents *are* aware of the importance of education but are suspicious of the system, of the results when "goodwill" and history clash. I wanted to tell Dan that one of the values of Latino culture is family. And when a system, like school, has consistently failed the parents of these students—and possibly these parents' parents—a natural response would be to question the value of that system.

A Final Word

I have done two things in this chapter. First, I've told a number of stories about my nephew and about students I have taught in the past, and second, I've framed those stories in terms of the process of self-reflexivity, unpacking the assumptions of teaching. I realize that by telling these students' stories and unpacking my own teaching I cannot make claims about all students. The students in our classes come from diverse backgrounds and orientations; sometimes these backgrounds and orientations conflict strongly with our own. They come into our classrooms with all sorts of levels of preparedness and unpreparedness. They come with coping strategies that resist erasure of their *selves*—approaches to learning that require teachers, I argue, to interpret, understand, *and* adapt, approaches, moreover, that require changes in teaching for which we may not be prepared.

And although I *am* telling individual stories, about individual students I have taught—even my own story of uncovering a process, of peeling back layers of epistemologies, is a personal one—to read these simply as individual stories is to miss an important point, for it was such a reading that prevented Ramon's teacher from recognizing her own complicity in teaching methods that alienated him in her classroom. These stories do speak to larger social and pedagogical contexts; these stories, like Karen's story, are about individual pain, but they are also about communal pain, about why certain peoples are victimized again and again by particular institutions. Ramon's story is our story as young Chicanos—so is Dennis' and Karen's, just as Ramon's teacher's story and even Dan's is the story of other teachers. Ramon's teacher's blindness prevented her from seeing how she participated in larger systems of oppression. Although I am critical of this teacher, I am also aware of how easily blindness happens. An unwitting complicity, I think, easily gets worked into daily acts, into acceptance of pedagogical models, especially when these go unexamined.

And although there is much I can say about the tensions within the stories themselves, I want to make an argument about connecting stories to the material conditions of people's lives. I want to connect the discursive practices of, say, defining *switchman* in a good sentence to the little boy (now almost a man) crying because he's hurt. I am suggesting that in academic institutions we privilege discursive practices without connecting those practices to materiality, to "the minds and hearts of young people" (Baldwin 1988) or to their experiences, their pain.

Yet another part of my argument is about language use in classrooms and the need to examine from whom we as teachers learn. This kind of examination, I argue, is significant, for when I turned the gaze upon myself, my teaching, my own assumptions, all sorts of issues arose—one being how (and by whom) the composition theory I subscribed to is articulated. The materiality embodied in that canonical composition theory is of white, middle-class, heterosexual males, and the discursive practices they advocate are based on assumptions about teaching, learning, writing, and schooling that grow out of their experiences. Preparing ourselves to go for broke also means including "other voices" in constructing canons and theories that grow out of these "other" experiences. Enlarging this discourse community invites multiple ways of knowing into composition theory, including those conveyed in the early language and schooling experiences related in autobiographies and biographies of people of color. But I also mean understanding the material existence of peoples, which translates into the pain of living in a culture of domination, the pain of participating in institutions that don't intend for certain peoples to survive, much less succeed. I also realize that to embrace what I am proposing means encountering resistance from privileged and comfortable students and no doubt from the powerful.

Finally, inquiry into complex pedagogical questions such as the dropout problem and complex social issues such as violence often requires receptivity to additional questions that seemingly have no answers. Questions of "how-to" educate become increasingly complex when we consider marginalized, oppressed people or when we realize that what we do as scholars and teachers does have potential to affect the lives of people we love—like Ramon, Karen, Dennis, and Valerie. To oversimplify pedagogies, or even the problems that students bring to schools, is to run the risk of replicating certain social dysfunctions in our own classrooms. To some extent, the answers lie in the process itself—of embracing conflict, of critically examining how we teach, and of recognizing the material conditions of people's lives—a truly revolutionary approach.

Notes

1. See bell hooks' *Talking Back* (1989) for a redefinition of "talking back." hooks writes about the danger of talking back to those with power—speaking about and naming honestly power relations—something that is punishable, and about the liberatory nature of talking back.

2. Certainly what I was valuing and what I wanted those teachers to value was my nephew. My feelings for him as a developing human being, a boy growing to manhood, a young Chicano maturing in a racist society could not be separated from how I as a teacher was also seeing him, something Baldwin alludes to in the epigraph.

3. See *Decolonising the Mind: The Politics of Language in African Literature* by Ngugi wa Thiong'o (1986). Ngugi argues that when one language with its cultural values is privileged over another, what emerges is a colonized mind.

4. See Shirley Brice Heath (1982, 1983); John U. Ogbu (1985); Susan U. Philips (1982, 1972); and Geneva Smitherman (1986). For narrative accounts of the clash between students' home language and school language, see Michelle Cliff (1988); bell hooks (1989); Gloria Anzaldua (1987); and Richard Rodriguez (1982) (although the split Rodriquez writes about between public and private language must continue to be dismantled and critiqued).

5. In the published version of "Desire and Power: A Feminist Perspective," Catherine MacKinnon (1988) includes comments she received from Gayatri Spivak after oral delivery of the essay, which "unpacks" the "rhetorical style of an address to an audience" and its grounding in male power. Spivak states:

> I would like to talk about the insistence, in the United States, on adjudicating freedom by rearranging the furniture or turning lecture sessions into town meetings. It is always Americans who pretend that they can be free in a completely structured situation. But I . . . think that history is stronger than benevolence and thus that there is a problem with authority that disguises itself as being permissive. (In MacKinnon 1988, 117.)

Spivak speaks to the problem I see with pedagogies that normalize power through benevolent gestures of "goodwill." As Spivak says, "history is stronger than benevolence," something to which people of color can attest, something schooling experiences reinforce over and over again.

6. Note the use of journals and expressive writing in process-oriented classrooms, which can expose students' vulnerabilities without interrogating power structures (between student and teacher, student and institution), while creating classroom spaces wherein things such as failure, risk taking, and experimentation are inherent to learning—things that early schooling experiences probably did not encourage *or* perhaps discouraged by means of punishment or degradation.

7. Ngugi (1986) states: "Berlin of 1884 [when Africa was divided into colonies] was effected through the sword and the bullet. But the night of the sword and the bullet was followed by the morning of the chalk and the blackboard. The physical violence of the battlefield was followed by the psychological violence of the classroom" (9).

6

Danger Zones
Risk and Resistance in the Writing Histories of Returning Adult Women

Anne Aronson

What validates us as human beings, validates us as writers.
Gloria Anzaldua

In 1973 I was seventeen years old and on the college market. At that time, several men's colleges in the Northeast were just beginning to accept women. I decided to apply to one, and I was notified that my interview would be in a hotel suite in New York City, where I lived. This interview was with two or three men, and I remember them sitting together behind a table or a counter; I was alone on the other side. Most of the interview was uneventful. I answered their questions about my academic and extracurricular interests, favorite books, and so on. At the end of the interview, however, one of the men leaned back in his chair and "confessed" to me one of his concerns. He said that the problem with having women students at the college was that women in general tend to enter college with strong records, but then decline in academic performance as they progress through their undergraduate years. He looked at me wistfully, hoping I would not be the type to repeat this fall from intellectual grace. I don't remember what I *said* in response to his comments (probably nothing). But I do remember that I *felt* terrified, terrified that my academic performance had indeed peaked, as this man indicated, and that I was looking ahead to a life of failure. I also felt a breath of anger somewhere inside of me, but I could not isolate it from the terror, nor identify its origin. His comment confirmed a suspicion, shared (I know now) by many women, that my success to that point had been lucky, tenuous, even fraudulent.

The story of my college interview would not seem to be a story about writing. But today, as I inch my way through this chapter, I meet the ghost of this interview again and again. Sometimes I stare at the hunched silhouette in my computer screen and see a shadow full of shortcomings, a shadow engendered by events like that interview from more than twenty years ago. For me the interview was a danger zone—a site where my identity as a woman placed me at considerable psychological risk. These danger zones pervade the lives of many socially disadvantaged peoples; they are artifacts of gender, class, race, and other hierarchies that shape the material and emotional well-being of those at both the top and the bottom. For many, the act of writing is itself a danger zone. Linda Brodkey (1989) says that writers who hold a central and powerful position within a discourse experience themselves as *speakers* of that discourse; in contrast, those at the margins of a discourse experience themselves as *spoken by* discourse. To be spoken by discourse—to feel that one's intentions, one's meanings, one's self are shaped by a powerful discourse—is to occupy a danger zone. Writers have begun to chronicle what it means to inhabit danger zones. Jane Tompkins (1987), for example, describes her anguish as a woman writing through "the screen of a forced language"—the patriarchal discourse of literary scholarship (174). Patricia J. Williams (1991) describes how her personal account of a racist experience, written for a law review, was savagely rewritten by the editors; at one point the editors argued that mention of her race—she is African American—was irrelevant to the article. In *Textual Orientations: Lesbian and Gay Students and the Making of Discourse Communities*, Harriet Malinowitz (1995) demonstrates how much current composition pedagogy—including, for example, the ongoing emphasis on personal writing—pose numerous dangers for gay and lesbian students.

These accounts of what it means to write and read within danger zones gain much of their power from their situatedness in everyday experience. Feminist scholars have long advocated for research that centers on the experience of women. Such research, says Dorothy Smith (1979), locates "our enterprises with knowers whose perspective is organized by exactly how it is they are outside [social] structures, how they are excluded from participation, what their concrete situation is, and its relations to the ruling apparatus" (151). Feminists in many academic fields have become interested in collecting and interpreting women's life stories, whether spoken orally or written down in letters, journals, memoirs, and autobiographies. These stories emphasize the rich and complex interaction of the individual with society. In the case of writing and reading, this complexity suggests that the meaning of literacy in an individual's life will not be determined by any single set of contextual "variables," but will emerge out of many interwoven contextual factors, including the historical moment, race, class, gender, disability, sexual orientation, age, family, school, and work, as well as the context in which a story is told. Studying the individual story allows us to trace the *relationship* among contextual factors, for example, the ways in which race/ethnicity, class, and gender mutually construct one another.

If such research were to become the norm, we would no longer read and hear about students who are assumed, without comment, to be white, middle class, twenty years old, heterosexual, and without disability. We would no longer read the articles of teachers and researchers whose own gender, class identity, and race/ethnicity would be rendered invisible. Instead, we would be exposed routinely to the contingencies of difference. The knowledge produced in any study would then be what Donna Haraway (1991) calls "situated knowledge," a limited, partial knowledge located in the selves of individuals who daily live the realities of power, privilege, difference, and oppression. Much of this knowledge would be constructed through narrative, the stories students and teachers tell about themselves not only as readers and writers, but also as lovers, daughters, sons, parents, workers, travelers, and friends. We would come to understand that literacy is forever embedded in the personal and social histories of readers and writers.

A Study of Returning Adult Women

This chapter examines how danger zones figure in the writing histories of one group of writers: women aged twenty-five and older who have returned to college after several years away from a formal educational setting. I chose to examine this group for several reasons. Most important, I believed that reentry women were a highly self-reflexive group of students who would be able to speak articulately about the relationship between their lives and their writing. I believed this because many returning students are in school as a result of a major change in their lives; these changes have prompted them to reconsider many things—their personal and professional goals, their relationships, their gender and class identities, and so on. I also chose this group of students because they have been virtually ignored within the composition literature.[1] The only time I ever heard about reentry women and writing was when teachers talked about how wonderful it was to have these articulate, mature individuals in their classes to enliven discussion. I knew that there was more to the story, however—that these women often faced enormous barriers in returning to school and completing their undergraduate educations. I also knew that returning adult women are a large and growing constituency within higher education; in 1990, reentry women accounted for 48 percent of all women in higher education, and 26 percent of all students (*Projection of Education Statistics* 1995).

In order to learn about danger zones in the writing histories of returning adult women, I interviewed in depth eight women attending or recently graduated from a midwestern Catholic women's college known for its programs for returning adult women. Participants included women from both low-income and middle-income backgrounds; African American, Mexican American, and white women; lesbian, bisexual, and heterosexual women; and women with and without learning disabilities. I questioned study participants principally about their histories as writers, but I also asked them about their identities as students, daughters, partners, workers, and so on. My goal was to understand more about what constituted a danger zone for marginal writers. I wanted to know why women feel disempowered in some writing situations. I also wanted to know how they resisted the dangers they encountered as writers. My assumption was that women's stories not only instantiate the effects of social hierarchies, but also reveal individual agency. I believed that women who have been damaged by dominant discourses can resist the discursive practices that oppress them, and thereby they can empower themselves as writers.

Danger Zones: Two Case Studies

In order to illustrate how participants in this study of returning adult women experience danger zones in their writing, I have chosen to focus on two women who clearly articulate how, at various points in their histories, they have been disempowered as writers. For Ginny, a white woman from a working-class background, writing and reading were most dangerous in her family of origin, in which her efforts at literacy were routinely ridiculed. For Rashida, a black lesbian, a friendship with a white, heterosexual man provided a danger zone for her writing. In each case, the experiences described here occurred before the women returned to college. But in each case, these experiences had a considerable impact on how the participants viewed themselves later as writers, both in and out of academic settings.

Ginny

Ginny was thirty-five years old when I interviewed her. She is white and comes from what she describes as a "lower-income, blue-collar" family in a small southern town. Her mother, who died when Ginny was ten, worked in a factory; her father is a trucker and a carpenter. Ginny married after finishing high school; worked as a waitress, a cashier, and a nurse's aide; and had three children before returning to school. She was divorced from her husband, a groundskeeper with a high school degree, shortly after entering the Catholic women's college. She graduated shortly after I met her, with a double major in English and philosophy. Ginny sees herself as a writer; she writes poems and fiction, and she was seeking a career in editing when I interviewed her.[2] Literacy, however, was not a central value in her home when she was growing up.

> It kind of makes me feel bad because some writers that you read about have always had pen in hand. But we talked before about my family background and that sort of thing wasn't really valued a lot. . . . It didn't occur to me that that was a possibility [to be a writer]. And there were times when I had done things for classes or certain pieces of work and I wouldn't mention it to my parents or anything because I didn't think that it would be important or that it would matter. And so I didn't. I just kind of kept it to myself and would just do the work and there were times when it did get attention from the instructor for something and I'd just you know, downplay it a lot. . . .
>
> And I know I had mentioned that my dad just always thought that kind of thing was silly. (What sort of thing?) Writing. It just wasn't concrete enough to him. . . . (What kinds of things did he value?) Things that were more secure, things that he could see a guarantee in money, a monetary return or something like that. I don't think that he was able to see a nurturing or the value in something that just made you feel good you know, like it makes me feel satisfied to write. And I don't think that he would see the value there or the usefulness. . . . When I was learning to read and we would have assignments to read out loud and things like that, I remember my dad would kind of chastise a bit if I was too dramatic with reading. . . .
>
> [My dad's] a carpenter and truck driver. He's pretty talented in things but I don't think he ever works to his potential you know. He's got a lot of potential that he wastes or has wasted—his carpentry and skills. He's really creative and he'll make things for friends and things like that but he doesn't commercialize it and I'm not sure what the reason is because there have been times when the family could have used the money you know. . . .
>
> I did enjoy letter writing. I wrote lots of letters to my friends so I think that was my path for writing, because that seemed OK, writing letters to friends. (What didn't seem OK, as opposed to what?) Well, poetry or short stories or something like that. . . . I guess I just think that the other stuff would have been sort of, I think my dad would have mocked it, poetry and fiction. And so my creativity could come out in my letter writing to my friends because that's very private you know.

At the heart of this account is Ginny's father's belief that writing is not a worthwhile activity for his daughter. At various points Ginny says that her father "chastised," "reprimanded," and "mocked" her, calling her writing and reading "silly." Years later, when Ginny was married, she encountered the same kind of ridicule from her husband: "I did a lot of reading, but my husband, it seemed like he enjoyed making fun of the things that I would choose to read."

In Ginny's mind, the ridicule and shaming she experienced when she engaged in literacy derived in part from her class identity. Identifying her father as blue collar, Ginny describes him as a man who did not value activities that simply made one "feel good"; there had to be some "concrete" outcome, specifically monetary gain. The irony is that, according to Ginny's account, he did precisely what he told Ginny she should not do; he was a carpenter who made things for friends without asking for any money in return. Ginny's father gave his daughter a double message; he modeled a behavior—doing creative work without pay—but ridiculed his daughter when she engaged in similar behavior. Ginny's father's creative endeavors may have opened up the possibility of writing for Ginny, but his verbal rejection of her experiments with literacy shut the door tight. His contradictory behavior may be due in part to the difference between carpentry and literacy. While both activities bring a kind of personal fulfillment to those engaged in them, writing and reading as community values may be associated in Ginny's father's mind with a more privileged social class in a way that carpentry is not. Ginny's attachment to writing may have seemed threatening to her father's identity, authority, and feelings of self-worth.

Ginny's interest in literacy may also have threatened both her father and her husband because of the interplay of gender and class dynamics in her personal history. She describes her father as the kind of "domineering male" typical of her small southern town. When she finished high school, he told her that college wasn't important for women. She says of her husband:

> He's I guess a lot more like my father than I realized or wanted him to be. Real stifling and dominating male. And somehow he had the attitude that his opinions were more important. . . . He didn't value education and stuff too much either. I think he felt intimidated by it, and that it was a put down to him for me to return to school. Because if I had tried to talk about things that I was learning in class, he took it that I was trying to show him up and be superior to him, which is a shame.

Her stories suggest that her attempts at fulfilling her needs for creative and intellectual expression and personal growth were particularly suspect in the male-dominated working class environment she grew up in and stayed in when she married. Like another participant, whose husband became jealous when she talked about returning to school, Ginny found that her pursuit of literacy and education threatened both the class and gender identities of her husband and her father.

The outcomes of Ginny's early experiences of ridicule and shame around writing are predictable. She describes how she "downplayed" her successes with writing at school and learned that her academic efforts simply weren't important. Ginny free-wrote about an incident in sixth grade in which she destroyed a piece of writing:

> Once in about sixth grade we had been asked to prepare speeches for some national contest. After delivering mine, I immediately returned to my desk and ripped it into tiny pieces. Later, the class voted mine one of the best and wanted to hear it again in order to choose a finalist, but of course there had only been one copy.

Like many women in this study, Ginny turned the messages she received from her environment inward. Having been ridiculed as a small child for reading aloud to her father, she learned to reject her own efforts at reading and writing. Although she had an early interest in writing, she decided not to pursue it as a hobby or career until she entered college, ten years after she graduated from high school.

Rashida

Rashida was thirty-two years old when I interviewed her. She grew up in an African American neighborhood in Kansas City, and went to a Catholic school for black girls. She identifies her background as "Afro-Cuban and lower-middle/working class." Her mother, a high school graduate, was a building custodian; her father, also a high school graduate, was frequently unemployed and absent from the family for most of Rashida's life. After graduating from high school, Rashida chose to go into the military rather than to college. In the eighties she returned to school to get an A.S. degree from a community college in Kansas City. She then moved to Minnesota and began work toward a degree in psychology and social work at the Catholic women's college. Rashida was living with her lesbian "partner-in-life" when I interviewed her. Rashida plans to earn a living as a psychologist, although she considers herself a professional writer. She had published one autobiographical piece in a book, and she was planning to publish a fantasy story when I met her. Her experiences of danger zones as a writer began when she was in the military.

> When I was in the Army, I was in the public affairs branch for a while and did a lot of writing. . . . I was writing stories, and there is a friend of mine, we call ourselves twins, who is like ten years older than me and white, but we had the same birthday. So we were twins. And he and I were on the paper together. . . . I was writing a story at the time. It was kind of a fantasy thing . . . kind of post-holocaust women's community type thing and I showed it to him. He was also an author, he was a published author. He did

some work for a heavy metal magazine and a book of his was published. So we were good friends and I respected his views a lot. . . . But I was writing this story, I showed it to him, I made the mistake of showing it to him because it was very—that was also the time I was coming out, so it was very lesbian—and also a bad time, because at the time I was having an affair with his ex-wife . . . and he knew about it, and that was supposed to be cool. But he ripped that story to shreds. And a lot of what he was ripping was that it was men-hating, da da da.

So I was crushed. I didn't want to show anything personal of mine again and I still struggle with that. It is very hard for me. . . . Showing it means putting myself out, exposing myself to be ripped apart. I put myself in the story, I've put myself in stories before and it's gotten ripped apart. . . . (Was the story explicitly lesbian?) Yes, very much so. And he freaked and then I freaked. And I respected him. . . . And I didn't think he would react the way he did. (Is it particularly what you're afraid of, is it being responded to as a lesbian, or is it other stuff?) It's just being ripped apart like that. I'm very comfortable with my sexuality and all that. I don't mind talking about it at all. But I just felt like I was ripped to shreds, my self personally, ripped to shreds. So that is the fear that lingers today. . . .

(So the thing with that guy in the service, that was a big turning point?) Yeah. That was a major blow. And it stopped me writing for several years—period. I mean I wouldn't write a letter to myself. . . . I was crunched. Crushed.

Rashida relentlessly uses metaphors of violence to characterize this event in which a friend brutally criticized something she had written. She uses the terms "ripped apart" or "ripped to shreds" six times in this passage alone; at one point she says it wasn't simply the story that was ripped apart, "but my self personally." Rashida talks about being "crunched" and "crushed" by her friend's criticism, and about how the event was a "major blow" to her. She interprets her friend's judgment of her writing as an act of violence which she experiences emotionally and even physically.

The power differences between Rashida and the man who degraded her work are stunning. He is white, straight, male, published, and ten years older than she. It was apparently the "man-hating" quality of her lesbian fantasy story that so irritated him. Such a reaction is blatantly homophobic, probably sexist, and possibly racist. Rashida is a highly resilient woman, who says she is not "the type of person to just sit back and let things happen" to her. The psychological impact of this event is so severe, however, that she cannot write fiction for several years. Even now, she says, the thought of showing her stories to anyone is "terrifying." Her account illustrates how those with authority and power have the ability to silence someone as resistant as Rashida. That silencing occurs in part because Rashida, like many women, people of color, and lesbians, is conditioned to need the approval of those with power. As a writer she naturally seeks the approval of a published author, but she has little opportunity to receive feedback from authors who are African American, female, and/or lesbian.

The stories returning adult women told me about their writing are fraught with experiences of disempowerment. Participants talk about how their ideas and forms of expression were stifled, their meanings altered, their efforts ridiculed, their texts the subject of violence. Writing, as the stories illustrate, is a site where dominant constructions of gender, race, class, disability, and sexual orientation are reproduced or resisted. In these stories, dominant constructions prevail. A lesbian is called a man-hater; a working-class child is deterred from pursuing her talents. These experiences effectively silence participants; the women stop writing, develop poor self-images as writers, or learn to accommodate to norms while sacrificing their own intentionality and agency as writers. Occurring in family and school contexts, each experience is shaped differently, reflecting the particular web of social relations in which it occurs. Writing is dangerous, in part because these women write from positions of subordination or marginalization. To write as a woman, as a person of color, as learning disabled, as a lesbian is to risk the same kind of degradation that one would risk in any number of other arenas.

While the social construction of gender, race, and other hierarchies plays a central role in participants' experience of danger zones, my interviews suggest that another issue is at play. Many participants expressed the belief that writing—academic and nonacademic alike—embodies the self. One participant, for example, repeatedly stated that her "self is on the line" when she writes, whether she's writing a journal entry or a scientific paper. Another said that writing is "so darn exposing. . . . It makes you vulnerable because each piece has to stand alone." Other participants felt dissatisfied with writing that does not embody the self; one woman describes a paper that she says improved as she revised it because "it became more me." The problem with a belief in writing as a window on the self is that writing becomes a site where the self can be damaged by overtly or covertly hostile audiences and discourse communities. At stake is participants' basic sense of self-worth, and more specifically their sense of competence and authority as knowers, thinkers, and language users. If they were to treat writing more as a game— a place to enact diverse personae, play with language, and persuade audiences—then writing might not prove to be so potent a danger zone. Experiences of disempowerment figure so prominently in participants' writing histories, then, not only because the culture they write in is indeed inhospitable, but also because they believe so strongly in the proximity of writing to self. While I honor this identification of writing and self in the women I interviewed and promote it to some extent in my classroom, I envision a second, alternative scene of writing; in this vision, writing is a site where language is treated experimentally, playfully, even sportively—writing is a site where the personal and emotional stakes of composing are low, where writing cannot become a danger zone.

Paths of Resistance

In the remainder of this chapter I explore the strategies used by returning adult women in this study to resist the damaging effects of writing within danger zones. I understand resistance to be a process by which individuals or groups oppose dominant constructions of race, gender, class, sexual orientation, ability/disability, age, and so on. Kathleen Weiler (1988), a feminist who draws on the radical education theory of Henry Giroux and Stanley Aronowitz, identifies resistance with what she calls "production theory." Production theorists, she says:

> are concerned with the ways in which both individuals and classes assert
> their own experience and contest or resist the ideological and material
> forces imposed upon them in a variety of settings. . . . These theorists . . .
> are concerned in varying degrees with the social construction of knowledge
> and the ways in which dominant forms of language and knowledge can be
> critiqued and made problematic. (11)

I use the term *resistance* in a broad sense to include all acts that defy the damaging effects of dominant ideologies. These acts may be conscious or unconscious, individual or collective; they may be deliberate efforts to change the system or survival tactics executed without political self-awareness. This is not to say that I don't make distinctions between these different acts of resistance. I have chosen, however, to cast a wide net in defining resistance because I believe it is important for educators to build on all evidence of resistance among students, not just those examples that seem to match our own political position at a given moment.

Two paths of resistance stand out in stories that returning adult women told me about their writing. The first is to control the environments in which one writes so that self-disclosure is safe, or alternatively to limit the degree to which one self-discloses in writing when the environment is potentially dangerous. The second is to write directly out of one's multiple identities and, in so doing, to make the very identities that endanger women and other oppressed groups into assets. In exploring these paths of resistance, I again focus on Ginny and Rashida.

Self-Disclosure and Audience

The paradox that participants' stories evoke again and again is that writing is at once most meaningful and most dangerous when the self is at the center. One of the strategies that participants use to reduce the danger of writing is to establish a kind of "writing space" in which they are free to write about

the self. For many, this space is a journal or other form of private writing.
The journal serves as a sanctuary in which the dangers of a hostile audience
are minimized (if not eliminated). [3] Rashida, for example, says that when she
encounters an injustice in her daily life (such as a racist incident), she often
chooses to write in her journal:

> When I'm in a hard situation like that, sometimes I would react and con-
> front verbally, but there are times that if I don't feel like it's safe, I won't
> say anything, but I go home and write about it, and that feels a lot safer to
> me because I can put that writing out there and let it talk.
>
>   (What makes it safer than letting it out in the situation itself?) Because
> there are times when for me as a woman of color it is not safe to directly
> confront someone. The Klan was beginning to come back when I was at
> home [in Kansas] and it's a good idea not to—just to survive, I think. So
> this is my way of doing it.

When I began this project, I had, like many other writing teachers and
feminists, become weary of journals. As a writing teacher, I had forgotten
what to do with personal journals—how to grade and respond to them, even
how to justify their place in a writing class. As a feminist, I had become suspicious of their intensely self-reflexive nature because they seemed to privilege thought over action. After talking to reentry women, however, I am once
again convinced of the importance of journals in women's lives. One participant put it rather dramatically when she said that journal writing "saved my
ass." Cinthia Gannett (1992), who has studied women's journals both historically and in contemporary composition classes, says that journals have
enabled women to "discover themselves as subjects, learn how to work
through language to inscribe themselves onto the world textually, and learn
to listen to their own voices and experience" (149). Usually a private or
semiprivate form of discourse, the journal liberates participants from the
damaging judgments of a hostile audience while relieving them of most discursive restrictions.

Even when participants are producing forms of discourse more public
than the journal, they often take steps to ensure that the wrong people do not
read their texts. Ginny, for example, is "guarded" about her writing. She lives
in a large house with several roommates: "I won't write out at the dining
room table if there are a lot of people in the house because then if I get up
and leave, my writing is there and I don't want anybody to see it." Rashida
describes how her sister used to read her writing before Rashida was ready
to show it. Now she is careful not to show her writing to anyone until she
feels ready to have it read.

Another method of minimizing the dangers of writing is to disempower
a potentially damaging audience. Participants often stop writing or develop
low self-esteem as writers when a hostile audience deprecates their writing.
Their stories suggest that this audience can become internalized so that it is

invoked when participants attempt to write, even when the real, addressed audience is friendly. Participants sometimes spook the ghost, however, by either reconceptualizing or discounting this internalized, hostile audience. Ginny has learned to discount her family as audience. She says, "I tell myself I'm writing it and if my family ever reads any of my work then it will be their problem to deal with their hang-ups. I'm doing my job and I'm doing it to the best of my ability and if they're offended, it's not my problem."

A final strategy participants use to negotiate the hazards of writing is to choose the extent to which they disclose themselves in writing. In most school and workplace situations, we do not have a choice about who reads our work. We do have a choice, however, about how much of ourselves we wish to risk disclosing in writing. Ginny says that when she is doing creative writing for "nonwriters" she is not as "revealing." She defines "nonwriters" as people who do not "bring a certain amount of understanding" and education to their reading. When writing for these readers, she does not "tend to go out on a limb as much and be as free with my writing style." Ginny's story about her current struggles with self and audience reminds me of her comments about how she was punished for her interest in literacy as a child and young adult. In holding back from "nonwriters," she may be protecting herself from readers like her father and husband who ridiculed her for attaching importance to literacy.

Although Rashida suffered the consequences of writing within a danger zone as a young adult, she had already developed strategies of resistance as a child. As a young girl, she used to write "hot, steamy" love letters for male friends to send to their girlfriends. The story is an interesting twist on the Cyrano de Bergerac tale: "[This guy] liked this girl and was scared to death to talk to her. And he wanted to tell her all these mushy things and he couldn't bring himself to write it. So I sat there with him and his sisters were around giggling and carrying on and I sat there and wrote this letter. And she loved it." Although Rashida says that she had not identified herself as a lesbian at the time, the incident reads like a surreptitious coming-out story. By placing her voice, her sentiments, her sexual feelings in the body of another, Rashida was able to write with her own intentionality without invoking any of the emotional and physical risks of being a young lesbian in a homophobic culture. Her strategy of "ghost writing" is something like the strategy of nineteenth-century women writers who published under male pseudonyms; in both cases, the writers disguise themselves in order to "speak discourse."

Managing Multiple Identities

Numerous feminists have theorized identity not as singular, but as multiple and often conflicted. Sociologist Patricia Hill Collins (1986), for example, writes about how her identity as an African American woman makes her an

academic outsider, while her status as an intellectual (which is closely associated with middle-class identity) makes her an insider.[4] Study participants
experienced similar conflicts. In Ginny's case, her gender identity, working-
class identity, and white identity, and her identity as a student at a private
liberal arts college place her in uneven and unequal positions with respect to
the dominant culture; while her identities as a working-class woman put her
at risk within the dominant system, her identities as a white college student
advantage her in the same system. Other participants experienced a conflict
between the white culture of the college and their home communities of
color. My interviews suggest that reentry women tend to revisit their pasts
frequently, bringing new knowledge and thinking skills to bear on their life
histories. In doing so, they confront the contradictions in their identities.
Those who feel alienated or estranged from one or more of their identities or
who have difficulty living with the tension created by conflicting identities
tend to see themselves as less empowered writers; those, on the other hand,
who are able to juggle, negotiate, and/or integrate their multiple and
conflicted identities tend to experience themselves as writers who can move
with ease and confidence among many discourses and writing situations.

For Ginny and Rashida, conflicts in identities are opportunities for,
rather than barriers to, voice. Ginny describes how, in her writing, she makes
the most of her dual identities as a college student from a blue-collar background:

> There's this whole thing about coming from the background that I come
> from and being in college and wanting to appear intelligent and that sort of
> thing. And my writing voice is still very colloquial and it's hard for me to
> accept that that's OK and that my characters can say important things with-
> out college vocabulary. And it's hard for me to let them do that. . . . And
> there's part of me that is struggling to separate from that [my background]
> and part of me that still cherishes it so it's a tough struggle. . . . I guess I
> want to separate from the part that would keep me from being all that I can.
> That would be the rigid little boxes that we're put into and how a lot of the
> people in small towns don't ever try to push beyond. And they're so accept-
> ing of things and that's the part I'm struggling against. And swallowing
> whole all the advice and feelings that my family presented to me without
> ever questioning. But on the other hand there's a close family and the loy-
> alties and that sort of thing, and the familiarity that comes from a small
> town that is very good. And I cherish that part.

Ginny's comments spin out a web in which conflicting identities are explored
and evaluated. Her identity as a student in a private college gives her the
freedom and capacity for critical thinking that were inaccessible to her as a
child. On the other hand, her rural, working-class roots give her the values
of loyalty, community, and groundedness in the concrete world that are

uncommon in an urban, academic environment. In order to feel comfortable with both of these identities, she has had to sort through them, picking out what is valuable in each. [5]

Rashida, too, has sorted through her cultural affiliations, in this case her affiliations to both a black and a white world. She says that she sees herself as belonging to "neither world. I'm not what most people think of as a black person, and yet there is no way that I can fit into white society either, so I'm kind of in the middle." Although Rashida is an outsider in both worlds, she is comfortable in both. Her conflicting identities spur rather than impede her creativity as a writer. She describes one of her fantasy stories:

> The characters are kind of like, they're a lot like me. One of the women is like the ruling caste of the planet and the other is from the lower caste. They come together and that's kind of like two sides of me. You see, it's the part that's very comfortable with being the only black in whatever and OK with that and there's the other part of me that can get down and talk with sisters and just get all crazy.

For Rashida, dual identities and dual languages are enriching rather than limiting to her self and her writing. bell hooks (1984) describes this enrichment as the ability to look from both "the outside in and from the inside out . . . a mode unknown to most of our oppressors, that sustained us, aided us in our struggle to transcend poverty and despair, strengthened our sense of self and our solidarity" (Preface). Like hooks, Rashida's position of being outside and inside simultaneously gives her an effective place from which to oppose systems of dominance. She has voiced that opposition in her academic writing, her fiction, and her nonfiction. She wrote, for example, an editorial for the college newspaper in which she analyzed white racism and called on the college community to take responsibility for eliminating intolerance: "You, as much as I, are victims of the effects of racism because its effects are mirrored in the ills of sexism, homophobia, and other 'isms.' No one is immune."

Rashida not only negotiates among her multiple identities, but she also confronts conflicts *within* her own identity as an African American person. In one paper for a social work class, she wrote about a site visit to a welfare agency. Rashida explores how her family programmed her to feel disdain for African Americans who took "handouts" from whites:

> I didn't want people to see me walk into that office. I would be just like *those* people. I'd be *another nigger* taking money from those who worked hard to get what they had. They would probably assume that I had lots of children at home. . . . I dressed too well, my clothes are not from the Salvation Army or some thrift store so I would probably spend all of the assistance money on new clothes every chance I got. The other "folk" in that

office would just know that I was different from them (because my manner
would be very aloof when speaking to them) and they would resent me for
it.

   I can see how internalized racism has me in its grip. It's like I couldn't
see the white people, Asians, and Native Americans walking through those
doors. I only saw the "lazy, good-for-nothing niggers" that my . . . family
seem to hate so much.

Rashida begins to demystify internalized racism—what Freire (1982)
identifies as the internalized oppressor—by examining the conflicts within
her own identity and personal history.

   These examples from Ginny's and Rashida's writing histories suggest
that in embracing their many identities and acknowledging the interrelated-
ness of these identities, participants can begin to resist the very systems of
dominance that create divided selves. Writing may still be a potential site of
danger, but it is also a site where dominant discourses can be challenged,
displaced, problematized. In exploring their many identities, participants also
come to terms with the personal histories that have often prevented them
from developing positive self-concepts as writers. Once participants decide
what to "cherish" and what to "separate from," they can leave behind the
danger zones in their histories without leaving behind the identities that constitute the self.

Discourses of Possibility

Participants in this study do not capitulate to the hostile environments that
often surround writers who do not hold privileged status within dominant
discourses. Consciously or unconsciously, they find strategies for asserting
their intentionality as writers and avoiding or defusing danger zones. They
find spaces where they are free to do the writing that is most meaningful to
them. They choose friendly audiences for their work, disempower hostile
audiences, and reconceptualize invoked audiences so that they can write with
voice. They carefully monitor the degree to which they self-disclose in their
writing. And they negotiate their multiple identities so that conflicts in those
identities nourish rather than paralyze them.

   In writing about these stories of hope, I cast participants as agents in
their own destinies. Their strategies for reducing the potentially damaging
effects of writing and increasing the liberatory effects, however, are not
autonomous acts of resistance, but occur within discourses—what Mike Rose
(1989) calls "discourses of possibility"—which confer on them the self-
esteem that is essential to the process of acting in their own self-interests.
The discourse of feminism, learned within the woman-centered context of
the college she attended, has enabled Ginny to dissect the gender and class
dimensions of her past. The discourses of feminism and antiracism have

enabled Rashida to embrace the goal of self-determination. The self-esteem that results from immersion in these discourses enables participants to "speak discourse": "What validates us as human beings, validates us as writers" (Anzaldua 1983, 170).

Notes

1. An exception is Greenwood's (1990) research on reentry women and writing. Connors (1982); Pomerenke and Mink (1987); and Sommer (1989) have written about adult college writers but have not addressed gender.

2. The questions I asked during the interviews appear in parentheses throughout this chapter.

3. Many of my students as well as these participants have talked or written about times when their journals were read by unintended audiences—that is, brothers, friends, parents, spouses. In most cases, the experience of journal violation is devastating; some describe it with language that evokes rape or incest (Aronson 1988). It may be that the journal provides only an illusion of safety.

4. See also Bulkin, Pratt, and Smith (1984); Harding (1991b); Mitchell (1982); Pheterson (1986); and Rich (1986). This is just a small sample of the rich feminist literature on women's multiple and conflicting identities.

5. Ginny's balancing act between past and present is echoed by bell hooks (1989):

Maintaining connections with family and community across class boundaries demands more than just summary recall of where one's roots are, where one comes from. It requires knowing, naming, and being ever mindful of those aspects of one's past that have enabled and do enable one's self-development in the present, that sustain and support, that enrich. One must also honestly confront barriers that do exist, aspects of that past that do diminish. (79)

7

The Unclaimed Self
Valuing Lesbian and Gay Diversity in the Writing Environment

Pamela J. Olano

"Must you write as a lesbian?" I've been asked this question so
many times that now it's the greeting that appears on my computer
screen every time I sit down to start a paper. It's the ghost that
haunts me in the hard drive, sits next to me in class, hides in my
notes.

—Pamela J. Olano

As researcher Jeffrey Weeks (1987) contends, "Identity is not a destiny but
a choice" (47). Identity choice locates us all on Pierre Bourdieu's (1984) map
of social positions, where locations serve as markers of cultural capital and
as either points of access or roadblocks to specific social spaces. In this
schema, lived experience constructs consciousness, and practices and properties of a lifestyle can facilitate entry into culturally perceived success or
can create the conditions that subordinate the individual and her or his social
group to the dominant culture. Having little cultural capital or influence, the
subordinate group possesses little economic or political capital.[1] Moreover,
when subordinate groups resist social "norms," they locate themselves politically in what Paulo Freire and Henry Giroux describe as the *other* camp—
those against whom the dominant culture defines itself.[2]

Lesbians and gays are located in a cultural category at the margins of
social acceptance. Consequently, as Weeks (1987) insists, "in a culture where
homosexual desires, female or male, are still execrated and denied, the adop-
tion of lesbian or gay identities constitutes a political choice" (47). Identity
thus creates for lesbians and gays a *politics of location*. This concept, first used

by Adrienne Rich (1986) to describe the claiming of her identity as a woman writer, applies as well to the experience of a writer who claims a lesbian or gay identity. Rich explains,

> To write directly and overtly as a woman [read lesbian or gay individual], out of a woman's [homoaffectional/sexual] body and experience . . . was something I had been hungering to do, needing to do, all my writing life. It placed me nakedly face to face with both *terror and anger,* it did indeed imply the breakdown of the world as I had always known it, the end of safety. (182)

Terror and anger are part and parcel of the struggle, fear, and anxiety we feel when we write from a contestatorial politics, when we write *outside* the discourse or run at it from another angle. In the case of the lesbian or gay student writer, identity choice and lifestyle practices and properties affect both learning and writing processes.

It is imperative, therefore, that we writing instructors and curriculum planners consider the ramifications of our students' choices of identities and our own, for it is at the intersection or collision of these identities that we experience the *politics of location* in the composition classroom. A sensitive composition pedagogy attends to the multidimensional realities—gendered, racial, cultural, and sexual—of the students who experience it. It also requires a certain circularity, a self-consciousness that makes us ask again and again *to whom are we teaching, how, and why.* In developing this sensitivity, we might take these questions as our starting point: How does lived *experience* affect teaching and learning? What do psychosexual structures (those of the student and those of the instructor) have to do with pedagogical effectiveness? What role does the politics of location play in curriculum planning, implementation, and reform?

Recent dialogues in the profession have focused on the role of the composition classroom as a site of political and social struggle. Vara Neverow-Turk (1991) claims that our assignments inevitably have political force (477), while Thomas Fox (1990) believes that our classes should promote "a tolerant understanding of socially diverse people" and expand "the world of those groups to whom our social structure has denied privilege, opportunity, and status" (5). For her part, Maxine Hairston (1992) warns that "the movement to make freshman English into courses in which students must write about specific social issues threatens all the gains we have made in teaching writing" since the 1970s (188–189). Hairston's objections arise from three convictions: that "students develop best as writers when they can write about something they care about and want to know more about," that they "develop best as writers when teachers are able to create a low-risk environment that encourages students to take chances," and that "injecting a prescribed political content into a required freshman course . . . severely limits freedom of expression for both students and instructors" (189). I would argue that Hairston's concerns inadvertently address the crux of the problems faced by lesbian and gay writers. In fact, these students cannot write about what interests them, do not experience low-risk environments, and already have their freedom of expression limited by pedagogical techniques and insensitivities that not only silence them but also negate their very existence.

In this chapter, I situate myself with Patricia Bizzell (1990), who urges that we "engage in a rhetorical process that can collectively generate . . . knowledge and beliefs to displace the repressive ideologies an unjust social order would prescribe" (670), and with Lillian Bridwell-Bowles (1992), who insists that "if we are to invent a truly pluralist society, we must envision a socially and politically situated view of language and the creation of texts— one that takes into account gender, race, class, sexual preference, and a host of issues that are implied by these and other cultural differences" (349). Composition and the research it fosters can be positioned on the frontier of social change. The first steps toward change lie in the research we conduct and the models we use for our studies. These steps, however, must be taken with an eye toward diverse discourses that run counter to mainstream cultural assumptions and representations. Sexual orientation is an important difference that produces another channel of meaning for the lesbian or gay writer, requires another set of composing strategies, challenges heterosexual privilege and thus places the writer at risk. We are not all the same.

The tacit assumption of some *generically human* experience drives most of our curriculum and pedagogy. But when providing neither role models nor accessible writing assignments, neither safe contexts in which to explore developing identities nor access to information, curriculum and pedagogy can help create a void in the lesbian or gay student's self-concept. That is to say, we ask lesbian and gay students to write *blindfolded* because we are unaware of the heterosexual assumptions that inform our course structures and content or because we are unconscious of the effects of our well-meaning but off-the-mark liberal attitudes. In what follows, I particularly investigate the lesbian and gay students' tactics and modes of resistance. How do homosexual writers cross the line drawn by heterosexual hegemony and how successfully? Most important, how can we, as instructors, facilitate and validate this process, turning it into powerful learning experiences for all writers in our courses?

It would be naive for any lesbian or gay individual or group to assume that she/he/they could engage peacefully and equally in academic pursuits on any college campus. Lesbian and gay students and instructors sense the wall of heterosexism whenever they try to incorporate who they are into what they do, especially whenever they speak the words *lesbian, gay*, or *homoerotic*. Often they become silent. About silence, however, I suggest that we recall Adrienne Rich's (1986) reminder: "Do not confuse it with any kind of absence" (17).

Lesbian and gay students and instructors represent 10 percent of the population. They are struggling for recognition as individuals, constructing identities that enable them to move through the university, making decisions to reach out, to come out, to stay out. Therefore, in a move inimical to postmodern theory and the purported impossibility of claiming any subject position, I offer here an investigation of *subjects*—subjects mediated by the culture's rejection and by the academy's ambivalence and fluctuating support.

The Research Model

The individuals in this study include undergraduate gay and lesbian students at a major midwestern research university, gay and lesbian instructors who conduct freshman and upper division writing courses, and gay and lesbian graduate students in several departmental and interdisciplinary programs. The study began as an investigation of both the options and the consequences of the academic decisions that lesbians and gays make as they encounter each new writing assignment or course project. In 1990, I began compiling data to determine the effects of the academy's policies and "common practices" on homosexual students at all levels of their postsecondary educations/careers.[3] Information was solicited through open-ended questions about such issues as risks taken or not taken because of lesbian or gay identity, effects of respondents' sexuality on scholarly work, and the atmosphere for gay and lesbian students on campus. Questionnaires were distributed in classrooms and by word of mouth through gay and lesbian organizations. A few students who were not members of target groups requested that they be allowed to join the study. Approximately two hundred questionnaires were distributed, and responses from seventy-five participants were returned. Graduates and undergraduates participated almost equally; thirty-seven undergraduates and thirty-eight graduates responded. Nineteen undergraduates identified themselves as gay males, sixteen as lesbians, and two as other; twenty-five graduates identified themselves as gay males, twelve as lesbians, and one as other.

With issues of personal privacy in mind, the survey was conducted largely among self-identified homosexual individuals who were "out" in some context. In the case of graduate participants, gay men were generally more willing to participate than were lesbians. After careful thought and much conversation with the group of older lesbian respondents, I attribute this reluctance to difficulties in separating the effects that their lesbian identities have had upon writing, studies, or careers from the effects their experiences as women have had. Undergraduate gay and lesbian students (usually aged eighteen to twenty-two) responded almost equally. These participants did not reflect the same concerns that graduate students did. Their comments revealed more anxiety about peer approval and less about discrimination in the job market or commitment to liberation movements. Most undergraduates were more "out" with family and friends. Many could not conceive of being closeted in these venues. All participants, however, reported strong undercurrents of homophobia and heterosexism at our institution. Their writing styles, choices of topics, career decisions, and senses of self are influenced by this environment.

The Importance of "Outsider-Within" Research

The research model for this study draws on Patricia Hill Collins' (1986) concept of the "outsider-within consciousness" that allows marginalized groups to be critically and self-reflectively studied by a member of that group. Collins claims that "at its best, outsider-within status seems to offer its occupants a powerful balance between the strengths of their . . . training and the offerings of their personal and cultural experiences; neither is subordinated to the other" (60). For gay/lesbian researchers, this means that our own academic training does not subsume or erase our differences from hegemonic cultural experience. Unarguably, we are indoctrinated by cultural assumptions; yet, we live in opposition (or at odds) with the mainstream, which creates an ongoing tension between gay/lesbian knower and hegemonic known. However, the outsiders within the academy can still employ their research know-how in order to make advances in their areas of inquiry.

"Outsider-within" research finds support among feminist theorists investigating methodological approaches. Donna J. Haraway (1991), for example, argues "for politics and epistemologies of location, positioning, and situating, where partiality and not universality is the condition of being heard to make rational knowledge claims" (195). Evelyn Fox Keller (1982), too, insists that "we need to add to the familiar methods of rational and empirical inquiry the additional process of critical self-reflection" (118). By becoming "conscious of self" as researchers, Keller says, we can become "conscious of the features of the scientific project that belie its claim to universality" (118).

It is exactly this claim to universality that we, as composition researchers, must interrogate. Too much research ignores the influence of sexual orientation on composing processes and invention strategies. Sexual preference does make a difference. Most critically, in the case of this research study, participants were more willing to admit those differences to another "outsider-within" facing similar struggles within the same institutional structure. My own place in this study was clear. Aware of the silent acceptance of (but little encouragement for) my own work on lesbian theory and distressed by the homophobia and heterosexism of the academic environment, I had long felt myself to be walking a delicate line.

This awareness had presented itself at major crossroads in my academic progress toward a degree. Where and what should I publish, what publications should be announced in the department newsletter, which fellowships and friends would entertain a lesbian topic, what would be the topic of my dissertation, what should be included on my curriculum? These questions plagued my graduate career. In fact, my decision to conduct this project grew from the writer's block I often experienced as I sat down to compose. If I was stymied by the privileging of heterosexual themes and assumptions, what might be happening to undergraduates and other graduate students as they tried to write papers, articulate theories, brainstorm ideas, plan classes?

Even as I searched for answers in composition research, I knew that the silences I found were part of the problem. While cultural diversity has been much on the minds of educators, the concept of difference has yet to be extended to sexual preference in any significant way. Work is only just beginning, and most of it is being conducted by lesbian or gay individuals. These two facts—the silences in the literature and the in-group nature of the research studies—provided the impetus for my study. It was time to listen to lesbian and gay concerns.

Diverse Individuals in Society: Composition Curriculum as Battle Site

John Fiske (1991) points out that "the difference between the meanings of the socially central and the marginalized is not one of liberal pluralist tolerance, but one of social and semiotic struggle" (6). The struggles between "secrecy or disclosure"—between resistance and accommodation, compliance and evasion—drive the daily drama of claiming a homosexual identity in the composition classroom and in the university. Lesbian and gay students and scholars are engaged in the politics of their locations—a politics that at times seems to provoke an assault on the carefully knitted fabric of homosexual identity. To grasp how the mechanisms of discipline are brought to bear upon lesbian and gay students and how these affect their writing competencies, we must first consider "the relation between diverse individuals and society"—a relationship, according to Henry Giroux, that is "steeped in domination and conflict."[4]

The academy presents us with a microcosm of our culture. The hegemonic assumptions that inform the institution and the social structure it replicates are those of the dominant group. Sexuality, in society and in the institution, is a dicey subject. The recuperation of any "body" in the academy is fraught with peril; the recuperation of a body not co-opted by heterosexuality is doubly difficult. Academe has never been simply an intellectual exercise. Rather, the institution operates within a system of monosexuality—if we are all assumed to be heterosexual, then we can eliminate that "constant" and move to other "more important" work. A lesbian writer and graduate student illustrates:

Ironically, I live in a de-sexed state academically. The assumed heterosexuality of our society is a safety net that I fall into. If I make my sexual orientation known, I seem to take on the responsibility for having sexualized everyone else in the room. In response to this, I have begun announcing my interest as *theorizing the body* . . . that's enough to make everybody squirm. If I'm feeling particularly brave, I'll insert the word *lesbian* before the word *body*, but I'm not always centered enough or strong enough to do this. There's a lot of guilt associated with not claiming my lesbian self. I've accepted it as self-defense.

The way one moves within or on the margins of culture constructs the world as an individual knows it. The world view of the gay or lesbian student requires a constant reading against the "norm." This world view also includes a sense of "outsider" status, whether one resides *in* or *out* of the closet. The outsider is always aware of the necessity to *camouflage* identity and is consciously selective when deciding to *come out*. If we examine all the skills needed by marginal groups to operate from their social positions— as members of the monosexual community and as members of a subordinate group that traverses the dominant culture—we begin to grasp the significance of the concept of a "whole way of life" for a homosexual. The lesbian or gay man is constantly reminded through her or his absence from almost all sources of mass "information" that she or he is an outsider—an invisible one or a strongly contested one. Her or his sense of identity is often conflictual.

Despite these marginalized positions, lesbian and gay students are still "operational" in the larger culture because they have the ability to decipher the dominant—actually are able to participate in it—through their ability to read and understand heterosexual hegemony. Poaching and fighting at every turn, they create a homosexual subtext. But at what price? They must always filter out compulsory heterosexuality in order to affirm their own culture's *meanings, pleasures, and values*. The lesbian or gay student's constant battle to decipher hegemonic codes while simultaneously shifting meaning to a more affirming opposition creates sites of "conflicting discourses and competing voices" (Fiske 1991, 237).

We might further understand the dilemma of the lesbian or gay writer by applying the term *polyphony* to the composing process. As Robert Stam (1987) writes, "polyphony calls attention to the coexistence, in any textual or extratextual situation, of a plurality of voices that do not fuse into a single consciousness but exist on different registers, generating dialogical dynamism among themselves" (229). Dialogical dynamism is present in all writers; however, for the lesbian or gay student, negotiation of social pressures, outsider status, camouflage, and social acceptance (or lack thereof), creates a polyphony that can disrupt the writing process and lead to a denial of the whole self instead of an embracing of multiple identities. There is both danger and consequence in claiming and/or denying a lesbian or gay identity. A graduate student writer and instructor noted her awareness of the risks:

> I actually have multiple copies of Curriculum Vitae, I suppose everyone does. But how many scholars have a queer CV and a straight CV? Probably every lesbian and gay man I know! I cannot tell you what it does to my ability to write, to theorize, to market myself knowing that I am at the mercy, not of my own abilities, but of someone's heterosexist biases.

Another lesbian graduate student disclosed her surprise at her own *reluctance* to work with the only lesbian faculty member. Her thoughts on this reticence are revealing:

> Maybe it's because I'd have to be too present—really all the way out of the closet. I wouldn't be able to move back and forth between my lesbian identity and my presumed heterosexuality. Guilt by association, or something like that. So now I'm challenging myself to risk—this is a personal battle for which, unfortunately, I get little in the way of visible support from anyone.

Another graduate student described the struggle of multiple coming outs:

> Each quarter, I stand poised on the brink of acceptance of rejection . . . or worse, of silence. We go around the room and introduce ourselves and our areas of interest. Each time, I have to decide whether I will be a lesbian in an unknown context or whether the closet door will remained closed.

For most homosexual students, ongoing personal struggle seems to be the order of the day—to decide in each new context whether to be visible, to seek acknowledgment, or to write from lesbian or gay identities and out of same-sex experiences. Many seem to feel that they have a choice; others feel passing as straight is no longer an option.

Here, we might call into play Bakhtin's understanding of the self as a "matrix of discursive forms, the site of multiple identities and identifications, a subject traversed by multiple discourses—which in no way denies the realities of class, gender and nation but only complicates them."[5] The homosexual's multiaccentual capacity as a member of a subordinate group in a dominant culture places her or his view both against the grain and alongside it. She or he "sees" both narratives (her or his own and any dominant reading/writing that will attempt to impose itself). As one undergraduate made clear, multiaccentuality can create tensions:

> I'm a good writer when I'm passing as straight. But I'm a terrible writer when I'm writing as a gay man. I fight within myself, my hands shake, the

words won't come. I go back into the closet. I am careful to edit out all references that might give away my identity. Then there was the time that I
inadvertently wrote "homosexuals, we . . ."

Composing Behaviors of Camouflaged/Out Writers

We, as writing instructors, can better decipher what we encounter in our
classes by considering Geoffrey Chase's (1988) three categories of student
writers. Drawing upon Giroux's *Theory and Resistance in Education* (1983),
Chase classifies the use of traditional discursive forms and strategies as
accommodating, opposing, or *resisting. Accommodating* students "accept
conventions" and do not ask how these "privilege some forms of knowledge
at the expense of others" (14). *Opposing* students behave in ways that break
"the normal progression of learning" (14–15). *Resisting* students, by their
"refusal to learn," move "against the dominant ideology" and "toward emancipation" (15). These categories can serve as starting points both in formu-
lating an understanding of lesbian or gay students' composing behaviors and
in developing pedagogical techniques to facilitate the writing processes of
these students.

How often do students write with *accommodation*, that is, accept without question the assignment, the instructor's expectations, or the discourse
community's ideology? Accommodation is at the heart of what Jenny Cook-
Gumperz (1986) calls *social reproduction* in the academy. Students are
expected to reproduce a discourse, to successfully eliminate any disparate
voices. Cook-Gumperz's term *metacognitive process* translates well to an
analysis of the lesbian or gay writer (3). If the assumption is that the successful learner arbitrates the myriad impressions and ideas that whet the critical
imagination and then focuses the possibilities into one coherent approach,
how might a "second layer of meaning" disrupt the process of accommodation to social "norms" in the assumptions that underlie many writing assignments and responses to student-generated texts? One lesbian writer, a graduate student and an instructor, explains her approach for accommodating
these demands:

> I try to think of myself as a student first and a lesbian second. Actually, as
> a *lesbian* only after about thirty other identifiers. I know this is unhealthy,
> but it's something I learned to do the hard way. After about the millionth
> time of being told that what I do in my private life is of no concern to my
> writing, I started to believe it. But I still wonder why it is that I feel so
> cheated, so off balance sometimes, when I write about the poetry of Adri-
> enne Rich and try to leave out the fact that she's a lesbian. What does it
> cost me to do that?

Lesbians and gays, of course, can and do compose simultaneously both in the discourse of the dominant culture and the discourse of their own subculture, but are they given the same opportunities as nonhomosexual students to record the self-affirming discourse of their own realities? Furthermore, if as Chase (1988) claims, "students learn to accept conventions" and do not ask how these "privilege some forms of knowledge at the expense of others," are we shoring up heterosexist and homophobic assumptions by providing instruction for some "universal" student, thereby entrapping the lesbian or gay writer in a writing environment that privileges dominant (that is, heterosexual) cultural "knowledge"? An undergraduate gay writer described his process of accommodation this way: "When I write, I am a shadow-figure. I have this out-of-body experience; I'm somebody else. When I read my papers, I often don't know how or why I wrote them. They are alien creations to me, especially if I'm passing as straight in the text."

Simultaneous Complications in Several Dimensions

Confusions and contradictions are apparent as lesbian or gay writers grapple to become (finally) the "subjects" of their language. While other students are practicing invention strategies, the lesbian or gay student is sifting through "simultaneous complications in several dimensions," thus disrupting the flow of the creative process—in effect keeping the writer outside the text. One undergraduate student's dislocation from the text was expressed this way:

> My writing instructor would ask us to discuss parenting. I'd talk about "turkey-baster babies" and artificial insemination. She would turn the discussion around to science and how men and women would one day be unnecessary in reproduction. Men and women! I was talking about lesbian parents who decide to have kids. I knew she didn't want to talk about it in class, so I had to switch gears and talk about how my parents raised me. Underneath, though, I was talking about how my partner and I were planning to raise our children—without men, for sure. Then I wrote my paper about parenting in the animal kingdom. The instructor was upset. I got a "C" and a note to rewrite the assignment for a better grade. I kept the "C."

When the assumption of compulsory, and therefore universal, heterosexuality confronts homosexual students, frequently *opposition* sets in. Several lesbian and gay students report writing papers on violent topics—perhaps a reaction to the cultural alienation experienced as a subordinated identity living daily life in the dominant culture. Others locate themselves in an even stronger oppositional position on the map of social spaces. They view their locations as outlaw identities, as lesbian or gay writers who claim "borderland" positions shared with other multiply marked, willfully disobedient women or men.

This oppositional placement of homosexual identity can disrupt the composing process. An undergraduate student described her alienation from and opposition to other class members: "In my small group, I read the first paragraph of my paper about a women's musical festival. One of my group members interrupted me and said, 'Are these women lesbians or normal?' How was I supposed to answer that? I threw the paper away and didn't do the writing assignment." Many other respondents report feeling "outside" the text, searching for a position from which to analyze material. Two undergraduates wrote similarly of their "outsider status":

> I am often afraid to speak out when day after day we are asked to read male/female narratives and respond in the appropriate gender-specific way. As a lesbian, I am much more focused on the female characters. At times, my interpretations of male/female interaction fall way outside of what the heterosexual members of the class perceive.

> As a gay male, I want to read stories with two male characters that are not war stories, man against nature stories, or solitary male stories. My culture repeatedly tells me that male bonding is either athletic, militaristic, brotherly, or men-against-the-land sort of things. I'm not surprised that gay men are now dying by the thousands because they had no role-models anywhere in their educations.

Finessing the Opposition

Interestingly, many lesbian and gay student writers report a growing finesse at avoiding ideological capture. Chase (1988) identifies this type of student as the *resisting* writer—one whose "refusal [to learn] grows out of a larger sense of the individual's relation to liberation." Student writers exhibiting this level of awareness are often what philosopher Marilyn Frye (1990) describes as "de-coders," constantly vigilant for attempts at erasure or silencing. Decoding (and coding) in the composition classroom requires students to undertake a number of composing maneuvers. A number of undergraduates laughingly spoke of using the journal as the "coming out" opportunity: "I hint around in my journal to see if my instructor will pick up on my clues. If she does, then I'll write a paper on a homosexual theme. If she doesn't, I bombard her with argumentative essays. I subvert her assignments in every way I can."

As instructors, how do we react to the destabilizing rhetoric of resistance? Resistance can be viewed as a positive struggle that grows directly out of the politics of the students' locations. What is the lesbian or gay student "refusing to learn" and how does that resistance reflect her or his relation to personal politics and liberation struggle? While instructors may see a student's repeated refusal to follow guidelines as a lack of cooperation or a display of anger, the writer may instead be exhibiting what Chase (1988) calls "movement toward emancipation." Several respondents said that they "tried to upset" instructors who seemed to have rigid political agendas. One undergraduate commented:

> I am NOT his disciple and I never will be. Just because he thinks homosexuality is 'morally and ethically wrong' is no reason for him to mark down my essays on AIDS. I wrote the worst papers of my undergraduate career in that class. I couldn't think, couldn't write ... I could hardly breathe!

Respondents who chose to compose from their positions as homosexual writers described a growing hostility and alienation from both community and text. Even those who experienced more affirming environments stated their constant awareness that they exist on the margins and do not occupy a validated social space from which to express a homosexual subject self. One male undergraduate described his reaction to assignments that placed him "so far off the beaten track that I was forever lost in the woods":

> I tried on more than one occasion to suggest to the instructor that we be allowed to write about "side-stream" topics. He just didn't get the message, so I wrote everything from a science fiction angle—you know, I'd end every paper with UFOs or supernatural stuff. I was known as the "weirdo from outer space" because my writing was so other-worldly.

What never diminishes for lesbian or gay writers are the risks. Even the momentary synchronicity of self and subject experienced by students who wrote as homosexuals does little to alleviate their anxieties about audience reception, social acceptance, and/or discrimination by peers or instructors. A gay graduate student instructor described his situation as follows:

> Every time I present an idea for a gay topic, I run the risk of a teacher saying NO. Then I'd have to examine the situation, try to decide whether the topic has no real feasibility, or whether the teacher is homophobic. Sometimes, by the time I've settled all the internal questions, I've lost my enthusiasm for writing. I just feel bored and frustrated. Imagine if a teacher ever said, "Write about two gay men who meet in a bar," or "Write about a gay man's reaction to his lover's death from AIDS." That doesn't happen.

The instructor who is aware of a student's struggles at this metalevel can intercede. One way to facilitate invention and composing processes is to provide scenarios that tap into the homosexual student's lifestyle patterns, but these topics must be related to a larger group experience that validates lesbian or gay identity. This can be done using strategies comparable to those that we now use to incorporate multicultural and racially diverse materials into our curricula. However, it is not sufficient to open the floor to discussions of issues such as the AIDS epidemic or the use of condoms. This type of "add gays and stir" methodology reinforces the idea that it is only sexual practices that create a homosexual identity. A broad, interdisciplinary investigation of alternative family structures, dating habits, financial implications, commitment ceremonies, and so on can add multiple dimensions to the possibilities for writing for all students. Too many instructors confine their inclusion of lesbian and gay issues to information related to social disenfranchisement. No wonder our homosexual students resist. We, in effect, intensify that disenfranchisement by highlighting it again and again.

Curriculum and Social Relations

Lesbian and gay students are struggling to come to terms with what it means to be a writer in a world not governed by sexual equality. For many, the politics of location is defined by what they deem to be their sexual identities. But the politics of homosexual identity is not one freely exercised. The politics of heterosexist hegemony encloses homosexuals in discriminatory practices and biased curricula. The politics of social relations must therefore be at the center of an emancipatory curriculum—a curriculum that promotes dialogue across diversity rather than opposition to difference. Gay affirmative texts and discussions, speakers, films, and ephemerae can be included to broaden both the homosexual student's sense of social space and the heterosexual student's base of knowledge. Units that investigate a variety of situations from a first person point of view help to eliminate the feeling that we are "all the same." Writing assignments that require students to *validate* an existence that they themselves do not claim (note: validate, not occupy)—homeless, gay or lesbian, imprisoned, white, person of color, corporate executive, environmentalist, emergency medical technician, domestic worker in a local hotel, mother, and so on—not only provide students with valuable information, but they also serve a liberating function: the world becomes large and diverse, not limited and universal. Assignments that focus on diversity validate difference instead of subsuming or erasing it. And, of course, lesbian and gay instructors can consider the value of coming out to their students, thus interjecting another discursive opportunity into the classroom.

Expectations: What Is Realistic?

Can we, realistically, expect that incorporating this type of experience into the composition classroom will bring equity within the academy? Can validation of lesbian and gay writers' sexual identities create the kind of open learning environments we wish to foster? Can a discursive community such as the university serve an emancipatory function? Like Paulo Freire (1982), Chase (1988) insists that we should teach students discursive strategies that "allow them to problematize their existence and to place themselves in . . . the world around them" (21). Further, Chase believes that students must be allowed to "affirm their own voices . . . to exercise the skills of critical interrogation . . . to exercise the courage to act in the interests of improving the quality of human life" (21–22). Whether identified as "resistance" or "struggle" against the prevailing social ideologies or against their continual reconstruction in the curriculum and pedagogy of the academy, a student's politics of location can and should be viewed as both a "sustained refusal" to accommodate and an acknowledged point of departure for social change (21). Giroux (1983) writes that "resistance must have a revealing function, one that contains a critique of domination and provides theoretical opportunities for self-reflection and for struggle in the interest of self-emancipation and social emancipation" (108–109). Writing courses seem to be appropriate sites for just this type of self-reflection and discovery.

I propose that we practice the "simultaneous complications in several dimensions" encountered by lesbian and gay writers, resist hegemonic assumptions, and view pedagogy *aslant.* To do so, it will be necessary to foreground the ideologies perpetuated by traditional concepts of knowledge, knowing, and literacy; to challenge the sociopolitical structures of the academy; and to develop an emancipatory curriculum that is both informed and mediated by the "two-track" discourse of dominant and subordinant cultures.

Not only must we interrogate the heterosexual biases of much of our curriculum, but we must also transform that curriculum at its core unit: the individual syllabus. Marilyn R. Schuster and Susan R. Van Dyne in "Syllabus Redesign Guidelines" (1985) offer us one way to implement such a review. To examine "the spoken and unspoken principles of selection that govern course structure and content" (279), they interrogate four areas of syllabus design: goal, content, organization, and method. Their schema also looks at the conventions of syllabus construction and possible transformations of those conventions. Starting from Schuster and Van Dyne's outline for making courses more gender fair, I have designed a set of questions on the "sexual orientation–sensitivity" of curriculum as this relates to syllabus design. The transformations specifically interrogate how well course content facilitates involvement by lesbian or gay writers. Aimed at making instructors more aware of overt and covert roadblocks to students' composing processes and written expression, the guidelines also call on instructors to consider larger cultural issues: social and ideological constructs that underlie content, hegemonic assumptions within course assignments that repress/ oppress students with differing perspectives, false concepts of universality in the student population, and so forth.

The guidelines further prompt pedagogical introspection on a number of levels: causes of student resistance, writing assignments that failed to evoke good student responses, limitations of the options offered to students. Through a combination of content interrogatories and pedagogical queries, the syllabus guidelines can help us begin unraveling the conundrums presented by the diversity of student writers who pass through our classrooms. (The syllabus guidelines appear at the end of this chapter.)

To Be or Not to Be: Some Conclusions

These questions offer starting points to examine the fairness and accessibility of our writing courses. As Chase (1988) reminds us, "discourse communities are organized around the production and legitimization of particular forms of knowledge and social practices at the expense of others, and they are not ideologically innocent" (13). Curricula based on assumptions that students automatically respect all forms of knowledge and give equal time to diverse opinions are doomed to failure. We live in a world in which domination and conflict are historically practiced. Composition studies can benefit from a deeper understanding of the nature of this dynamic.

The classroom environment should provide a positively valued way in for individual difference. Unfortunately, most college writing courses are not responsive to students' social, economic, sexual, and psychic diversity. The development and implementation of a cross-disciplinary approach that is at once a product of *lived experience* and *the politics of location* is best suited to achieve the greatest return on student and instructor efforts. As we begin to conceptualize such a curriculum, it is critical to think about the symbolic relationship between identity formation and lived experience, and to consider how a politics of location is influenced by this relationship. The pedagogical philosophies and teaching strategies that inform a composition program will either close off cultural spaces or grant students access to them. In a classroom where students are in the process of transforming thought into words, we have a tremendous opportunity to aid in the emancipation of all varieties of student writers. As composition instructors, we stand at the nexus of social change. Audre Lorde (1984) writes:

> Each of us is here now because in one way or another we share a common commitment to language and to the power of language, and to the reclaiming of that language which has been made to work against us. In the transformation of silence into language and action, it is vitally necessary for each one of us to establish or examine her function in that transformation, and to recognize her role as vital within that transformation. (22)

It is my hope that this transformation will open more social *space*—space in which to create other ways of knowing and being in the world, space in which the cultural capital of lesbian and gay writers is increased, space where resistance is recognized as the first sign of awakening consciousness, and space where steps toward personal freedom can be taken.

Composition research, in particular, represents an important venue for the valuation of lesbian and gay cultural capital. Sensitive composition pedagogy and research necessitate a self-consciousness that asks the question *to whom are we teaching, how, and why.* The politics of both student and teacher locations must inform the kinds of research we do and should require us to situate ourselves within that research paradigm. The outsider-within consciousness demands self-reflection and self-consciousness. Research methods that place subject and researcher in similar locations can provide us with important insights not available otherwise.

The factor of trust is of first importance in this type of study. I argue for a research paradigm that allows the embedded codes and transcodes of the marginalized subject to be understood by the researcher. Partiality, not universality, is especially necessary in this regard. The lesbian and gay experience is not universal, even within the homosexual community. Therefore, a research study that immediately discards a belief in "common experience" will be better positioned to discover the unique *situatedness* or *locatedness* of marginalized identities. The kind of research that we need in composition studies should be informed by our awareness of the politics of locations— student's, teacher's and researcher's.

I envision this type of research to be the basis of a more emancipatory curriculum that benefits all members of a diverse university community—a community in which we may one day have no need to decide whether "to be or not to be." When we can claim our identities and respect the politics of locations, the ghosts in all of our hard drives may at last be laid to rest.

Appendix A

The Syllabus Guidelines[6]

I: Goal

Convention What is the goal of this course? How can I best facilitate student access to writing experiences that are not oppressive, exclusionary, or assumptive? How does course content aid or block student composing processes? Does the course teach students to read, write, observe, interpret, develop informed opinions?

Transformation What material is used to stimulate student writing? What kinds of materials are generally most valued in traditional writing courses? Why? Who decides? How might the teaching of reading, writing, observation, and opinion formation change if the sexual preference or orientation of the writer/readers were explicitly taken into account? How might this syllabus help to create an emancipatory curriculum?

II: Content

Convention What issues are chosen for inclusion in a writing-based course? How is "importance" defined? Whose issues are these? Is there an assumption of universality associated with these issues? Do these issues affect all people in the same ways? What is the cultural context in which these issues are located? Does sexual orientation change the focus of these issues? What are the social and ideological constructs that govern these issues? Is ideology or hegemony built into these issues?

Transformation How does incorporating lesbian and gay responses enrich our sense of diversity and what it means? How does inclusion of lesbian and gay experience and self-expression extend the writing environment? How might implied hierarchies and heterosexual hegemony be challenged by openly including lesbian and gay issues in writing prompts? What population of students will be served by including lesbian and gay issues in writing assignments? Does resistance by some students indicate that course materials are oppressive and assumptive?

III: Organization

Convention What is the underlying principle of organization or selection in the syllabus? What are the assumptions about gender, race, class, *and sexual orientation?* What "norms" determine selection? Are these "norms" based upon assumptions that are hegemonic and/or exclusive?

Transformation Does the principle of organization or do the "norms" for selection obscure or distort lesbian and gay experience? the experiences of other minorities? What other organizing principles could be devised to include issues for diverse student populations? Could groups of thematically related topics that cut across hegemonic assumptions be considered? Are alternative responses to a topic given equal value? Do writing assignments provide opportunity for emancipation by oppressed groups?

IV: Method

Convention What methodological and social assumptions underlie both the content and organization of the syllabus? of the writing prompts? Do social assumptions affect instructor response to alternative points of view? What issues are suitable for writing assignments? By whom are these issues considered suitable? What issues are not addressed or introduced? Why? What issues are assumed to be universal? Are they? What assumptions are made about composing processes, especially in regard to individual access to information on a topic? Who is excluded/included in the topic? What assumptions are made about lived experience, especially with regard to the relationship between the individual and the social context? Where do these assumptions come from?

Transformation What writing prompts might be designed that open the field of responses by students? What surprises, baffles, perplexes us in responses to writing assignments? Why? How might these challenges lead to new questions and new writing opportunities? How are our assumptions about universality challenged when sexual orientation becomes a category of analysis?

Notes

1. See Bourdieu (1984).

2. Both Freire and Giroux develop the concept of "otherness" in their analysis. See Freire (1982) and Giroux (1983).

3. All participants were promised anonymity; therefore quotes are attributed by the designations "undergraduate student," "graduate student," or "graduate student instructor."

4. As quoted by Myron C. Tuman (1988).

5. Mikhail Bakhtin as paraphrased by Robert Stam (1987, 237).

6. I would like to thank Professor Lisa Albrecht of the University of Minnesota for inspiring this revision. She is using a similar set of questions to interrogate multicultural content in courses.

8

The Role of Response

Sally Barr Ebest

Recently, members of the English department's writing faculty decided to make cultural studies the focus of freshman and advanced composition courses at the University of Missouri, St. Louis. By cultural studies, I mean social, political, and multicultural issues, such as the increasingly violent battles over abortion, suicide, and euthanasia; censorship and artistic freedom; racism, sexism and homophobism; in sum, the growing intolerance for those whose lifestyles or views differ from the "mainstream." We chose this focus "to enable students to define themselves as empowered individuals with a political will that is resilient in the face of social control" (McClelland 1991).

The writing classroom may be one of the few places where students can express their opinions, explore new ideas, defend their beliefs, or question the assumptions of the authors they read. In other words, the writing classroom would appear to be the ideal place to introduce social issues. Both within and without the English department, of course, many would argue that the purpose of writing courses is to teach "skills." I have been told that undergraduate students didn't know enough about social issues to say anything intelligent, that they shouldn't be forced to deal with what their instructors consider relevant social issues, that the writing course is not the place to teach "political correctness."

This is not, however, the stance taken by the English Coalition. In his account of the proceedings, Peter Elbow (1990) reports that the participants—teachers of English from elementary school through college—called for "a more frankly activist, political, Jeffersonian view of education . . . a language-oriented teaching and learning" designed to help make our students "better citizens." These goals would best be accomplished in "an atmosphere of free thought where all ideas are invited to compete; [in] talk-rich, interactive classrooms where students are invited actively to make their own meanings, form their own hypotheses, and test them autonomously and in open discussion" (32).

I believe that this is what writing courses are for: to help our students make meaning and to enable them to reflect on that process. Such a focus requires a different mode of response to student writing. If we want students to explore their beliefs about social issues, we must focus our response on what they say, rather than on how they say it. And if we are responding as a reader rather than as a "teacher," we must also do away with grades.

This chapter reports on research conducted to determine the effects of such an approach in an experimental freshman composition course. In conducting this research, I wanted to find out how students would respond without the motivation—or the penalty—of grades. Would they take risks and explore their thoughts and prejudices? Would they be honest in their discussions and thorough in their responses and analyses? Were they mature enough to recognize and analyze their traditional prejudices about race, sex, and homosexuality? Would writing about these issues influence the students' ability to reflect critically? Would lack of traditional writing instruction affect their fluency, style, and mechanics? their ability to think logically and critically, to write clear, concise, and well-supported essays? In sum, I wanted to discover how the lack of grades and the writing instruction implicit in the circles and red marks of a "graded" paper would influence the students' ability to think critically and to write honestly.

To answer these questions, I conducted both quantitative and qualitative research. I established baseline data by comparing my students' final essays with those written by other students enrolled in regular sections of freshman composition that semester. These data showed that a nongraded, nonskills approach did not adversely affect the students' writing. But quantitative data can only go so far. To determine the effects of this approach on my students' beliefs and self-understanding, I had to look beyond anonymous, aggregate scores; I had to look at individual students. To do so, I conducted ethnographic research: I observed the students in our writing classroom during each meeting, questioned them, listened to what they said, wrote with them, gave them feedback on their spoken and written ideas, and collected all of their writing samples. As both teacher and researcher, I was a natural part of the study and the setting, a factor that contributes to the reflexive nature of ethnographic research.

This approach enabled me to go beyond quantitative data to ask crucial questions about the effect of writing instruction on students' attitudes about themselves and others. Part I of this chapter establishes the environmental context for this study, as well as some baseline data, to demonstrate that a "nonskills" approach is not detrimental to students' writing ability. Part II presents a case study of one student, Bill, to show in detail how a student can grow as a result of a pedagogy that recognizes and values diversity.

I

This experimental section of freshman composition focused on three social issues—sexism, racism, and homophobism. In this class, there were twenty-one students: twelve males and nine females. Three students (two males, one female), or 14 percent of the population, were black. Students' average age was nineteen; only two were in their late twenties. All but three were local residents who had spent almost their entire lives in the St. Louis area. The only exceptions were two students who had served briefly in the military.

We had two texts in this class: a reader, *Re-Reading America*, and the students' own essays. The students read essays about sexism, racism, and homophobism and composed free-written responses to the readings and to related topics. Following an introductory, informal paper (used to place them in permanent gender-mixed groups of three students with related interests), assignments led gradually into the specific course themes. Essay 2, for example, was ostensibly on family traditions, while Essay 3 asked students to discuss the effect of school on their creativity and conformity. In both cases, the topics led the students to reveal their attitudes toward and treatment of people differing from them in race, sex, or sexual orientation. Following these, students wrote two papers on sexism, two on racism, and two on homophobism.

There was no emphasis on writing as a process. Instead, I had the students free-write in response to prompts and turn in their papers without worrying about being mechanically, or politically, correct. There were neither lectures nor small-group work on grammar or style. We used class time to discuss individual students' essays, focusing on how their language use revealed their ideas and prejudices; we used small groups to analyze their peers' language features. By language features, I mean elements of language use, such as preferred topics; family relationships; relationships with teachers, with peers, and with strangers; expressions of feeling; essay structure and length; preferred sentence type; preferred words and phrases; technical proficiency; and other features that might recur regularly, such as the use of humor or sarcasm.

My role in this class was as teacher-writer-researcher. I made this clear the first day when I outlined the course and explained how it would differ from the other freshman comp courses. As the teacher, I was responsible for the curriculum, daily format, and final grades. Grades were based on the students' ability to analyze and explore their use of language, as evidenced in their midterm and final essays, papers that differed from the personal experience papers that constituted the bulk of the semester's work. For these formal papers, students analyzed and explained the language features revealed in their informal, personal experience essays. In doing so, they came to understand not only how they used language, but also what their language revealed about them and their beliefs. Because these papers entailed all the elements of a research paper, they were graded on traditional criteria—clarity, organization, development, use of illustrations and explanations, and synthesis of ideas.

The majority of the class, however, focused on the students' free-written responses. I did not grade these papers because any type of critical response would have quickly eliminated the possibility of further open or honest pieces. Similarly, an emphasis on style or mechanics would have shifted the focus to these matters. Instead, I used an alternative method of response based on theories of reader response and involving analysis and description of recurring language features. According to David Bleich (1987), such a focus shows:

> how our habits of writing are tied to our habits of speaking, that we have a more or less general way of handling language, and this way of speaking has come from, and continues to grow in, the variety of interpersonal relationships and wider social belongings in our lives, particularly those pertinent to our memberships in a gender, ethnic group, or economic class. (*Guidelines*)

If we want students to write about and understand their social attitudes and prejudices, this type of response seems most appropriate.

To emphasize the importance of open responses, to decenter the classroom, and to facilitate development of the class as a discourse community, I wrote with the students. I completed all assignments, shared them with the students, and took a turn at having my writing analyzed and discussed. My participation in the writing process coupled with my method of response encouraged the students to trust me.

My participation was an essential element of the research process. Ethnographers Hammersley and Atkinson (1983) maintain that "there is no way in which we can escape the social world in order to study it; nor, fortunately, is that necessary. . . . How people respond to the presence of the researcher may be as informative as how they react to other situations" (15). If I had not been writing, I could not have intelligently responded during group work or discussions, nor would my response have been accepted—or rejected—as a member of the students' discourse community. As a writer, however, I was on neutral ground. Students could take or leave what I said; neither action would affect their grade. Moreover, since we were all involved in the same mode of response, my voice was not the only one they heard. My comments on students' papers were often echoed by their peers during group work and class discussion.

To determine the effect of nontraditional response on their writing, I had students write the state-mandated assessment essay required in all freshman and advanced composition courses. Students at both levels were given a short reading (on smokers' rights) and asked to write an argumentative essay that agreed with, disagreed with, or critiqued it, supporting their argument with examples from the reading and from their own experience. This assignment was similar to those written by students in other sections during the semester. The composing process, though truncated, was also similar to work done throughout the semester in traditional classes.

Prior to the last week of the semester, the students in all freshman and advanced composition sections were asked to read and free-write a response to the "smoking" essay over the weekend. During the last week of class, they discussed the reading and brainstormed ideas for an argumentative essay. They spent the rest of that week drafting and revising in class, then returned to class during the two-hour final exam period to revise their drafts and write a final version. During that period, the students were allowed to participate in peer evaluation groups to get feedback prior to writing the final draft.

This entire process was unfamiliar to my students. Nevertheless, as members of a freshman composition course, they were bound to participate. When my students had turned in their final drafts, I coded their papers and integrated them with those from all the other freshman composition sections. These papers were then evaluated by readers trained and calibrated to rate the essays holistically using a 1–4 point scale. When all the papers had been rated, a statistician determined mean scores and degrees of significance between the freshman and advanced classes. She also determined the mean scores of the students in the experimental course and compared them to those of the students in the regular, graded freshman comp courses.

The findings surprised even me: Students in the experimental course had a mean score of 2.28; students in the regular courses averaged 2.27. These similarities suggest that grading does not make a difference. But grading per se is not the issue here. The problem is with the types of response that grading elicits. At its worst, grading elicits critical responses. At its best, a teacher's response focuses on the finished product and how it failed or succeeded. Such responses direct attention outward, to the paper rather than to the student. They do not affect students' self-knowledge or understanding of their language use. To illustrate the difference that response can make, we trace the progress of Bill, the subject of the following case study.

II

At the time of this study, Bill was a nineteen-year-old freshman. I chose him for this study for a number of reasons. As a subject, he fit the description of our typical undergraduate—white, first-generation college student, born and raised in St. Louis, still living at home. As a writer, Bill clearly had room for improvement, as you can see in his Essay 1, "Who Are You?"

> My name is Bill S. I have lived in St. Louis all my life. I am from a large
> family of nine, six brothers and two sisters. All are married except for my

younger brother. He's seventeen. On my dad's side he has twelve brothers and sisters and my mom has three brothers and sisters.

I attend[ed] Bishop DuBourg High School and now attend UMSL. I played soccer and baseball all four years of high school and received many awards. I am also the Scholar Athlete of DuBourg. I'm not bragging just facts. I was recruited on the UMSL's baseball team and received some Scholarship money.

I enjoy hunting and fishing for fun and my hobbies. I hunt and fish all year round and yes; I wear all that camouflage stuff. Besides baseball and soccer, hunting, fishing, and markmanship are my favorite sports.

I want to major in Criminology. I want to be a policeman but I want to be a detective or obtain some position in the Federal Department of the government. I'd rather play Major League Baseball and hope to play it one day if not I have my college career to fall back on.

This summer I worked as a maintenance man at two different schools. Besides painting and stripping and waxing which I already knew, I learned some things about electrical work and plumbing. This summer has been a knowledgeable one for me. I guess as you get older things are easier to learn.

For this essay, as with all subsequent ones, the students were to free-write for one hour. These free-writes were directed—that is, students were given a topic—but they were encouraged to write without concern for grammar, mechanics, spelling, or organization. Despite a comma splice and a misused semicolon, Bill appears to have little trouble with technical proficiency. Nevertheless, it seems fairly obvious from the essay's length (originally seventeen lines) that he was not very fluent and was not an experienced writer. The preponderance of simple sentences also suggests that he was an inexperienced reader, since variety in syntax is usually assimilated from reading prose models.

A traditional response might have praised Bill's organization but focused primarily on the comma splice, semicolon problem, and syntax, and pointed out the need for paragraph development. Overall, given the lack of development, this might be a *C* or *C+* paper. The nontraditional response used in this class, however, focused on language features (in italics).

You wrote an interesting, if short, essay. *Relationships w/ family* are hard to determine. Who's your favorite? Who do you avoid? How do you like coming from such a large family? There are few *expressions of feeling* just, as you say in par. 2, the facts. About the only one is "I enjoy." You are slightly more specific in the paragraph on your career, repeating "I want" three times, which suggests this is important. But why do you want to do this? There's also nothing on *relations w/ peers*. Do you hang around with other jocks or are you a loner? Who do you hunt with?

All of these lead to some inferences about *relations w/ peers, strangers, and teachers.* Either you don't like to write, or you don't reveal much about yourself to people you don't know. Which is it?

Essay length could be due to either or both, since its shortness is because of a lack of details. *Essay structure* is clear, though: introductory paragraph giving background, followed by 3 equally developed paragraphs and a concluding one of the same length. That last paragraph can be identified as a conclusion because of your last couple of sentences, which sort of make a statement about life, which is a nice way to end. Since there are 2 paragraphs on sports or sport-related activities (hunting & fishing), these would qualify as your *preferred topics. Technical proficiency* is okay—no glaring misspellings or punctuation problems. *Preferred sentence type* is simple: subject-verb-object. Note how the majority follow that pattern. I didn't notice any *preferred words,* though I'd guess that your preference is, as you said in paragraph 2, for just the facts.

Hopefully, as the semester progresses and you get to know your readers and get used to writing, essay length will develop.

As you can see, this type of response is descriptive and fairly neutral. It points out areas of strengths and interest; it does not judge, criticize, or penalize, which might inhibit further involvement in writing or in the class itself.

It was hard to gauge Bill's reaction after he received this first paper. He was fairly quiet, rarely volunteering in class discussion unless it was his turn. During his group work, he appeared slightly more outgoing, interacting with his group members, giving them descriptive feedback on their essays, and generally acting at ease. His second paper, on family traditions, was not noticeably different from Essay 1. Essay 2 had one less paragraph, but it was two lines longer than Essay 1. There were some typographical errors, some misspellings, and misused semicolons. Again, there was the repetition of facts, although this time, there was also an inkling of feelings: "We are all excited an [sic] can't wait to go [on vacation], because we know around a month before where we are going. Everyone has something to look forward to while being busy."

Following this introduction, establishing the context for their annual family vacation, Bill tells how he and his dad work to get everything packed and ready to go. The third paragraph is the most developed. It is here that we begin to see the dynamics of family relationships:

Well her [sic] is the time when we start to run late and if we don't leave by a certain time my dad isn't going. My mom is rushing. I'm packing and my brother aoways [sic] manages to slip out and disappear for awhile: so he doesn't have to work. My dad starts yelling at my mom. My mom yells at him and they decide that we are not going on vacation. Then I get yelled at for not doing something right. Then I yell at Matt for not helping me. When we arrive, the unloading of the car and getting settled is the start of a new argument.

My comments began with a remark that our family vacations often resembled his; then I noted Bill's increased essay length, clear structure, variety of syntax, and primarily correct punctuation. I also raised questions regarding family relationships and expression of feelings:

> Since [paragraph 3] is the focus of the essay, it makes sense that the arguments on the day of departure make this paragraph the most developed. At the same time, however, since it is the focus, why aren't there more details? What is said? Where does your brother go? What do you say? How do you feel about these arguments at the time, and in general? Later, how are the bad feelings resolved? Do they go away once you're in the car and then start up during unloading, or is the whole drive uncomfortable? Again, how are the arguments resolved? Since we're focusing on language, it makes sense to include those details.
>
> Lack of details = lack of feelings. In paragraph 1 you say you are all excited because of the impending trip and you conclude that the whole thing is "kind of funny." But how do you feel about this tradition? Do you think such arguments will continue when you have a family, or would you try to avoid them? Lack of details also offers little information on *relations w/ your family*. From pars. 1 and 2 I can infer that you and your dad are closer, since you work together for the trip. True?

Again, this method of response included no criticism of language use—just description and questions about the relationship between language and relationships. The questions were posed not out of any voyeuristic interest, or even with a particular concern for fluency or essay length; rather, I wanted Bill to become aware of his language use and its possible sources.

This type of response, coupled with the noncritical classroom environment, seemed to have a positive effect on Bill's writing. His next essay, on school relations, was thirty-six lines long, consisting of eight paragraphs. In his first paragraph, preferred topics of sports and resulting competition recur: "The guys I played ball with and some other friends would always criticize each other and try and out do each other by getting the highest grade. 'I usually won.'" Bill goes on to tell how his coaches always checked up on his grades. This was no problem until his senior year, when he took Pascal Programming, a difficult course that took up extra time and cut into his sports practices. Moreover, despite his hard work, Bill wasn't doing well. He got a *D* when he thought he deserved a *B,* so he told his teacher:

> ... if I don't get out of her class that she better pass me or I would go to the Vice Principle [sic]. ... I ended up passing with a "D" and I know I failed the class and I wasn't worried about it. If we failed any class in the

last semester we couldn't graduate Mr. Meatrici [the vice principal] told me don't worry about it. So I didn't and passed.

At this point, there seem to be some language patterns emerging. Just as Bill's father "yelled at" his mother and declared he wouldn't go on vacation in Essay 2, Bill tries to bully his teacher into letting him drop the class. If I had been grading this essay, his actions and attitudes might have affected the grade I gave him: despite his improved fluency, paragraph development, and sentence variety, his attitude toward women and the apparent complicity of the male faculty, coaches, and administration touched a nerve. I felt angry at Bill and at the stereotypical and preferential treatment of male athletes. However, the descriptive mode of response provided a buffer and a more positive outlet for my feelings. After commenting on the fact that sports was a preferred subject that seemed to have a positive effect on his success in school, and that this essay was moving away from a factual presentation, I wrote:

> I think this is the first time for *relations w/ teachers* and *peers*. For the most part, relations w/ teachers seems good. Was that only w/ teachers who were sports fans or only w/ male teachers (maybe the same thing)? It is interesting that your only problem occurred w/ a female teacher. There are no *expressions of feeling* regarding her. However, the fact that you didn't use her name suggests a lack of communication and respect; more obvious is your threat to her on p. 3 and the fact that you didn't even worry about her, since you knew the "higher-ups"—male teachers, administrators, and coaches—would take care of you. So what does this say about relations w/ females, or female teachers?

Apart from brief comments when I sat in on the students' group discussions, I received little feedback about my responses. Bill rarely said anything in class; however, I could see the effect of my feedback through the changes in his writing. The next essay assignment asked the students to write about an incident in which they were the object of sexual discrimination, and then to write about a time when they discriminated against someone on the basis of that person's gender. Bill wrote the following:

> Believe it or not, sexism is still here. It will never change. Although there are things men are better equipped for like the Military. I'm not saying women can't do it. But women aren't suppose [sic] to be rough and tough. Sexism isn't just against women, I can tell you I've been at both ends of the stick.
>
> There is this store, I don't know where because my girlfriend won't tell, that I can't go into. "It's only for women," she said. Then I said, "Bologna, guys probably work there." She said, "Nope, only women, because it has everything that women need." I said, "So does Grandpa Pigeons [a local version of K-Mart]." Now that's sexist! And we both got into an argument and then her mom jumped in. This all started because she

needed a dress to wear to a wedding, so she wanted to buy a new one. I was like, I'll come and see what your [sic] getting and see if it's pretty. She said, "Fine." A couple of days later she said she was going out to get a dress. I said, "What about me. I thought I was going." She said her mom was taking her to this store where she got her Prom dress and men aren't allowed in. I said, "You're crazy, you just don't want me to come." And her mom said no she wasn't, it is because it's an old fashion [sic] store. This place must be a whole [sic] in the ground. I never heard of anything so ridiculous. I was mad. I wanted to find this place and just walk in and see how long I could stand there until they threw me out . . .

Women playing soccer is a joke, all they do is complain and cry. I referee women's soccer because I got control over them, also the money's pretty good. But I get more of a kick watching them complain. I ref at Forest Park; and one day the game started off fine, for the first minute anyway. A girl was screaming at me because I called a goal back, because of offside. The funny thing is that it was going to be there [sic] ball because of a foul committed after the goal. It was going to be a penalty shot. Being sly, like I love doing when reffing, I said, "Who's [sic] ball is it?" Real nice to her. She said, "It's their's." I said, "No it's a penalty shot, and by the way you've got three strikes." She said what and I said you're out and I gave her a red card. I never had to [sic] much trouble with any other team, once I showed those women who was boss. Unlike this one woman ref, man was she terrible. She wouldn't call fouls or when she did they'd say something back to her. One day she started crying, it was pretty funny, because she called a foul and they started arguing. I guess it wouldn't of been funny if I were in her shoes. But give me a break, she was too emotional. Like my dad says, "Play the game or go home you little girl."

There are ways to overcome sexism. I don't mean to sound like a sexist pig but women should do women jobs, and there are women that agree with me. But I've seen how it is to be treated at both ends to [sic] the stick because of my gender.

As a woman, I was offended by what I considered Bill's blatantly sexist attitudes as revealed in his actions and his language. If I had been grading this paper, my feelings might well have affected his grade. Even if I could have separated the two, I would have felt the need to disagree or to point out the error of his thinking. But neither preaching nor penalty would have necessarily made Bill conscious of what his language illustrated and might only have strengthened his views about women. By responding to his language features, however, I was able to discuss Bill's writing without questioning his intellect or quashing his openness.

Whew! Is this unconscious, or are you aware of these attitudes? Since you quote your dad, I can see that some of it comes from *relations w/ family.*

And maybe playing sports exacerbates it. Research has shown that athletes are more sexist than the average male. What do you think?

So how does your attitude affect *relations w/ peers* esp. females? How does it affect the relationship w/ your girlfriend? Does she stand up to you often? Your *expressions of feeling* in this paragraph are very direct, more so than in previous essays: *women aren't supposed to be rough and tough; women playing soccer is a joke; I was mad; . . .*

It's interesting that this essay is your longest so far. Was *essay length* related to the topic, are you getting used to writing, or is it related to the strength of your feelings? Your *essay structure is* also interesting. In paragraph 1, p. 1, you say sexism "will never change." But in your last paragraph, you say there are ways to overcome sexism. Yet your next sentence implies that sexism can be overcome by people doing gender-specific jobs. Is this what you mean? You seem to contradict yourself. Your 2 middle paragraphs are about the same length, but Part I is longer than the other side. People seem to focus more on the wrongs done to them and to excuse their own. . . . *Relations w/ strangers* seems to be based on their gender—would you agree?

Bill received stronger comments than this from his group members—Frank, a fairly sexist male, and Becky, a conservative female—who also based their responses on his language features. Bill said little in response, so I asked him what he thought of his group's reaction. He summed up their conversation succinctly: "Becky really let me have it," he said. "She couldn't believe the things I said about women." And then he laughed.

Because this paper was so outrageous and more outspoken than any of the other essays I had received, I felt that it needed a wider response than what I or Bill's group could provide, so I distributed it to the class (with Bill's permission) for discussion. This resulted in one of our most lively discussions. Bill's statements provoked responses from practically everyone, even from students who hadn't spoken much all semester. The women were outraged, while the men were surprised (and amused) at Bill's directness. His group members contributed to the discussion by pointing out certain trends in Bill's writing. He had already exhibited this need for control, they said, in his paper about the computer teacher. They supported their opinions by pointing out that Bill wanted to be a police officer. As for the source of his attitudes, the group said he was close to his dad, so it made sense that he would quote him.

The group's input gave us a fuller picture of Bill and a better understanding of the reasons for his language use. Simultaneously, the class discussion helped Bill to see how his language affected his audience. The discussion focused on his language rather than on his personality. Consequently, Bill did not feel the need to edit or constrain his opinions.

In subsequent essays, Bill's writing showed many of the same traits: he became gradually more open, revealing clearly sexist acts and feelings. As he became more open, Bill's fluency increased. Both essays on sexism were twice the length of his first paper; essays on racism were an additional 25 percent longer. His syntax also matured, changing from primarily simple sentences to a mixture of compound and compound-complex. Recurring topics were sports, fighting, his relations with women, and his relationship with his father.

The only alternating language feature was Bill's expressions of feeling. While he had been quite direct when discussing sexism, he became circumspect in his essays on racism. However, when we began the unit on homophobism, he became suddenly and inappropriately direct. It seemed that because Bill felt superior to women, he did not need to curb his sexist tendencies. His feelings about blacks were not so evident. Perhaps because he had played sports on integrated teams, he was not prejudiced. Or if he was prejudiced, he respected his black peers enough not to insult them with his true feelings.

However, Bill was not so careful when we began to discuss homosexuality. Bill and his male peers viewed gay men as completely different; therefore, they felt no constraint in expressing homophobic fears and prejudices during class discussion and in their writing. The latter surprised me somewhat, as I had tried to design this essay assignment so that the students had a personal stake in it, so that they would become aware of, and write from a sense of, their own sexuality (see Berg et al. 1990 for more specific advice).

I began the assignment with the story of a family friend who "came out" to us and then told us how his father had reacted. The assignment then raised the following questions: Have you ever been in a similar situation? If so, tell how it occurred, what you said and did, and how or if the revelation affected your friendship. If not, tell what you would say if one of your friends or family members "came out." Bill's essay was one of the most offensive I received.

> At my high school there was this group of people that hung around together. By the way they dressed and talked, I knew they were homos. I was friends with this one guy for two years. We double dated a few times and went to some parties together.
>
> Junior year in high school he started to talk to that group of gays and I told him what I thought of them. He kind of agreed, and I told him that I don't think it's a good idea to talk to them. . . . I was still friends with him because I didn't think he was changing until Senior Year. (I was friends with him over the summer and still did things with him. But he seemed a little strange. He didn't tease the girls like we used to.)
>
> During the second semester he started going out with the gay group and [I] stopped talking to him and hanging out with him. He would talk to me and say "Let's go out this weekend and I'll bring a few new friends." I would say "No" right away and walk away.

Well, this year he goes to UMSL. He told these girls who I am friends with also, that he was gay. My friend Mike told me and I said "I knew. Couldn't you tell that he was gay when we were going to high school." He said maybe but he never said he was gay.

He is in one class with me and I told him outright. "Don't even talk to me. Stay away and just go in your little gay corner and play your games. You are a sick and discusting [sic] individual, touch me or come near me and die." I was serious and he knows it. He isn't a friend of mine and as far as I'm concerned, he never was. If [a] girl was gay, it wouldn't bother me.

My parents would disown me real quick and kick me out of the house. They both would have the same reactions. "Get out." My mom gets sick anytime I start talking about homos, because it makes her so upset. We had a couple of guys living down the street from us who were gay and my dad used to write death threats to them. They moved about 2 months later. My brothers and sisters would act the same way. For sure!

If any of my brother or sisters or parents told me they were gay, I wouldn't have anything to do with them. I wouldn't treat them ignorantly. By not talking to them and having nothing to do with them. My attitude wouldn't change at all. I'd feel sorrow for them, and tell them, then say "See Ya!"

It would be very easy—and very tempting—to give this paper a bad grade. When I showed it to other teachers, they found a number of reasons to justify a grade of C, D, or F. Their comments told Bill to *make it more clear, rewrite . . . and elaborate, be more specific with your description and detail, don't make generalizations, work on transitions, work on organization,* and *be specific.* But the comments did not stop there. They also criticized Bill personally—*[your essay] was hard for me to handle because it showed so much prejudice; you are not open-minded; if you had thought about why you feel this way . . . I would have respected your opinions; you kept my interest, even though I don't agree; did you really invest time in analysis, in thought?* These teachers had tried to be neutral; however, their feelings about Bill's prejudice, coupled with their natural inclination to critique his thinking and writing, led to a series of commands (rewrite, be specific, work!) and condemnation (I can't handle this, you didn't think, I don't respect you).

I believe these comments are fairly typical, for they reflect how we were taught to teach writing. Despite the move toward portfolios and delayed grades, this tendency is still very much with us. Pat Bizzell (1991) has pointed out that we cannot help promoting our own political views through our presence and our pedagogy. I would take that a step further: we cannot help promoting our political views through our responses to students' papers.

We have long heard, and believed, that writing aids thinking. Yet despite the focus in many writing classrooms on writing as a process, the emphasis is still on the final product. The bottom line, the ultimate goal, is the grade.

We want our students to do what these teachers encouraged: add details, develop ideas, use smooth transitions, work on organization, be specific. If the students think along the way, that's a bonus. But how much are critical thinking and exploration of ideas encouraged when the emphasis is on style, on writing that traditional essay? This problem is even more serious when students write about social issues. While college may be a new environment, the students bring with them eighteen years of borrowed and unexplored prejudices and beliefs. They are unlikely to risk exploring them if they are writing for a grade.

We can teach students to appeal to an audience, to write the traditional essay, cleaned up for a good grade—or we can let them really express themselves, then teach them to look at what they are saying and ask why. Where did this come from? Why do I feel this way? What does my language say about who I am and how I feel? What effect would the teachers' comments on the homophobic paper have on a student's willingness to express and explore his ideas in future papers, or to consider why he felt this way? Contrast these with a descriptive response:

Bill—

I can see where you got this attitude. It's interesting that examples or quotes from your dad come out on subjects dealing with prejudice. . . .

What do your last two paragraphs say about *relationships with your family?* On the one hand, you share ideas and beliefs, but almost because of these, you all seem willing never to see one another again if one of you differed from the rest.

Relationships with peers is stated directly, as are your feelings about them. These *feelings* are expressed both directly and indirectly. The fact that you walk away from your former friend, refuse to talk to or be seen with him, or with your family if they were gay, are all indirect expressions of fear. The most direct expression for your family comes at the end: "I'd feel sorrow for them and tell them." You say gays are "sick and disgusting," but your actions suggest great fear: it's not good to talk to them or to be seen with them; it's even dangerous to live down the street from them. How has Laura's association with them harmed her? Why are "lesbians O.K."? Why was this former friend safe to hang around with and double date with before, but not now? How does sexual preference affect real friends? Have you ever thought about why you feel this way?

Your *essay structure* basically answers the questions. The *length* is more than usual, which seems to reflect the strength of your feelings. *Technical proficiency* is good with quotations, but suffers some with word omissions and misspellings, perhaps because you were writing fast or focusing on feelings. *Syntax* is mixed, maybe smoother than usual, perhaps because you had a great deal to say. *Preferred words* are gay and "homo": the recurring action is avoidance. Why?

Needless to say, if this had been the first paper in the class, I could not have written so much in response, made the connections with family, or even raised some of these questions. I was able to do so because I had read all of Bill's work, spoken with him during group discussion, and responded in this manner to each of his papers. My analysis was furthered by insights from Bill's group members who had discussed his papers with him, and the feelings behind them, in even more detail. Finally, I was able to proceed in this fashion because I was neither a grader nor a voyeur but participated fully in the writing and responding process of the class.

III

Most teachers can accept the idea that this type of response will help students think about their prejudices and beliefs; nevertheless, they still feel that students need more specific guidance. How can a series of ungraded, unmarked free-writes improve students' writing skills? How can we send students out of a writing course without calling attention to and working on matters of organization, development, style, and mechanics?

One way to answer that is quantitatively—to recall that on a four-point scale, the freshmen whose papers had been graded, marked up, and gone through numerous revisions scored 2.27, while the students in the experimental section, whose free-written, ungraded essays had received descriptive responses from me and their peers scored 2.28. These scores do not, however, show the difference that this type of writing and response can make in students' knowledge of themselves and about their language use. To do that, I will quote from Bill's final essay—thirteen pages long—in which he analyzes his use of language and what he has learned.

> I definitely know why I write the way I do. It's mainly because of my competitive nature and the influence of my dad. Being around my dad has rubbed off on me and it's noticeable in my writings. Being competitive is also shown throughout my essays. This has always made me push and work hard for what I want. Showing my emotions became more and more apparent. . . . This took some time because opening up isn't my style. But through talking to Mrs. [Ebest] and group members I became comfortable and opened up. . . . My state of mind reflected in my writings would have to be 'rebellious.' Throughout my essays, except one, I display some kind of dislike or argument, 'fighting.' If I'm not beating someone up, I'm putting down their personal life . . . or telling others what to do, my sexist view. Being competitive, I think right away makes me [seem] rebellious because I'm always trying to outdo others.
>
> Being rebellious relates to college but stems off of my peers and Mrs. [Ebest]. If I don't force myself above all my peers so that Mrs. [Ebest] notices me, then I failed. I have to try and do better to make myself noticed,

like getting into arguments on the views I have with Mrs. [Ebest], which we have done on a regular basis, and to get her advice. This class has helped me see how important it is to show your feelings so readers can and will understand you and your material.

Bill would not have written this type of paper in a traditional classroom, nor would he have been able to. A number of factors contributed to his ability to think and write about his language use. Chief among them is the freedom engendered by the descriptive response and the lack of grades. As David Bleich (1988) notes, "the change in relation to the teacher entails a change in what kind of writing is done" (244).

If we value diversity, we have to establish a context in which students can explore their opinions and feel safe in expressing them, no matter how extreme. If we ask students for honest opinions, we cannot punish them for what they say, or how they say it. If we want to help our students think and grow, we need to rethink and refocus our responses to them and their writing. In doing so, we may begin to change our students' attitudes about writing, about themselves, and about others.

9

The Morrises
A Study of One Family's Writing

Constance Chapman

It was a warm, sunny Sunday afternoon. I watched as six children perched, crouched, or sprawled on the furniture and the floor with pencils and crayons, happily producing everything from lines and squiggles to a sophisticated character named Freddy who donned sunglasses and wore a cigarette hanging from his lips. The cigarette-smoking character had been drawn by Burt, the only boy in the family. After his picture was completed, he wrote a story. His creation complete, Burt ran to the bedroom, got a basal reader, told his twin sisters to sit on the overstuffed chair, sat between them, opened the book and began to read. I was elated! "This is going to be a wonderful study!" I thought.

It was my first day as a participant-observer in the Morris home.[1] The scenario I watched turned out in the end to belie the old saying "What you see is what you get," for, as it turned out, the relationship between this family and school, along with reading and writing, was much more problematic. The Morrises live in Dalver City, a city in the deep South, where I was collecting data for my ethnographic study of the writing in African American families, the last phase on my road to a doctorate. Traveling to this point had been a long road, paved with triumphs and disappointments. Teaching had been one of my triumphs. I had more than twenty years of experience, most of them in elementary and secondary schools. However, the most rewarding years for me had been those teaching composition to college freshmen.

I had begun teaching this course in a special program created by the New York Board of Higher Education to serve low-income students, most of whom were deficient in their basic skills. All were either African American or Hispanic. Teaching them was a pleasure for me because they learned so quickly. Sadly, however, many of them worked hard on writing only because it was a required course. One of them told me that he would never write after he graduated, not even letters. That would be his secretary's job, he said. It

106

troubled me that many of my students had the same attitude, and I often wondered why. My chance to find some answers came when I met a disappointment on my career road.

Open enrollment programs were beginning to be strangled by those who no longer wanted to bear the burden of paying for developmental courses for the underprivileged. College teachers, like me, who had neither doctorates nor certificates of continuous employment (CCEs) were forced into adjunct positions. It was then that I decided to return to graduate school and earn a doctorate.

Finally, it was time for me to focus on a dissertation. The quantitative research reports I had read during my course work had left me with the question, "So what?" The questions I had about my students' apathy toward writing still concerned me, but I could find no answers in the esoteric articles I read by researchers who focused on multiple probes, standard deviations, ANOVA, and the like—researchers who cared more about *what* than *why*.

In ethnography, there is emphasis on direct personal and holistic involvement in the community. These methods are especially useful in the field of writing when the purpose of the research is to discover what is there rather than to prove or disprove a particular theory. According to Beach and Bridwell (1984), "The writing ethnographer studies the context as it exists in the real world. From these observations and from interview data, the investigator begins to determine subjects' perceptions—of themselves as writers, of their audience, and of the situation—and how these perceptions influence their writing performances" (16). I patterned my research after Shirley Brice Heath's (1983) work, and since the purpose of my study was to find out how another group of people use writing in their everyday lives, I chose to use participant-observation techniques in order to examine "phenomena in their naturally occurring contexts" (Goetz and LeCompte 1984).

My plan was to stay with a family and take notes on all incidents of writing that I observed and then ascertain, through questioning or careful observation, the writers' purposes for writing, their feelings about the task, whether they completed the task with ease or with great pain, whether they revised the writing or seemed satisfied with first drafts, whether writing was done only for special events or was an important ingredient in their everyday lives, and any other data that would help me to describe writing and writing events in a southern African American family. My aim was to discover how the family members dealt with writing in their everyday lives. I reasoned that if I discovered whether they wrote and exactly what they wrote, I could suggest ways to reshape writing programs to help students to enjoy writing and to encourage them to use it in beneficial ways as they use reading and math.

When I told a classmate about my research plans, she suggested that I collect my data in Dalver City. Her husband taught there and would be glad to find families who would agree to participate in my study. He found three families for me (see Chapman 1991), but in this chapter, I will focus on the

Morris family, a family of seven—the mother, Della, twenty-eight; and six children: Stella, twelve; Rita, eleven; Burt, nine; Edna, six; and twins, Tina and Sheena, three.

Della and Her Writing

Della became pregnant when she was in the ninth grade and dropped out of school. Consequently, she spent her adolescence and young adulthood raising children. Her first child, Stella, was born when Della was fifteen. The others arrived in rapid succession: Rita when Della was sixteen; Burt when she was nineteen; Edna when she was twenty-two; and the twins, Tina and Sheena, when she was twenty-five.

Except for signing her name, Della did only two short writing tasks during the time I spent with the family, neither of which was self-initiated. The first occurred in a shoe store where she and I had gone to exchange some sneakers that were too small for Burt. The saleswoman gave her a return form to complete. Della filled in the portion asking for her name and address but left blank the lines asking for the reason for the return. The saleswoman informed her that it was essential that she complete that section also. Della picked up a pen, moved it back and forth in the air, and stared through the window, punctuating her silence with sporadic utterances of "What? What?" She finally wrote, "To big." Since the shoes were too small for Burt, I could only assume that she could spell neither *small* nor *little*.

The second writing task that Della completed was a receipt for the money I had given her for room and board. I asked for the receipt four or five times before she gave me one. Although there was plenty of writing paper around the house on which she could have written a receipt, she got a receipt form from someone and filled it in. The receipt provided some clues that Della might have difficulty with reading. She filled in the date and my name in the correct places and crossed out the word *address* and wrote *paid*, indicating that she knew those words. In the place headed *description*, she wrote her name, the amount of money I gave her, and the word *rent*. Also, the line at the bottom of the receipt reserved for the person writing the receipt was left blank. While this is not conclusive evidence that Della is only functionally literate, there were other clues that seemed to substantiate this inference. Della never bought or read the newspaper. Problems with reading surfaced whenever Della had to follow written directions to make or alter something. On these occasions, she asked Rita to read the instructions for her. Della never read notes from the children's teachers, even if the children told her that they were important. The children frequently suffered negative consequences. For example, Burt's teacher told me that Burt often had to sit in other classrooms because Della had not responded to notes about trips his class planned to take.

The children also used Della's inability to read to their advantage by not mentioning or showing her certain letters sent from school. For example, Della was unaware that it was the custom of Ms. Nancy, Edna's teacher, to send a form to parents each Friday that reported the child's conduct for the week. The form was to be read, signed, and returned to school on Mondays. Ms. Nancy said that Edna always "forgot" her report.

One of the most significant consequences of Della's feeling of insecurity about her literacy skills is that it may have prevented her from participating in a training program designed for welfare mothers with dependent children. The program provided computer training, transportation to and from classes, a stipend, and job placement at the end of the training. Della told me that she intended to sign up but had no one to keep the twins and would wait until they were old enough to go to school. However, a neighbor told me that the program also provided child care for preschool children. The reason Della made excuses about signing up may have been that she did not want people to discover her difficulty with reading.

Stella and Her Writing

Twelve-year-old Stella was the oldest child. A seventh grader in middle school, Stella was an average student. This was quite a drop from her elementary school performance; in fifth grade, she won an award (a plaque displayed on the living room wall) for earning all *A*'s. Like Della, Stella was also taciturn around me. Stella wrote often but always refused to show her work to anyone in the family. The first time I had a clue that she was writing was one evening when she came into the living room and announced that she had written something. I asked her what she had written and she said it was "something like a journal." However, Stella was full of discrepancies. Several days later I asked her whether she wrote in her journal often. She replied that she would not start one until she was thirteen (her birthday was three months away). To insure privacy, she kept her "journal" in her handbag. Since I was unable to convince her to share any of her writing with me, I did not know whether she felt that what she had written was too private to share or whether her journal, in fact, contained any writing at all.

The only thing that Stella did let me see was a page of sentences that said, "I will not talk in school." I asked her whether she had been given that for punishment. She said no, she was just writing it because she knew she was going to have to write it. Consequently, she was doing it so she would not have homework the next day. "So you know you're going to talk?" I asked her. "Yeah," she replied. She carefully numbered lines on a pad and wrote one hundred sentences, two on each line.

One day I sat in on Stella's morning classes. She was rude and talkative in all of them except language arts. There, her behavior changed completely.

She was quiet, attentive, and did not speak unless she was called on. I talked with the teacher, Mrs. Evens, who told me that Stella was a good worker in her class. When I explained my research and told her that Stella had refused to let me see any of her writing, Mrs. Evens gave me a copy of a story Stella had written.

When I told Stella that Mrs. Evens had given me the copy, she replied: "Oh, I copied that. I always copy my stories." Later, during an interview, I asked her about the story again. This time she said she had not copied the story, just the idea for it. As I read the story I saw evidence that both her statements were mixtures of the truth. The story, entitled "The Night of the Comet," told about a girl whose grandfather had taken her to Central Park to see the Leonid. Clues that Stella had written the story herself were run-on sentences and the omission of *ed* and *s* endings on verbs and nouns, common patterns in Black English. Clues that she had copied parts of the story were pronoun references to the narrator's grandfather—sometimes *he* and other times *she*. Switching gender pronouns often happens when a person tries to alter a story as she or he copies. Another clue that Stella had copied parts of the story was her use of a sophisticated metaphor in one of the sentences: "a hallway of sky" between buildings. Stella's teacher told me that she also suspected that Stella had copied parts of the story, but because she was sure that, if questioned, Stella would react negatively by refusing to do subsequent assignments, she had decided not to pursue the matter.

Rita and Her Writing

Rita, who wants to be a doctor when she grows up, enjoyed doing crossword puzzles and caught on quickly when I showed her how to solve cryptograms. Her science teacher said that she was a good student and would perform better if she got encouragement from home. On several occasions, Rita used her writing skills to create documents that had nothing to do with school. One was a contract written for Della's boyfriend, Gene, to sign. Rita got the idea for the contract after a Dalver City philanthropist announced that he intended to "adopt" the school Rita attended. In order to encourage the students to earn better grades and remain in school, he promised to pay students five dollars for each *A*, two dollars for each *B*, and five dollars for perfect attendance. Rita felt that this remuneration was inadequate and unfair, so she decided to ask Gene to sign a contract that would pay more money. However, Gene did not agree to the contract. He wrote a large "No" on the appropriate line and the contract was tossed aside. Rita also used her skills to forge a note for two of her friends who planned to arrive in class late. I was present when Rita wrote the note. As Rita proceeded to the class for which the note was written, she dropped it to the floor unnoticed and I retrieved it. The errors made in the note (the missing date, the crossed out *e* on *excuse,* the lowercase letters on *monica* and *wykisha*, the signature with no title (or first name) were obvious clues that the note was written by a student and probably would have caused more trouble for the students than arriving late to class.

A bright student, Rita appeared to be losing interest in school, probably because her studies were not challenging enough. Her interest in writing was not stimulated by her teacher, Ms. Brown, who was unaware of Rita's interest in composing legal documents such as contracts and promissory notes. Moreover, instead of being pregnant with compositions, poems, and notes, Rita's writing folder was empty except for some fill-in exercises. Ms. Brown said that she had asked the students to write poems on several occasions but Rita had not submitted hers. However, Rita explained that Ms. Brown would not accept her work because it was late and so she had become disgusted and destroyed it.

Ms. Brown also required that her students write in their journals during the first fifteen minutes of class. She told me that the students often complained that they did not know what to write about, so she resorted to assigned topics. Ms. Brown may not have known that her students had few books or reading experiences, no current magazines, and thus no easy store of "literate" topics. I knew, though, that her students, like Rita and her siblings, were filled with questions: "What is the Holy Ghost?" "If you drop a bullet, will it explode?" Learning answers to questions such as these can help children begin to think critically, to solve problems, and to find the answers to subsequent questions on their own. This can also be done by encouraging children to explore these questions in their journals. Unfortunately, Ms. Brown seemed not to have thought of these possibilities.

On the day I visited Rita's class, the subject for journal writing was the cartoon cat Garfield. The teacher said it was chosen from a list of suggestions the students had made during a brainstorming session. On this particular day, Rita wrote nothing in her journal. She told me that she did not want to write about Garfield but could think of nothing else to write. A quick glance through her journal later revealed dates but few entries, sentences that stopped midway, and unfinished anecdotes. The idea of journals is for students to write in a nonthreatening genre, so that they can develop their fluency without worrying about mechanics and grammar. However, Rita's teacher used journal writing to keep students busy while she was on hall duty during class changes. She, like many teachers I have observed, provided time for students to write, but never wrote with them. It is clear from research and from practice that students respond well when teachers model the literacy behaviors they want students to adopt. Many classroom teachers, however, still do not do so. In fact, none of the teachers of the children I observed in this study wrote or shared their work with students. We need to understand why. The reasons may be various, ranging from increasing noninstructional duties to lack of confidence in their own writing. Teachers may not be familiar with this advice, or they may lack a clear sense of how to implement it.

Burt and His Writing

Often the only boy in a family of all girls is spoiled and doted on, but this was not the case in the Morris home. Burt, a nine-year-old, was treated with disdain. On one occasion, after looking at his spelling test, Stella told him, "Boy, you don't know how to spell *reading*? And what's this? You should be ashamed!" He was often called *stupid,* and because he was always made to wait until last to fix his plate at dinnertime, he sometimes did not get one of the dishes prepared.

Burt seemed to want to write, but his performance in writing was tempered by the ridicule he often received from his siblings. As reported earlier, on the first day I arrived at the Morris apartment, he was drawing a picture of someone he called Freddy. Freddy, with his sunglasses, a black hat with a red hatband, and a cigarette dangling from his lips, was the epitome of what some would call "cool." In fact, Burt wrote the words *Cool Play Boy* on every side of Freddy's portrait (see Figure 9–1). Next to Freddy's portrait was a man whose feet and hands had been nailed to the wall. From these extremities dripped blood. I asked Burt why Freddy killed people. He shrugged his shoulders. I thought the reason might be revealed if Burt wrote a story about Freddy, so I encouraged him to do so.

Writing the story about Freddy was difficult for Burt. There were many pauses in his writing, some lasting for five or six minutes, during which he played with the other children or watched the cartoons on television. His efforts were punctuated by comments and criticism from his siblings. Rita told him that Freddy never killed anyone and that he spelled *once* and *Freddy* wrong. Stella snatched his paper and sneered, "*There* and *Killer* ain't suppose to have no capital letters and that's not the way you spell *people*," and threw the paper back at him. Burt seemed to lose interest in the writing, but he continued when I told him that I would like to have the story when he finished. As I reflect on the first scenario I witnessed in the Morris home, I surmise that Burt's performance had been an effort to show a new person in his life that he was not stupid. But Rita and Stella's ridicule had, in his mind, negated his attempt.

I discovered that Burt was interested in mechanical gadgets. The first of his "inventions" I saw was a present he made for me—a twenty-one-inch pencil. He had used a hollow rod and stuck a pencil in each end so that one end had an eraser and the other had lead. He secured the pencils to the rod with masking tape. Another "invention" materialized one day when he told me that he wished he had a battery because he wanted to make something. I gave him one of the batteries I had for my tape recorder. He took one of his sister's broken dolls, retrieved a part, connected it to wires and the battery, and made the part spin. The spinning part was so small that I could not see it, so he attached a piece of paper that whirled like a fan when he touched the wires to the battery. On yet another day, he made a sophisticated slingshot using a piece

Figure 9–1
Burt's story

Ouce upon a time There
Was a Killer His name was
Freddy He go aroud the world
Killing popel

of wood, glue, rubber bands, and a clothespin for a firing pin. Burt also loved to go crawfishing. On a shelf in the Morris living room was a trophy he had won for catching the most crawfish in a contest during a church outing.

Often, especially with students like Burt, teachers must reach beyond the required curriculum to stimulate them to learn. Many teachers and researchers have reported remarkable success when they have done so. For example, regarding one student, Atwell (1987) reported, "Just as soon as I knew his interests, I started feeding Tom books about the natural world" (255). Soon, Tom found books about his favorite subject on his own. Eventually he wrote a letter to the author of a book he particularly enjoyed. Yet Tom was a student whose mother had reported that he disliked both reading and writing and probably would refuse to exert any effort in these subjects. Unfortunately, Burt's interests and talents were unknown to his teacher.

Edna and Her Writing

Edna, a six-year-old, appeared to have a learning disability. She had a great deal of trouble with reading and math. Her reading was slow and hesitant and her inability to master basic math concepts made it necessary for her to use her fingers to compute. At home, part of Edna's problem was that she was easily distracted and the Morris home was full of distractions—the blasting television, noisy visitors, screaming siblings. While the other children were able to complete their work in this atmosphere, Edna was not. She stopped after each mark she made on a page, listened to what was being said, or watched something on television.

Edna enjoyed writing stories and often used invented spelling. Her teacher said that this spelling illustrated that Edna had not mastered word attack skills. This might have been because she either did not hear the sounds or had yet to learn to associate the sounds with corresponding letters or blends. For example, Figure 9–2 shows a story about a girl who went (wns) swimming (simin) and saw a fish.

One day, Edna told me that she wanted to write a "l-o-ong story" to "fill up the whole paper." This was the first story she wrote that did not accompany a drawing. She worked for a long time and produced a list of yes/no questions beginning "Do I like. . . ." and "Do you like. . . ." She gave it to me proudly and said that I should keep it. A week before I left the Morris family for the last time, Edna gave me another piece of writing that she said was a present for me. Edna is an example of what can happen if teachers elect to use real life experience to teach writing. In contrast to the students in Burt's class, the children in Edna's class had many opportunities to write. They wrote class stories that were related to experiences that they had had—field trips, current events, curriculum. Although Edna had reading difficulties, I heard her read one of the class-written stories, "Space Astronaut," with ease.

The Twins and Their Writing

Tina and Sheena, aged three, were fraternal twins. Tina, who was one hour older, was also the smaller. Sheena, who was taller and larger-boned, could easily pass for five years of age. Tina was precocious and friendly; Sheena was average and shy. However, Sheena was calmer and more independent than Tina. The twins were loved and petted by everyone. In fact, they were the only children Della hugged, kissed, and told of her love for them.

Sheena and Tina enjoyed drawing pictures and dictating captions. Sometimes their desire to draw and write was stimulated by seeing their siblings do so. At other times, they initiated writing events themselves, particularly when they were tired of playing outside or on inclement days when everyone had to remain indoors. When they could find no paper, they asked for it, and they used

Figure 9–2
Edna's story

See The girL wns
sImin Fish Like
water

whatever writing implements were available, sometimes pencils, sometimes felt-tipped pens, and sometimes crayons. They would offer their drawings to someone in the family as gifts. I received many of them.

Della seldom took the time to take the twins on excursions, partly because she did not have a car and public transportation in Dalver City was extremely poor. For example, a trip that would take one hour by car would sometimes take an entire day by bus. During my second month with the Morris family, I asked Della if I could take Tina and Sheena on a trip. Dalver City is the state capital and, since the twins had never been there, I decided to take them to the State Office Building. When we returned, Sheena drew pictures of what they had seen and asked me to add captions. The twins found all kinds of things to draw, using their surroundings to stimulate ideas. For example, whenever it rained, large worms would come out of the ground to get air. Tina used this as the subject for one of her stories.

Some Observations and Possible Recommendations

Even though writing was painful for Burt and nonexistent for Della, writing in the Morris family was frequent. None of the children expressed negative attitudes about writing, although Burt had to be prodded to complete two of his writing events. The children also made time to write, often squeezing it in between playing outdoors and watching television. They wrote pieces other than their school assignments. Rita, for example, wrote a contract and a promissory note; Edna composed a "lo-o-ng story"; and Sheena and Tina gave gifts of their writing. All of the children, with the exception of Burt, seemed to gain great satisfaction out of writing. Writing seemed to give them a chance to express themselves in nonrestricted ways. Ironically, the data reported here seem to identify age as an important determinant to indicate whether or not people enjoy writing. This observation concurs with a National Assessment of Educational Progress (NAEP) report that comments that "students seem to lose interest in writing as they get older. Fifty-five percent of fourth graders said they like to write, compared to forty-two percent of eight-graders and thirty-seven percent of eleventh graders" (Conciatore 1990, 4). This notion implies that by the time the Morris children reach the eleventh grade, they probably will have lost their enthusiasm for writing. Since interest in writing seems to diminish as people get older, some answers that explain this phenomenon might be found by a closer examination of the writing of the Morris children who seemed to enjoy writing the most.

If we begin with Sheena and Tina, we discover where the enchantment for writing begins to dwindle. Both of these girls enjoyed drawing and getting someone to write captions for their artwork. Calkins (1986) writes: "The wonderful thing is that within this kind of context [drawing], growth happens very quickly." She further contends that drawing is the beginning of transitions to more and more conventional symbols for ideas. The twins were often stimulated to draw when they saw their siblings writing. They were eager to explain their drawings, and to tell stories about the lines and squiggles they sketched on their papers. They had plenty of stimulation to draw but almost no encouragement until I lived with the family. Who records the stories of young siblings in the homes of families like the Morrises where literacy expectations are very low? In the Morris family, the oldest children were not interested in helping the twins to translate their drawings, and Della's lack of skills made it impossible for her to do so. Does this mean that the twins will lose their enthusiasm for creating? Is there anything that can be done about this? Perhaps there is.

We cannot continue to try to teach children like Della's without offering education to Della and parents like her. One way to do this is to provide training for parents in the school setting. However, getting parents like Della to go to such classes is difficult. They feel uncomfortable in the school setting. They realize that their own skills are deficient, that they do not speak what some call "proper" English, so many of them avoid visiting their children's schools. One way to alleviate this discomfort is to return to "the basics"—not "the three Rs" but home visitations. Years ago, teachers were welcome visitors in the home. They felt comfortable there, and in familiar settings, parents could feel at ease sharing their concerns about their children's education. Another way to get parents to take an active role in schools is to replace parent-teacher conferences, which seldom attract the parents of students who are performing poorly, with hands-on workshops. During these workshops, parents could be engaged in the same type of writing activities that their children are asked to do. Parents and teachers could not only engage in writing activities during the workshops but they could also learn from each other. Parents and teachers could share some of their concerns, fears, problems, achievements, and goals, and they could share insights that would help both groups to improve their own and the students' writing skills. In this way, the two groups could begin to understand each other's problems and concerns and make giant steps toward their mutual goal—providing quality education for students. In fact, such workshops are provided on Saturdays at an elementary school in a low income area in Atlanta, Georgia. The day begins with exercise and breakfast after which parents and teachers meet for collaborative activities in reading, writing, and math. Child care is provided for parents who have young children. The principal reports that sixty percent of the students' parents participate each week. In Della's case, the workshops could provide her with an opportunity to learn how to record the simple language of the twins' drawings and thus to stimulate both their reading and their writing progress. But most important, she could not only improve her own skills but also lift the "shade of shame" that now covers her because the skills she has are inadequate.

What about Della's children? Rita's and Burt's teachers illustrate Goodlad's (1987) notion that teachers have their own agendas and that these agendas seldom coincide with students' daily lives, needs, and concerns. One factor that stood out was Burt's and Rita's lack of interest in the subjects their teachers asked them to write about. They either refused to write, as the empty pages in their notebooks and journals indicated, or they substituted alternative activities (talking, passing notes to other students).

Freeman, Samuelson, and Sanders (1986) and Szwed (1981) suggest that tasks like those given to Burt and Rita are assigned to students because teachers make assumptions about students' literacy needs without considering the relevance of these assignments to students' daily lives and the functions of writing outside the classroom. Therefore, assignments are separated from real writing and students begin to feel an indifference toward writing.

Ways that might stimulate Burt to write have already been discussed. As for Rita, the enthusiasm with which she told about incidents occurring while the Morrises lived on a farm gives us a clue about encouraging her imagination enough so that she will continue to enjoy writing. We can imagine the pleasure she would get by finding out what city her grandfather's farm was in, how to find it on the map, how many miles away it was, and how long it would take to travel there. Additionally, since she seemed to have an interest in legal documents, she might be interested in finding out where to look up ownership of the farm and whether or not her family had any legal claim to it. And finally, Rita could record the whole process in a journal.

The reader might wonder, then, whether I am saying that we should give up teaching essay and creative writing in schools. On the contrary, meeting people's needs does not mean making a foolish decision similar to the one made by the builders of the luxury liner *Titanic* who reasoned that, because the ship was unsinkable, it only needed to carry a few lifeboats. The solution is to *add to* rather than subtract from the writing curriculum. Elbow (1991) said it well: "In my view, the best test of a writing course is whether it makes students more likely to use writing in their lives" (136). The goal here is to make a concerted effort to help students retain their interest in writing so that they will not become like Stella, who copied others' work to submit as her own, or like Della, whose inadequate skills prevented her from writing at all.

Writing is a powerful tool, perhaps the most powerful skill taught in school because, unlike other disciplines—reading, math, and science, for example—it allows students to deal with their own thoughts rather than those of others. We must lead a campaign to encourage students to write about their ideas, needs, fears, and desires. Then, perhaps, we can reverse the trend reported in the NAEP study, a trend that seems destined to describe the children in the Morris family and others who become disenchanted with writing and, by the time they complete college, plan to "leave it to their secretaries."

Note

1. In order to protect the participants in this study, all of the names of the people and places have been changed.

10

Item 50
Dialect Diversity and Teacher Preparation

Ted Lardner

Is it at all possible to teach students that they need Standard English and that their own dialect is beautiful without making them feel even just a little bit inferior about their own dialect? If it is possible to teach both then how do we do it?

Stacia Smith[1]

Oddly enough, conspicuously absent are the voices of the students themselves.

Keith Gilyard, *Voices of the Self*

The older ones go on and on in a curbside social philosophy session. It's about 1972. In a few days, the two-thousand-student public high school that serves our town will be closed by race fights. As the police sweep the campus, some girls will throw down another girl in the hall, then let her up. "Let her go," they'll say, "She's allright." There are "Jim Davis for Mayor" signs in some yards. He'll be elected the first African American mayor of this town, but the neighborhood youngsters spare little interest for such matters just now. They ride off, hissing rules for a game that absorbs them completely.

Fast-forward to 1985: I begin at last to wake from that childhood game the day I walk into a college writing class in Detroit. As a part-time instructor, I come "trained" for this work. I am by some measures an experienced teacher. But I am lost. The history I bring to my teaching and that provides me with a way to think about learning and writing leaves me ill-prepared, and as

I begin to discern the consequences of living inside this history, I begin to suspect how much I don't know, to feel the pull of questions that might awaken me to a world bigger than the one in which I'd grown up. In the faces of the students who look up or don't as I talk from the front of the room, in the sounds of their voices, in the figures and stories that inform their writing, I begin to catch glimpses, as if by reflection, of the differences that divide us, and that I'd preferred, and been able, until now (how?) to neglect.

Fast-forward to 1990, when I sign on to help teach an English Methods course. The relationship between social dialects (specifically, African American English[2]) and the teaching of writing have remained a concern to me. It seems the more I look for answers, the more questions I come upon. Of course, some questions are purely practical: I want to know "what works in the classroom," but as I struggle through the research and through what Steve North (1987) calls "lore" for answers, I find other questions lurking beneath these. They point to the underlying rationale for practice. What do we know, for example, about the phonological or grammatical or rhetorical dimensions of African American English? About the relationship between spoken and written language? About the role of language attitudes in classroom achievement?

My intent in this chapter is to examine the ways the group of preservice teachers in that 1990 English Methods class talked about the professional, pedagogical, and personal politics surrounding African American English. Their conversation was recorded as an optional discussion item numbered "Item 50" on our course computer conference. Setting the context for the discussion that developed in Item 50, we assigned students a set of readings that included Zora Neale Hurston's *Their Eyes Were Watching God* (1990), the CCCC proclamation "Students' Right to Their Own Language" (1974), and Jim Sledd's "Bi-dialectalism: The Linguistics of White Supremacy" (1969). On the one hand, we wanted the Methods students to develop lesson plans anchored in Hurston's novel. On the other hand, Hurston's novel masterfully blends oral storytelling forms and Black English Vernacular, and we wanted to consider the classroom implications of these expressive forms rooted in a specific cultural tradition in her writing as well as in the speech and writing of significant numbers of black students. We wanted finally for students to reflect on their own experiences as language learners as they considered their responsibilities as future teachers.

The topic of dialect diversity in the classroom became a site of reflection and contest. Competing discourses (disciplinary discourses and the extradisciplinary discourse of personal reflection and anecdote) situated these preservice teachers in conflicted relationships with one another, and to their sense of their future obligations in the classroom. Against the background of these contending discourses, I became interested in the ways these Methods students seemed to orient their responses to one another and to the paradox that Stacia Smith's question names:

Is it at all possible to teach students that they need Standard English and that their own dialect is beautiful without making them feel even just a little bit inferior about their own dialect? If it is possible to teach both then how do we do it?

The lively, at times passionate, exchange in Item 50 absorbed the attention of most of the students in our class for the better part of the semester. Though the degree of participation varied, eleven of the thirteen students in the course took part in Item 50. When they finished, the participants in Item 50 had generated 128 responses and 6 related discussion items. Addressing the ins and outs of dialect diversity in Item 50, the voices that Keith Gilyard (1991) alludes to, "the voices of the students themselves," became audible.

As I reread the printout, I hoped to discover how these students' ways of thinking fit into, clarified, or complicated established views on the topic. The first excerpt that I will cite, from Rachel Gupta, is typical of many of the students' entries, in that it begins retrospectively, framing the issues in autobiographical terms. This move to autobiographical terms is in my reading the most common and most significant move evident among the participants in Item 50.

What does it mean to talk different ways in different cultural contexts? To have different cultural contexts? To belong to cultures with different "languages"? To in some ways be living between, when these cultures don't overlap—to realize that the experiences I've had make me seem in some ways too X for the Ys and too Y for the Xs. This has been my own experience in some ways.

In Rachel's representation, the social realities attendant on language variation compel an individual to make serious choices. In Rachel's experience, education changes not the community that is left behind, but the individual:

I believe that real education changes us. It changes our thinking and our language, and leaves us misfits to some degree. The place where we used to fit comfortably starts to feel in some ways too small, and we might seem odd to our old friends as well as to our new. We conform less; we become more independent; sometimes we become lonely, like Langston Hughes.

While independence undoubtedly has its virtues, it has its risks as well. There is neither a clear identity nor a recognizable community into which the newly educated individual moves.

In one of her initial entries on the conference, another student, Michele Mills, approached the topic of dialect diversity through similar references to personal experience. In doing so, she echoed the tensions that Rachel gives voice to, but Michele drew on a communal, African American cultural perspective rather than on an individual one:

We as black people will speak very differently from the majority of students at this school. What I look for when I think about how society deals with our language is whether they are understanding of our right to speak in a way that defines us as Black Americans. Many people that I know feel that to hold onto the BEV or whatever you want to label it, helps them to hold onto their culture and the experiences they have had growing up as a black person. To me, it is very important when I enter a place like this university, because I believe that it tries to condition you to conform to the norm. There is nothing wrong with knowing Standard English because as has been suggested in other items, we all must know it if we want to get ahead in this world. Yet, I maintain that it personally is better for society if people recognize and understand that different dialects of language define the people who speak them and help them to hold onto the culture that has also helped to define them.

By linking her experience to a communal identity through references to black culture, Michele raises the stakes. The issue of dialect diversity becomes not a matter of individual adjustment, but of cultural politics in which survival is linked to community identity and power. Michele continued:

I say as a young black woman, I am willing to play the game for all that it is worth. But, I will never put much emphasis on winning if I have to give up my language which ties me to my fellow black students, which ties me to my family, which ties me to my ancestors.

Like Rachel, who included a reference to Labov's "The Logic of Nonstandard English" (1973), Michele also referred to her knowledge of linguistics: "After taking a class on the English language last term, my views on this subject are very strong," she wrote. But because she represented her experience as a black woman who had negotiated the demands for linguistic conformity throughout her educational career, the force of her conviction, her authority, seemed linked not to technical knowledge of her home language, but to lived experience.

Nearly everyone who participated in Item 50 included a story of encountering dialect diversity, of crossing the boundaries of language communities. In some of these cases, questions of conflict and struggle became displaced. One student, for example, described "swapping every kind of dialect, accent, and . . . 'slang' you could imagine" with her friends at summer camp. The image of summer camp as a polyglot utopia is appealing to me; I wish classrooms could be like that. Another student, Cathy Sheets, described the linguistic milieu at the social services agency where she worked. "As a white person," she said, "I am a minority":

I am immersed on a daily basis in the language you all are calling BEV. . . .
If someone told me I HAD to begin speaking BEV in order to work there,
I would feel torn in two. I could do it, but it's not who I am. Throwing in a

few colloquialisms here and there, appreciating the diversity in the language we hear and write, is not the same as changing our whole speech pattern.

Cathy's gesture, of trying to put herself in someone else's shoes, to imagine what it would be like to be forced to change her "whole speech pattern," is admirable, but Cathy was quick to point out that she knew she would not, in reality, be "forced" ever to change her way of speaking. Stacia described feeling like "a hick" coming to the university: "I have definitely felt that my dialect is inferior to the dialect which I found here," she wrote. In each case, it can be argued that as much as a technical analysis of their speech might reveal about its structural and functional features, the subjective experiences reflected in Cathy's statement, "I would feel torn in two," or in Stacia's sense of herself as "a hick," would be removed from view. Removed from view, but not erased. And while it may be true that real education changes us, the changes are emotionally, socially, and, dare I say it, spiritually more costly for some than for others.

Over the past thirty years or so, the educational issues surrounding African American English have necessarily been addressed through the technical discourse of linguistics and sociolinguistics. Teachers have continued to struggle to make this information speak to their situation in the classroom, and researchers continue to acknowledge the depth of the problem of language attitudes as these shape teachers' expectations and, thereby, student performance. In the face of this history, one hypothesis suggested by the data in Item 50 is that the road to changed attitudes lies in personalizing the issues, moving from the dry objectivity of the research report to the reflective (and emotionally volatile) process of locating oneself in relation to others and in encountering one another across differences of power. For this encounter to have real significance I think there can be no substitute for live dialogue, where one perspective can answer and be answered by conflicting perspectives. In nearly every turn she took, Michele testified to the antagonistic effect of being confronted as linguistically and culturally "other" in school. In the next excerpt, this antagonism is depicted as a power struggle played out in impersonal but, paradoxically, intimate terms:

> My problem with this whole notion is when students are asked to put aside their native way of speaking and conform to the status quo. The language that a person speaks is part of their culture that shapes each person into the individual that he or she is. I strongly disagree with a society or for our purposes a school district that side by side tries to mold the accepted language into these students while pushing down a part of them that will help them to sustain who they are in the midst of life's ups and downs.

The agentless syntax of power shapes Michele's sentences here. It is evident in the passive constructions and in the corporate subjects: "students are asked to put aside" their language and to "conform"; "society" and "a school district" will try to "mold the accepted language into" students while "pushing down a part of them." In her responses on Item 50, Michele identifies the stakes involved in this struggle as maintaining a sense of identity within an encompassing African American culture. The goal of assimilating into the norms of academic literacy can and often does conflict with this, Michele asserted. While her observation tracks with the accounts of others, it was, I think, her act of witnessing to the truth of her experience that was most persuasive to her classmates. It was certainly most persuasive to me.

Everyone who participated in the discussion in Item 50 acknowledged the need to learn Standard English. Michele stated: "You can't get anything more than sympathy and handouts if you do not familiarize yourself with the English language." Several spoke of making language variety an explicit topic of reflection in the writing classroom; others described an approach that would foreground the decisions writers must make based on the subjects, purposes, and audiences for their writing. Furthermore, as I read the printout of Item 50, it occurred to me that the practical and philosophical questions surrounding African American English and the teaching of writing had been put to rest, prematurely perhaps. For some of the students in the Methods class, as perhaps is the case for some number of teachers of writing today, the means and ends are straightforward—to help all students to master standard written English. Acquiring academic literacy expands students' language options; it does not deny anyone's "home" language or sense of identity. Speaking of options rather than prescriptions, the Methods students seemed to wish for their students "a kind of political savvy about writing."

In some circumstances, I'm sure I would name a similar-sounding goal for teaching writing, but I also resist it. First, I resist especially the way such a formulation works to close discussion. Second, when talk turns to teaching students to be savvy, I distrust the sort of determinism that creeps in, in which audience seems to exercise undue control over the rhetorical choices a speaker or writer might make. Third, I'm prodded to doubts by my experience, in which teaching writing never seems as simple as simple slogans make it seem. Fourth, I think what happened at this point in the discussion in Item 50 is what has often happened in the profession at large in the conversation about African American English in the classroom: We zeroed in on the goal, say, mastery of standard written English, and, having agreed on that, we quit thinking very carefully about the means to that goal. When the conversation in Item 50 seemed to settle toward closure here, a quiet violence, a kind of unspoken pain, remained to be acknowledged. Not surprisingly, Michele was the one who turned these tables around again. In one particularly forceful move from a generalized "other" to a specific "you," she challenged one of her classmates:

> People in society who hypocritically stand by the notion that they respect the
> right for individuals to hold on to their native selves, yet teach that this native

aspect (whether it be language or dress) should be second to what is the status quo here in OUR country, are the type of people who will ignorantly condition these young people to deny themselves to be who they are. I respect your right to disagree with my idea . . . but I question whether you would stand behind the same things if you were one of those people who are socially and academically forced to minimize their native heritage and culture.

Michele consistently reasserted the connection between her sense of self and her culture, but her purpose seemed not so much to dispute the need, as she put it, "to know and speak English well," as much as to argue that we all should consider "the more prevalent thing," that is, what "message we are sending" when we "insist on Standard English":

> I have personally witnessed people who have told me that if I want to be a good public speaker, I should pretend as if I have forgotten how to speak Black English Vernacular. As I went from high school to college, I was slowly but surely conditioned to believe that Standard English is correct and good and anything else is bullshit. Well, I think any type of argument like that is nothing more than BS. We all should realize that it is necessary to know and speak English well in the U.S. to get a job, make money and have a future. Yet, I believe the more prevalent thing should be what type of message we are sending to people like me and others when we insist on Standard English—as the culturally blind people have established and stand behind—as the correct way to speak and learn in order to be successful.

Michele answers here, in a sense, the question Stacia Smith asked. It's delivered as a challenge, really: as teachers, "we all should realize" that the "more prevalent thing" is "what type of message we are sending." That message, I think, is that we must question whose best interests we have at heart as we teach what we teach, to whom we teach, in the classroom. But how do we become conscious of these subtle, "more prevalent" messages we as teachers are sending? Can we know how our students will construe our intentions toward them? As a mainstream teacher of mainstream discourse, can I avoid making nonmainstream students feel "even just a little bit inferior" about their home language? The problem with the straightforward approach that sees language variation as comparable to a dress code is that it continually proves inadequate to the task. Farr and Daniels (1986) point out that school literacy most closely resembles middle-class standard speakers' ways with words (42), and that the majority of nonstandard-English-speaking students fail to master standard written English (24).

As answers to questions both practical and philosophical, prospective teachers have traditionally been offered a kind of foundational information from research—positive knowledge of social dialects; variable rules; and the history, structure, and functions of African American English, to name a few of the prominent topics. There is no disputing the value for teachers of this information. But critics of conventional teacher-preparation programs have pointed out the flaws in this system. On the one hand, it tends to portray teaching as an "applied science" (Zeichner 1983, 4). On the other hand, it can treat language as a "neutral vehicle of communication" (Lu 1991, 27). Dialect diversity presents a complicated picture because in it, writing teachers confront ideological questions of race, difference, and power that cannot be resolved in terms of disinterested empirical information. Further, as Jim Sledd (1988) has argued, to ask only "what works in the classroom" implies that underlying questions of motives and goals need not be addressed. As valuable as they are, technical analyses of "nonstandard" English and their yield of facts cannot resolve the ideological dilemmas entailed in teaching writing to "nonmainstream" students, and the activity of teaching writing can neither be adequately reflected on nor practiced without considering these politics.

Scholars who have interrogated the historical and social construction of standard languages and literacies situate the African American struggle for literacy in a matrix of power relations, recognizing literacy's liberatory possibilities. These possibilities have been realized by writers from Frederick Douglass to Malcolm X, Harriet Jacobs to Alice Walker. Because literacy may be an instrument of domination or liberation (Sledd 1988), a principled practice must acknowledge the functions that literacy and schooling (and students and teachers) fulfill in the reproduction (or revisionary recreation) of social reality. Such value-laden issues encompass and extend beyond matters of managing "what works in the classroom." Though it ultimately shapes what we do as teachers, our understanding of these encompassing value issues is not determined through the acquisition of more "information," that is, the product of "research" as we conventionally think of it. It is just this engagement with values and commitments that constituted the incisive edge of the dialogue in Item 50. In a computer conference consisting of seventy-eight discussion items, in a printout that exceeded two hundred thousand words, Item 50 cannot easily be passed over as just another question the English Methods students took up. The intensity of the conversation in Item 50 indicates the significance this topic held for the students in the course.

In "The Uses of Diversity," Clifford Geertz (1986) argues that valuing diversity presupposes of us a willingness and an ability to exercise a certain kind of imagination. Difference no longer begins across the water, on some distant colonial shore, Geertz writes. It begins at one's skin, the mouth, with one's word. Our response to difference ingrains itself in the quality of our day-to-day lives. Therefore, Geertz writes,

> comprehending that which is, in some manner or form, alien to us and
> likely to remain so, without either smoothing it over with vacant murmurs
> of common humanity, disarming it with to-each-his-own indifferentism or
> dismissing it as charming, lovely even, but inconsequential, is a skill we

have arduously to learn, and having learnt it, always very imperfectly, work continuously to keep alive. (122)

Dialect differences, and the educational and personal politics associated with them, posed no barrier to my own education, since, for most intents and purposes, my teachers and I spoke alike. Having experienced no bumps on that road, to fail to notice how others could be tripped up was easy, as natural as breathing. I keep trying to think about that—what was so easy to fail to notice, to respond to—as I think about teaching.

Notes

1. Stacia Smith was a student in the English Methods course that is the focus of this chapter. With their permission, I have used participating students' real names.

2. "African American English" is the most recent term academics have used to name the social dialect also commonly referred to as Black English. I follow Keith Gilyard's (1991) lead in using these terms interchangeably.

11

English—Yours, Mine, or Ours
Language Teaching and the Needs of "Nonnative" Speakers of English

Yuet-Sim Darrell Chiang

I cry when I think that I cannot speak my own mother tongue as
well as I can speak the English language.

> Nehru, quoted in Alex Josey,
> *Lee Kuan Yew*

Claiming English as my own was my first step out of the iron
cage and into a voice. And who is to say it is not my language
and not my voice?

> Shirley Geok-Lin Lim,
> "The Scarlet Brewer and the
> Voice of the Colonized"

In the world of the tradition, I was unimagined. I would have to
imagine myself.

> David Mura, *Turning Japanese*

I stare at the long, blue aerogram. Its lined page seems foreboding. How will
I fill up the page? Aunt MeiLing looks at me. I pick up the ballpoint pen,
fingers tightening round its narrow neck; I sit poised and ready—acting as if
this is part of my routine. Everybody says I am good in English, but how does
that make me a letter writer? Aunt MeiLing begins, her choppy Cantonese

128

words vibrating in my ears, "Yes, first ask them if they are well." Hmmm. I pause. Do I start with "How are you?" or do I write "You are good?"—the way Chinese normally phrase their greetings. This is the way we talk with each other, so just write it like that, I reason. But that's not right, I counterargue, that's not how an English-educated student like me should write; I would sound uneducated. Aunt MeiLing hovers over my shoulder, her eyes expectant and eager. I clench my pen and stare at her acne-scarred face. My hand begins to sweat and I wonder if Aunt MeiLing can hear the drumming in my heart. I look out the kitchen window into the verandah where Dad sits visiting with Uncle Chong. I wish Dad had not told everybody that I could write. I look at the empty blue lines, torn between "How are you?" and "You are good?" English or Chinese? Which should I choose? But I want both, I mumble to myself.

That scene took place more than thirty years ago, but the struggles I faced as I tried to integrate these two languages are etched deeply in my mind. My dilemmas as a child learning to think and write in English, and the agony of being caught between two language worlds, have left me with many questions about what it means to be English-educated. What was my place in the language world where I was labeled "nonnative" in the only language I had to define and conceptualize my world? What did it really mean to read and write English for someone like me—labeled a "nonnative" speaker, whose literate life was lived in English? And how was I to make important connections to my roots and heritage with a language whose terms and concepts were at times alien to the complexities of my Asian upbringing?

These questions grew even more pronounced when I became a composition teacher and found myself needing to bring my experience and understanding of the English language to those I taught. How has my language experience as a "nonnative" speaker but one who is literate only in English shaped the way I think of myself as a reader, writer, and now a teacher of English? What are the social, political, and emotional effects upon the lives of people whose conceptualizations of the world are defined in English terms and concepts, but whose "nonnative" roots separate them from the historicity of the Western world? What does it mean to say, to echo Shirley Lim's (1991) words, that "claiming English as my own was my first step out of the iron cage and into a voice" (8)? It is this process of searching for a social and cultural place for myself within the English-speaking world that my chapter seeks to address.[1]

Our Voices, Our Experiences

Having been sent to an English school in Singapore at the age of seven, I learned very early in life to identify with the English language and with its thoughts and philosophy. English was the only language in which I became literate; colonialism did not make learning my own language "profitable." In fact, I tried very hard NOT to "learn" my home language for fear that it would dilute my connections with English. English became my thinking language as well as my school language. But in spite of my facility with it, I never thought I could claim English as my language nor that I could use it to talk about my Asian background or upbringing. My negatively prefixed status, "nonnative," applied to me by teachers and mainstream "native" speakers, kept me from feeling that I was an authentic language user.

The need to assert one's worth in the English-speaking world is captured by David Mura in his autobiographical novel *Turning Japanese* (1991). Mura, a third-generation Japanese American, talks about his need to "prove" himself to the Anglo American teaching assistant assigned to assist him in teaching Freshman English to a group of Southeast Asian refugees. He writes,

> When my teaching assistant first entered the class, she . . . saw my face, and thought, Oh, God, not only am I going to have to teach English to nonnative speakers, but the teacher's also a foreigner. As a way of getting back at her, I made jokes about her mistakes in grammar, as if to prove my superior command of English. Somehow I needed to prove that I had the same rights to the language that she had. (75)

Mura, a third-generation American, was obviously far from being a "nonnative" speaker, but his "nonnative" roots visibly marked him as different. Chinese American writer Maxine Hong Kingston (1977) echoes a similar experience: ". . . when white demons said, 'You speak English very well,' I muttered, 'It's my language too'" (154).

When talking with a colleague one day about "native" and "nonnative" speakers, I remarked that the burden of proof is so pervasive in "nonnative" speakers that even I, with my increasing understanding of the politics of language, had to consciously and constantly fight against it. I told him about how conscious I was about my language whenever I talked to "native" English teachers and how I felt this "burden" to prove that I was capable of teaching the language, albeit as a "nonnative" speaker. John pursed his lips, thought for a while, and said, "Yeah, the first time I met you? Well, the first three minutes I was really listening to you, and I think if you had made any mistakes during that time, I would have thought differently of you." Not too surprised, I continued, "Would you have the same expectation if you were talking to a 'native-speaking' English teacher?" John looked at me, and a full moment passed before he answered, "W . . e . . ll, now. [Pause] Come to think of it, I don't think I would. Hmmmm." Stroking his chin, John pondered aloud, "I wonder why."

It was to John's credit that he confronted his own prejudices, but I think his response reflects the unspoken, often prejudicial, assumptions people have about "nonnative" speakers. For three minutes in my initial interaction with John, I was frozen. In his frame of reference, consciously or unconsciously, my language became an object to be evaluated. I was not seen as someone using language to articulate her world, but as someone who needed to prove her credibility. If I had "failed," John would not have taken me seriously as a participant in his world. I believe my non-European appearance and accent contributed to John's assumptions about me as a language user, and I would argue that ingrained in John's assumptions was the uncontested belief that English was a "white man's" language. Because I was using "his" language, I had, by nature of the hierarchy, become his "evaluatee" and he my "evaluator."

I saw this subservient posture toward the English language frequently in the many "nonnative" students I worked with as a writing teacher and researcher at the University of Nebraska. Radha, for example, was from India and learned English as a child when she first attended school in England where her father pursued his doctorate. In one of my participant-observer interviews, Radha expressed surprise that her small group, all of whom were Americans, were interested in what she was writing.[2] She said, "I never thought that I had anything to share. I thought I'd bore them, you know." Radha's "you know" was more than a cursory gesture; it was like an act of alliance between us—an "unspoken" bond of being "nonnative" speakers. Instead of describing herself in terms of her own writing, Radha used her "native-speaking" peers to measure the value of her own writing. Throughout the semester she was conscious that she was "nonnative," notwithstanding the fact that she had grown up in English, and that her writing, according to her composition instructor, was better than many of her Anglo peers.

The unconscious and unspoken authority Radha attached to her "native-speaking" peers, especially in writing, is echoed by Theresa, a South American student in a teacher-researcher project:[3] "Yah, I have a friend, an American friend, and I used to ask her to please read my paper. And she said, 'I don't know what to do in this line.' And I said, 'No, you are an American, you should know! Well, if you cannot do it, I cannot do it either.'" Theresa's last phrase illustrates the assumed sense of authority that "nonnative" speakers ascribe to "native" speakers. Underlying that off-handed remark is the disempowering assumption that she is not capable of creating her own authority. Her example made me recall my own fears when I was learning English. I thought that if I were a "native" speaker, I wouldn't make mistakes because the knowledge I needed to accumulate would have been "ingrained" in me by virtue of my "nativeness."

This "deficiency" mentality, and the equating of learning English with knowledge-telling rather than with knowledge-processing, prevented me from stepping beyond the boundaries of the safe and prescribed rules of language use. Those unspoken fears made me write in ways that left very little room for errors. I saw myself not as a participant in language making, but as a follower; my job was to imitate or parrot whatever I was given. That way

I freed myself from the troubled thoughts that I was really not "one of them." The impression I soon developed was that I really had nothing to say or contribute in the English language.

This yearning for English and yet fearing English created a love-hate relationship with the language. It was like the "abusive mother" of Nourbesse Philip (Owomoyela 1992, 88). I felt an urgency to "master" the language, to accumulate this "vast knowledge," while at the back of my mind I knew that no matter how hard I tried I would still be seen as "the other," not as a natural language user, much less as a creator of language. I recall the time I was preparing a paper for a national language teaching conference. I wanted to use the word *inauthentic* to help me describe this feeling of not belonging, but for some reason I could not remember if it was "in" or "un" authentic. Too lazy to verify it in a dictionary, I turned to one of my colleagues and asked, "Hey, tell me, is it *unauthentic* or *inauthentic*?" Mary was not sure what I wanted, and so I explained what I was trying to say in my paper. Then without so much as a pause, she said, "Oh, Sim, it doesn't matter. You're a foreigner. Nobody is going to care. Just use any word you like; they'll think it's cute." Embedded in Mary's off-handed remark was the assumption that English was really not "my" language. Not only was my place in the English-speaking world exoticized by my "native-speaking" colleague, but by arbitrarily assuming that "it doesn't matter" she had positioned me as the "other"—not a language user using English to articulate her world.

It is this need not to be dismissed as "the other" that often forces many of us to make choices that are alien to our cultural or linguistic backgrounds. I remember how, as a child, I used to sit in front of an aged and coffee-stained Sony radio listening to the BBC news at night, trying to imitate the way the broadcaster pronounced the words. Somehow I thought that by developing a BBC English pronunciation I would be more authentic—not so much with my Singapore peers but with "native" speakers. It did not matter that by doing so I was seen by my peers as fakey—a "yellow banana"—for the need not to be dismissed as "the other" in the language world seemed more important than the acceptance of my peers.[4]

For many "nonnative" English speakers, this wanting to be "like them" often leads to unquestioned Westernization, as communicated in my student Eng Soon's self-revelation about wanting to be like his American contemporaries: "I want to be like them, I even comb my hair like them so that I don't stand out. I just want them to accept me." When asked why it was so important to him to be accepted by his American peers, Eng Soon commented on "how clever" the American students were with "their" language, and how "natural" they sounded. Encapsulated in Eng Soon's impressions about his American peers' language acts was the unspoken assumption that English was more naturally "their" language.

The myth that the English language is "innate" to the English people is illuminated in "The Scarlet Brewer and the Voice of the Colonized," in which Shirley Lim (1991) describes her psychological journey of demystifying the notion of who owns the English language:

> Brewer's book of forms demythologized once and for all that literary culture the English taught colonized native children to memorize and fear. . . . The simple naming of craft as craft unweighted the imperialism in English poetry and sent it floating deliriously within my grasp. What [it] proved to me was that the English language was not a *natural possession* [my emphasis] of the English people. . . . Instead they were mindful things constructed out of reading, observation, care, learning, and play with language and form. . . . English poetry was socially constructed, not innately inherent in race and genius. (4–5)

Even though Eng Soon's and Lim's language experiences are separated by a generation, the internalized notion that English is "their" language is still deeply rooted in the consciousness of the "nonnative" speaker.

For many people, demystifying the notion of who owns the English language is the only option. The alternative is to be forever chained to the "burden of proof"—to feel that one's only "rightful" place is to imitate rather than to use the language in a process of discovery or meaning making. For me, the claiming process started with relearning my place in the English-speaking world and reflecting upon my own language experiences. It was in a process-oriented writing workshop that I first learned not only to challenge the alienating myth of myself as an imitator of "pure English" (read "native"), but also that I could use English to tell my stories, my wants, and my aspirations in a public way. As my voice began to shake free from the manacles of the "nonnative" bondage, I discovered that English is really not a relentless master but a companion to my language self—enabling me to voice my needs and realities. I began to learn to write from within, rather than from without. I began to discern that the label "nonnative," imposed upon me by society and institutions at large, is a socioeconomic and political separatist tool, not an embodiment of my literate experience. When I found that my rights and the spectrum of my language experience could, and should, extend beyond the limitations of the negatively prefixed "nonnative" status, I learned, like Shirley Lim, to "step out of the iron cage and into a voice" (8).

Rewriting Ourselves: Obstacles and Struggles

The process of reclaiming my language experience is, however, not without challenge. Many English teachers continue to subscribe to the notion that there is only one worthy English to teach, the so-called Standard English. The reduction of language learning to mere knowledge of the correct use of verbs, adjectives, pronouns, and so on, not only harbors a prescriptive English curriculum, but restricts "nonnative" students to a singular "native" speaker code. As Kachru (1986) notes, "The urge for prescriptivism has been so strong that any innovation which is not according to the native speakers' linguistic code is considered a linguistic aberration. If one makes too many such 'mistakes,' it is treated as an indication of a language user's linguistic deprivation or deficiency" (93).

Furthermore, seldom, if ever, is the unspoken and unquestioned authority conceded to "native" speakers challenged, either by English practitioners or researchers.[5] This unchallenged authority is perpetuated when learning English is viewed as an acquisition of literal language acts—something that can be easily imparted from those who "have" the language to those who "have not," as an advertisement in *The Chronicle of Higher Education*, February 20, 1991, indicates: "English as a Second Language Teachers . . . Minimum Qualifications: M.A. in TESL . . . native English speaker . . ." (B20). Advertisements with similar stipulations have also appeared in other issues of the *Chronicle* and in the *Modern Language Association Job Information List*.

Often the unspoken assumption is for the "have-nots" to wait on the "haves" to tell them what to do, despite the fact that of the 750 million users of English, barely half speak it as a mother tongue (McCrum et al. 1986). In spite of the predominance of "nonnative" English speakers, much of what is printed, argued, debated, or asserted in English teaching journals (such as *TESOL Quarterly, English Education, College English*) is often between and among "native" speakers. Even in North America, where the changing demographics indicate a growing population of speakers of non-English-speaking backgrounds, the complexities of language learning are frequently filtered through the monolingual experiential lens of the mainstream "native" speakers.

The emphasis on "how to" rather than on "what is" is further attested to in a review of articles published by *TESOL Quarterly* between 1989 and 1991: out of fifty-nine articles, forty-one were aimed at curriculum development (such as improving placement tests and curriculum models), nine were on student's learning processes (such as strategies used by unsuccessful language learners or metacognitive strategies for reading), while the remaining nine centered on the political and social aspects of language learning.[6] Even within these nine articles, the social, cultural, and emotional realities of what it means to learn English in a "nonnative" setting are scarcely addressed. This lack is observed even in research that seeks to "verify critical assumptions about second language learning" (Vann and Abraham 1990, 177). For example, in a case study of Mona and Shida, two "unsuccessful language learners," researchers Vann and Abraham evaluated their learning strategies based on Mona's and Shida's think-aloud protocols and performances in "four typical classroom tasks": an oral interview, two fill-in-the-blank exercises (verbs and articles), a cloze passage, and a composition (180). Of the cloze passage, Vann and Abraham say that "To fill the blanks correctly, subjects need considerable knowledge about cross-cultural differences in proxemics and attitudes toward time. This could be obtained from the passage itself, but for students of low proficiency, reading a *mutilated* [my emphasis] passage for meaning was not easy" (186). Yet, in their evaluation of the "unsuccessful" performances of Shida and Mona, Vann and Abraham did not consider this significant variable. Instead, interpretations of Mona's and Shida's language facility were reduced to measures of discrete units such as "grammatical knowledge," "low-level strategies," or failure in "attending to form" (188).

The homogenization of the "nonnative" speaker is further evidenced in the way "nonnative" speakers of English are regularized under the ESL category even though for many "nonnative" speakers, particularly for foreign-born immigrants or refugees in the United States, English is more than just a "second language."[7] This growing group of language users, as Ann Raimes (1991) points out, not only "need[s] to be able to write in English for the rest of their working and earning lives" but "[also to] . . . forge their place in it" (420). To further complicate the blanketing classification, there are also, in Shirley Lim's (1991) words, "generations of colonial peoples (who) are writing in English, warping it into their own instruments, producing other traditions . . . replacing the hegemonic and hierarchical world view of the imperialists" (7). Nonetheless, the needs of these people, whose English is part of their identities, are subsumed under the "nonnative" label. Underlying this deceptive and politically charged classification is the faulty assumption that there is a generic "nonnative" speaker.

The complexity of the "nonnative" label is further illuminated in the writing experiences of my immigrant students labeled as ESL students by the university and the English Department. For example, May Ling, a student in my teacher-researcher study, sees writing as more than a transactional activity. For May Ling, writing is also a way of understanding her thoughts and her realities. When reflecting on a piece of writing that she did at the end of a writing workshop course, May Ling wrote, "My purpose of writing is not only for the grade but most importantly, I'm writing it for myself and my grandmother . . . I started to think more carefully and evaluate what and how I actually think/feel and why I think/feel that way. I finally have the answer and I eventually understand. . . . Writing creates questions, thoughts, understandings and conclusions." The dialogical component embedded in May Ling's English experience is succinctly captured in an earlier description of herself as a language user:

> Well, I talked about thinking in Chinese and writing in English. In fact there is still another problem that I have, i.e. I think in English and talk or write in Chinese. What I mean is it happens both ways. For example, I communicate with my boyfriend in Mandarin but when it comes to arguing I find myself speaking in English. Or when I try to explain something, I would

speak in English. The only time when I think in Chinese and write in English is when . . . I'm writing a formal paper, where I'm so unfamiliar with the ways of writing. Writing research is different than when I write or how I normally talk.

The assumption that May Ling only writes with a "translation" mode (thinking in Chinese but writing in English) is counterbalanced by her ready use of English in her personal and intimate life. Her writing portrays a person whose language experience in English is more than just a "second" language. More important, May Ling's articulation of her integral links with English signifies the social, cultural, emotional, political, and psychological realities of the "nonnative" English speakers.

The limitations of the labels and their inability to capture the multiplicities of English learning are further accentuated when May Ling's language experience is juxtaposed with mine. In spite of our common "nonnative" status, my language experience is different from May Ling's. My working-class background, coupled with an education steeped in colonialism—one that resulted in my being literate only in English—forced me to develop and attach a significance to English that is even more acute than May Ling's. "Mastering" English was not only my key to a better and more secure future, it was also my way of "standing up" to the "white man," a bargaining tool I felt I needed to have. How else could I be visible to them if I could not get them (meaning my colonizer) to listen to me, a "nonnative" English speaker?[8] But in the process of "mastering" English, I was also socialized into a way of thinking, a worldview that oftentimes stands in opposition to my cultural heritage.[9]

Critics who argue that the special needs (so-called lack of intuition) of "nonnative" speakers require special instruction often use this excuse to treat "nonnatives" as "the other" instead of seeing them as language users who have the same need, and right, to see writing as a way of constructing the world.[10] This is epitomized in my encounter with one of the administrators in the English department who expressed concern when I requested to teach an ESL class. When I queried him about his misgivings, he said, "Don't forget, Sim. These students did not come all the way to North America to learn English from you, a 'nonnative' speaker." His response not only repudiated my professional training and experience as an English teacher, but it also denied my affinity with the English-speaking world.[11]

Even Ann Raimes (1987), who has been a leader in the movement to revision the "nonnative" English-speaking writer to the TESOL community and who claims that "nonnative" speakers are not that different from "native" speakers in their writing process (459–460) appears to be guilty of this "equal but separate" treatment in the introduction to her text *How English Works* (1990): "As we teachers know only too well, even advanced students who speak and understand English with apparent ease can still make many errors when they write and can still have surprising gaps in understanding" (ix). The emphasis on "errors" and "gaps" in understanding English prevails throughout Raimes' book. The idea of understanding writing as a process, or as an act of discovery and meaning making, was overshadowed by Raimes' need to reduce language learning to a methodological and linear system as suggested in her introduction:

> *How English Works* is based on the premise that students can't really work on improving their grammar while they are speaking. . . . So in each chapter, reading leads to analysis, which leads to study of principles followed by practice, which then leads to writing and editing, that is, to the application of principles of grammar. (xi)

Raimes is not alone in her "equal but separate" double standard. I too am guilty of this language segregation. I remember the struggles, self-doubts, and bouts of anxiety I experienced when I first taught a group of advanced ESL students. In spite of my personal and academic goals of debunking the notion of the "nonnative" speaker, I found myself journaling in my teacher-researcher logbook about how "desperately" my students needed to be taught grammar. In my reflections on the first week of the workshop, I wrote:

> Right now I feel overwhelmed . . . worrying abut their sentences . . . worrying about the way they're using the language. Some of them can't even put together a decent sentence! . . . I fear this workshop method will backfire . . . maybe 1) students do not have the basic grasp of the mechanical aspects of the language to work on their own. 2) Students need to be shown/"taught" elementary rules governing the English language and my workshop style does not have enough time to address these issues . . . How will I ever be [able] to go beyond what they're sharing here to writing when they're so, so down with deficiencies?

Even as I reflect upon my journal entry written that first week, I am shocked at the way I have defined my "ESL" students as the deficient "other." With them, I equated writing with teaching them "the basics" while with my American students ("the native speakers") teaching writing meant teaching them the "real thing." I was a living embodiment of that equal but separate double standard! That semester of teacher-researcher study was a painful and humbling experience as I learned to decolonize the hierarchical and imperialistic thinking embedded in my language assumptions and practices. The study forced me to do what I have attempted to do publicly, that is, to deconstruct the notion of the "nonnative" speaker within the language consciousness of the English-speaking world.[12]

Our Needs and Our Wants

The political, social, and cultural domains governing the use and learning of English involve more than just an "either-or" question. As I have attempted to illustrate, my own language experience was significantly affected by my colonial background. I could not separate from my literacy those images that crossed my daily life—images that equate learning English with the unchallenged imitation of rules and unquestioned Westernization. I was fully aware that prestige and power often went to those who "had" the language. Like Eng Soon, I too had subscribed to the myth that English was more "natural" for the "native" speaker and, therefore, by analogy, my "nonnativeness" had made me less "natural." I held on to the internalized linguistic imperialism and believed that the "white man" was more knowledgeable, more intelligent, and more capable with the language, and that the nonwhite man and woman were "the lesser," forever constrained by that "burden of proof."

However, I see this in a more complex way when one of my colleagues, a "native" speaker, points out to me that much of what I have described is also representative of her experience both as a language user and writing teacher. She never thought she could write; she never felt "connected" to the language. Like me, she felt in many ways "the other" in relation to her writing world. She is just as conscious of the way she presents herself whenever she introduces herself as an English teacher, just as nervous about the way she talks when giving a public speech, knowing that she is being evaluated, rightly or not. But as I have said to her, "It's precisely because you share my experience, it's precisely because your needs are similar to mine, that I am challenging this restrictive compartmentalization!" It is the way the language needs of "native" and "nonnative" speakers parallel one another that makes me question the current practices of assuming or blanketing the "nonnative" speakers as "the other" and approaching them in a separatist and prescriptivist way.

What I see is a spectrum of language users—not an "either-or" division. There are those who are learning English for special purposes—scientific inquiry, business contacts, travel, and so on, but there are also those who are "living" in the language, albeit as a "nonnative" speaker. The segmented "native" and "nonnative" labels do not capture the complexities experienced by this continuum of language users. The labels, instead, diffuse what it means to read and write English, especially for people like me. My "nonnative" students and I are not that different from our "native" counterparts; what we need from English is similar to what they need: we too need the language as a way of making meaning, of understanding our worlds. We too need to use language to articulate our realities, whether it be our love for our grandmothers, writing letters on behalf of our parents or aunts, or teaching English as a "nonnative" speaker.

But this is when the paradox sets in. It is precisely because of our "nonnative" background that I see a need to examine and challenge our traditional assumptions of what it means to learn English. Does learning English mean unquestioned assimilation into the Western world? Can I hold on to my Chinese heritage and feel I am a valid member in the English-speaking world? What is my personal response (both as a language user and a writing teacher) to texts that do not embody my lived experience or that arbitrarily subjugate my needs? How can we be thoughtful and sensitive to the language needs of "native" and "nonnative" speakers without falling into stereotypical or tokenized responses? What should be included in our research and pedagogical practices in order to more democratically respond to the complex social, political, and cultural issues of language teaching?

Reconstructing Our Literate Selves and Voices

Our needs and experiences in English can no longer be only presented and filtered through the "native" speaker's lens. "Nonnative" speakers must too be accorded a place where people like me can, as Mura (1991) describes,

> learn to write out of my sense of duality, or rather plurality, to write not in slavish imitation of the European tradition but to use it and combine it with other elements of my background, trying to achieve a difficult balance. In order to understand who I was and who I would become, I would have to listen to voices that my father, or T. S. Eliot or Robert Lowell, did not dream of. Voices of my family . . . of my own wayward and unassimilated past. In the world of the tradition, I was unimagined. I would have to imagine myself. (77)

We must reconceptualize our understanding of the "nonnative" speaker. The negatively prefixed "nonnative" status is an injustice to people like me who have chosen to "live" in English; and its "gate-keeping" use serves only to deter us from confidently participating in the English-speaking world.

As Peter Elbow (1990) states, "[to] walk down the streets of our cities and towns and down the halls of our schools is to see that differences and heterogeneity are givens" (40), and if this is so then it is time that we ask what English is and what it represents to us. If English learning is to help us make meaning and become active learners who construct knowledge, then it is imperative that we ask ourselves *whose meaning* we are making, and *whose knowledge* we are constructing. It also demands that we reexamine our assumptions of *what* English is and *whose language* we are teaching or using. English is no longer the "prerogative" (Quirk 1968, 5) of the "white man" whose rules and dictates traditionally have formed the yardsticks by which language users are judged. And if this is so, then it is critical that this new understanding be reflected both in our pedagogical and research practices, for to do otherwise is to continue to deny the experiences of those who, for personal, social, or political reasons, have chosen to think and live in English. It is far easier to talk about theories of language or theories of learning than to talk about our realities. It is hard to reflect on our language experiences, to admit our fears. It is even harder to believe that we can rewrite ourselves when we have always been written. Confronting these moments not only means a heightened political awareness of our place in the English language world but also a greater appreciation of the journey we have undertaken. Ultimately, I believe, it is the embracing of our duality, or plurality, that will give us, language learners and users, the power to claim, rather than be claimed, and the power to shape, rather than be shaped by, the postcolonial English-speaking world.

Notes

1. My discussion will center on people whose literate life is lived in English. This group includes people from former British colonies and speakers of World Englishes (see Kachru [1986]; Strevens [1982]; and Smith [1983]) as well as immigrants and natives learning English as a "bi-language."

2. As a research assistant in the University of Nebraska–Lincoln Pilot Composition Project, I interviewed students about their English language experience. Radha's hesitancy and self-doubts were consistent at the beginning and middle of the semester. Toward the end of the semester, both interviews and self-reflections in her process log show her beginning to see herself as "owner" of her language.

3. The teacher-researcher project was part of my dissertation study of the transition of eighteen "nonnative" speakers of English in my process-oriented writing workshop. The study explores contextual factors related to the development of teachers as writing instructors and of students as writers in a workshop where both teachers and students are viewed as writers.

4. For a comparative analysis, read DiPardo's (1993) case study of Al, an African American. Note Al's conflicts and struggles with Black English and how he "felt both proud and defensive about his linguistic background" (144).

5. I would further argue that the "unchallenged authority" is fortified by linguistic imperialism inherent in English learning. Read Robert Phillipson's provocative book *Linguistic Imperialism* (1992) and the symposium on it in *World Englishes* (Kachru et al. 1993), 335–373, and Marc Deneire's (1993) essay "Democratizing English as an International Language."

6. More recently, there has been a gradual increase of articles that critique the social construction of literacy in a pluralistic society. For example, see Auerbach (1993) and McKay and Weinstein-Shr (1993), or the special issue on adult literacies in *TESOL Quarterly* 27.3 (1993).

7. For further insights into the political nature of the enculturation process of English in the lives of "nonnative" speakers, read Tollefson (1989) and Pennycook (1989). See Ogbu and Matute-Bianchi (1986) for discussion of the sociocultural factors in schooling minority language students.

8. Similarly, one of Canada's native Members of Parliament was told as a child that he must master the "white man's" speech so "he could talk to him on equal terms" (see Ashworth 1991).

9. See Ferdman (1990) for an excellent discussion of the link between language and cultural identity. For a contrasting analysis of language and identity, read Shen (1989); also see Barrera (1992) for insights into the cultural gap in literature-based literacy instruction. For a deeper appreciation of the sociopsychological impact of English on cultural identity, read Hoffman's (1989) autobiographical novel *Lost in Translation.* Also see the NCTE Grant-in-Aid Research Report on the English literacy and language identity of Asian American students by Chiang and Schmida (1996).

10. For more on the mainstreaming of linguistic minority students, see McKay and Freedman (1990) as well as Peirce (1989). Also read DiPardo (1993) for a critical understanding of language learning and linguistic minorities.

11. I want to add that I did get to teach the class, but only after I had shared with him my language history and convinced him of the validity of exposing students to "nonmainstream" language users who not only have succeeded in learning the language but who also have learned to thrive in it.

12. For further insights, read my unpublished dissertation, "The Process-Oriented Writing Workshop and Nonnative Speakers of English: A Teacher-Researcher Study," University of Nebraska–Lincoln, 1992.

12

Multiple Languages, Multiple Literacies

Alice Roy

Students in composition classes participate in a large social system, of which the class is only a small part.[1] Besides being enrolled in other classes, they are members of social groups and families as well. They use literacy in these environments in response to various demands, in ways that suit their needs, and within constraints imposed by individuals or institutions.[2] Students who use English as their second (or third, or fourth) language may have an even more complex literacy life because they think, learn, and interact socially in more than one language.

Elizabeth Chiseri-Strater (1991) has written movingly in *Academic Literacies* about the lack of fit between the intellectual needs and goals of two white middle-class students and the apparent goals for them of the institution that they attend. In Chiseri-Strater's account, these students, intelligent and talented, are discouraged from continuing their education by the hierarchical, competitive, and isolative nature of the academic environment, which asks and provides what one of them calls "abbreviated learning" (146). But what about nonwhite, non-middle-class, nonnative English-speaking students? What strategies do they bring to the academy and how does the education they receive serve them?

An examination of a student's writing, in and out of class, can show us whether the abilities and knowledge she already has are being drawn upon and whether her academic needs are being met in this encounter with North American culture as encoded in the English language university. We can also consider whether a university should attend to these needs and if so, how composition courses can contribute to the academic development of such students. Further, we can consider to what extent the responsibility is distributed throughout the academy.

To investigate how nonnative speakers of English negotiate their education through literacy in a second language, I interviewed six Asian-born students enrolled in a large urban state university once a week during a ten-week quarter and collected copies of all the writing they produced both in and out of class during that period.[3] Here I report the case study of Linh, a young ethnic-Chinese woman from Vietnam. I examine the literacy demands of her classes, note ways in which the instructors' student-related literacy practices affect her development, analyze some of the actual writing she does, and consider her non-school-based writing.[4] From this description emerges the profile of a speaker of English as another language, coping with the demands of getting an education, having friends, and helping her family—sometimes in her native language, but mainly in a language not her own. What also emerges is a partial picture of the education this young woman is experiencing. Though our view can only be fragmentary, it will lead to some unsettling questions about higher education and nonnative speakers of English.

Two principles appeared during my discussions with these students and from subsequent analysis of the data. The first is *familiarity*. This somewhat folksy term is related to more formal terms such as *schema theory* or *acculturation* or *scaffolding*. It is a word used often by the student described in this study. Simply put, we only learn if there is something in our previous experience and understanding for the new thing to attach to, or at least we learn more readily in such cases. From the point of view of the learner, enough of the context must be familiar enough for the learner to go on learning. Thus mathematics, for instance, may be easier than literature or social sciences for a speaker from another language because there are fewer culturally embedded links that have to be made or gaps that have to be closed. Linh has a strong sense of the role familiarity plays in her academic successes and difficulties during the period of our discussions.

A second useful principle is that of *collaborative learning and the zone of proximal development*. In *Children's Minds*, Margaret Donaldson (1978) demonstrated that when adults showed children how to transfer what they already knew into more abstract situations, the children were able to do things that Piaget had claimed they couldn't do. Donaldson linked this transfer made possible through adult assistance to Vygotsky's (1986) "zone of proximal development," that mental area in which a learner, with the help of an adult or knowledgeable peer, can negotiate tasks that she might be unable to perform by herself. This principle is related to the principle of familiarity because material accessible to the zone of proximal development operates within a range of familiarity and becomes usable through the assistance of an adult or knowledgeable peer. Linh from time to time draws on such support, seeking the counsel of her more advanced peers.

Family and Educational Background

Linh, a quiet, soft-spoken young woman, was born in Vietnam. Her family were the only ethnic Chinese in town so the children spoke Vietnamese

early. Her schooling was in Vietnamese. Linh and her family left Vietnam in
a boat and spent more than a year in Indonesia before arriving in the United
States. Linh entered school in Los Angeles in seventh grade. In junior high
school, Linh was in special ESL classes. She had cooking class in English.
She was not in separate ESL classes in high school. She often couldn't
understand the classes and relied on reading the textbooks.

Linh speaks both Vietnamese and Chinese. She writes in Vietnamese,
for example, in letters to friends. She speaks Chinese with her family and
with Chinese friends, but she does not write it. She can read Chinese for
things she is interested in, such as teen magazines for makeup, skin care, and
advice. Occasionally she looks at similar articles in English, but she doesn't
have much time for reading in English.

Linh has eleven brothers and sisters; she is the next to youngest child.
All of the family is here in Los Angeles. Her father finished elementary
school; her mother had a private tutor, but Linh doesn't know how far her
mother's education extended. In Vietnam her father was a businessman, her
mother a housewife. Neither parent is currently working. The father is taking
English language classes at adult school. Linh's mother reads the Vietnamese newspaper. She doesn't have many friends and stays in the kitchen much
of the day. She is not lonely, Linh believes; she likes to take care of the children. There are not a lot of Chinese or Vietnamese where they live. Her parents do the shopping in Chinese stores.

Linh's older brothers and sisters work. Linh doesn't work; although
most students at this urban working-class university do have jobs, it is not
unusual for young freshman women, especially Asian, not to work yet. At
the time of this study, Linh is nineteen, in the third quarter of her first year
of college.

Getting Started

During the quarter I interview her, Linh is enrolled in three courses: a
required philosophy course in critical thinking; post–Civil War history
(fulfilling a general education requirement); and a sophomore-level mathematics course for business and economics majors. She is not currently taking
a composition course; she took and passed the first level of developmental
writing, where she had been placed the previous quarter on the basis of a
system-wide placement exam. In that class, Linh wrote about her own experiences in response to readings about U.S., white, middle-class culture and
about experiences of writers from other cultures.

What Do Syllabuses Do?

To our first meeting Linh brings course descriptions and schedules from
her classes for this quarter. Although intended to be self-explanatory, such

communications are deeply embedded in the culture and discourse of higher education. They thus present challenges to all students' literacy capabilities, but perhaps especially for those students for whom English is not their native language. Syllabuses also set the framework for literacy activities throughout the quarter.

The Philosophy/Critical Thinking syllabus presents a weekly schedule and course requirements—tests, homework, reports—with evaluation weights. The information is laid out clearly on the page, with various sections spaced or indented for visual distinctiveness. Sentences are straightforward, not short, but relying mainly on coordination, with a few self-evident passives: "attendance will be taken."

The description of the history class is more discursive. The instructor emphasizes that the course will deal not just with facts but with themes that emerge in the past and affect the future. He stresses the importance of independent, self-motivated work. There will be two midterm examinations, one paper, and a final exam, all weighted equally. The second page of the history handout describes the writing assignment, a review of a book that all of the students will buy. The instructor provides guidelines in the form of four questions that they may use if they wish to focus and organize the report. Linh says, "It's *like* a book review. He gives you some questions to help you see—it's like if we don't know how to do a book review—."

The syllabus for Linh's math class comes in two handwritten pages. The instructor is Middle Eastern, not a native speaker of English himself. There is no textbook. The course will consist of lectures and problems. There will be a midterm and a final examination. I ask Linh if math is a good subject for her. She nods and smiles, "Yes."

How Do Class Notes Work?

Ideally, class notes form a record of material the instructor focuses on and provide a basis for review. Note taking for the nonnative speaker of English is a complex literacy task, since the listener must process material that will probably include new concepts and vocabulary. Even if the instructor is discussing material assigned as reading before the class meeting, it may be the first time the student has heard the terms spoken aloud. Usually, too, the terms are embedded in a speech stream of definition and example and relation to other concepts.

Linh's notes from the first week of her critical thinking course show the instructor laying the groundwork for the course content with technical definitions: *claim, critical thinking, deductive* and *inductive, argument* and *explanation, valid* and *sound, ambiguous* and *vague, semantic* and *syntactic.* In our discussion of her notes, which are orderly and thorough, Linh says the vocabulary is hard and the examples go too fast for her to see the relationships clearly. She hopes the book will help, a strategy she relied on in high school.

Linh brings several pages of history notes, both from class and from her reading of the textbook. In class, the instructor puts an outline on the board for the day's lecture. This outline supports Linh in her note taking: it gives her the spelling of key terms and lets her see hierarchical relationships of periods, events, and concepts. She makes a few errors in writing: "In the South, whites were supremacy"; "Southerners dealt with Hayes." Occasionally, Linh writes in the margin the Vietnamese for a new term, such as *Vagrancy Act.* By linking new terms to known concepts in her first language, she exploits a strategy that increases her familiarity with the new material.

Linh's math notes show that the instructor puts mathematical definitions on the board, combining both prose and examples. He puts up problems that they are to do for homework. The material appears to be self-contained and definite; it does not depend on cultural information.

Homework

The role of homework is ostensibly to give the students experience with the material of the course; if turned in and evaluated, it also gives the instructor material for determining a final course grade. Students must read and comprehend the text of the homework, respond with some sort of writing, and monitor their response. If the instructor writes anything on the homework for specific problems or general comment, the student may need to understand such messages as guidance for future work.

Linh's writing log for this week shows her answering questions and doing exercises based on her reading of the philosophy text, taking notes on the history reading, and solving quadratic equations and graphing for math homework.

The first homework exercise for critical thinking consists of eight one-word answers, *syntactic* or *semantic,* referring to types of ambiguity. For example, Linh correctly identifies the announcement, "Volunteer help requested: Come prepared to lift heavy equipment with construction helmet and work overalls," as containing *syntactic* ambiguity, where the hearer cannot be sure whether "with construction helmet and work overalls" goes with "prepared" or "lift." Of course, pragmatics takes over where syntax fails; no one really thinks the writer of the advertisement might have intended volunteers to use a helmet and overalls to lift heavy equipment, nor are respondents to the ad likely to imagine such a scenario. However, Linh is an experienced and willing student: she accepts the artificiality of the exercise and responds appropriately. However, she fails to identify two sentences with pronouns as *semantic* ambiguity, as in "We were invited to go to the movies yesterday." Linh's class notes show that the instructor had said that pronouns are always ambiguous.[5] A pragmatic reading would assume that the speaker and hearer of such an utterance would know from the context what the referent for "we" must be, and Linh, as a communicatively competent speaker of English, seems to have been reading that sentence as a cooperative participant. She does not achieve the metalinguistic distance needed for this acontextual task.

The writing task of these exercises is undemanding, calling for one-word or short phrase responses, chosen from those provided by the text. The reading task is more complex, in that it provides highly decontextualized prose situations that need interpretation and analysis. On this homework Linh receives an 88, but on the next philosophy homework she receives only a 50. In this exercise, the student must read a statement or short passage and say whether each contains an argument or an explanation. Linh has not been able to apply the distinction to new examples drawn from mainstream American culture or, in some cases, British literature. Both the method of discourse and the material used for analysis are unfamiliar, "foreign" to her.

In math, Linh has already turned in some homework problems, and I ask how she knows if she's done it right. She says (as the syllabus did) that if they have any problems they can go and talk to the instructor. I ask how she knows if she has a problem. She looks at me gently and says, "You can tell if the answer comes out."

Sometimes she checks the problems with friends. So far, she had most of this work in high school, so she feels fairly confident. She says she probably will not go to the instructor very much—in an earlier math course she spent a lot of time waiting to see the instructor. In math the problems are clearly right or wrong, and Linh can draw on the knowledge of her peers when she needs to. In doing so, she uses collaborative learning to extend her understanding.

When Linh's early math homework is returned by the instructor, she receives a 98 for the three pages of solutions and graphs. At one point the instructor crosses out her "we have" as an introduction to the prose part of the solution and elaborates her statement to the proper discourse form: "the 2×2 determinant associated with the given system is given by . . ." He then allows her page-long solution to stand. Although her notes show that he says "We have" when he talks through problems on the board, he teaches her here the preferred text for written discourse in mathematics.

Nonacademic Writing

Linh's writing log shows her writing a letter in Vietnamese to a friend, telling her about her college life. She also writes a business letter, in English, for her older sister regarding financial aid. The sister was sixteen when she came to the United States, an age when many immigrants find it difficult to acquire English literacy. Most of their time is spent with family and friends using the native language; they often take jobs in offices and companies run by compatriots where they continue to use their native language, at least behind the scenes when not dealing with English-speaking customers or clients. In "Learning to Read Culturally: Literacy Before Schooling," Schieffelin and

Cochran-Smith (1984) show how children function as translators or interme-
diaries in English for their parents; Linh appears to be filling this role for her
older sister.

Midterm Activities

Preparing for and Taking Tests

Preparing for tests invokes literacy demands and strategies; tests are literacy
events. For Linh's history midterm, there is a study guide: a list of some
twenty specific topics with subpoints, along with six more general topics. For
these last six topics, the students can prepare their responses ahead by writing the identification and significance of each. Linh's writing log shows that
she spends several hours over a few evenings taking notes and writing in
preparation for this test.

To prepare for her history test, Linh reads the text and writes out the
identification and significance of the six special focus topics. The summaries
are supposed to be in the students' own words; most of hers are, though one
is transcribed directly from class notes. In this way, Linh perhaps learns
unconsciously how to say the material in a way that is appropriate for discourse in history. There are a few errors; like many native-English speakers,
she hears and writes *Klu* Klux Klan rather than the correct but less predictable *Ku*.

Examinations are interpretive events for native as well as nonnative
speakers of English. Multiple-choice questions are designed not to be too
straightforward, to require some sifting and selecting among possibilities.
Essay questions require comprehension of the question and evaluation of
what will be read as a satisfactory response. Examinations also require interpretation of results for use in performing on later tests in the course.

On both of her history tests, Linh does well, although she was worried
after taking the second one because the topics for which she was writing
identifications and significance were more complex than before and she had
to do more reading to discover them. Linh values the chance to prepare the
lists of study topics provided by the instructor: "If I write it myself I don't
have to memorize it, I know what I wrote." The history course constructs
familiarity for Linh because it is "about itself": that is, while the material is
certainly culturally American, it investigates that very material, thus giving
Linh time to become familiar with the events, concepts, and vocabulary
peculiar to it. The opportunity to write out the definition and significance of
various items helps her to increase this familiarity.

Linh has a copy of the math midterm. She was to choose five out of
seven questions. Two she wasn't sure of; the others she knew well enough.
She knows she made a careless mistake on one. Her log shows she prepared

for the test by "re-doing all the H.W. problems." When the examination is graded and returned, it shows that, as she predicted, she missed one part of one of the questions. Linh has the knowledge and skills to evaluate her own performance in math. The instructor writes in the correct procedure for the part she forgot to include. He demonstrates a known procedure that the student can use to monitor her work and verify new problems that she can identify as ones done before. She receives an *A* on this test. Linh's familiarity with mathematics, some of which she has already had in high school, and her competence in what is essentially a fourth language for her, enable her to proceed successfully.

The Dropping Strategy

Linh withdraws from her philosophy class. She failed the multiple choice test; the high score was 85, the average 65, and hers was 53. However, her percentage of correct answers on those questions she answered, the first forty, was high. Linh says: "If I have enough time, if I have time to think—see [pointing to lower portion of Scantron form], I missed all the last part because I didn't have time to think." She wishes she could talk over the questions or write out why she thinks a particular choice is correct. Linh didn't discuss her decision with the instructor; she doesn't feel confident that she can manage the class. In critical thinking, in contrast to the history class, the American cultural material was used as a basis for identifying and analyzing arguments but was not itself the object of study. There was not enough time for Linh to comprehend both the culture-bound material base of the course *and* the analysis and production of sound arguments that constituted its aim.

Writing Papers

Linh begins preparing her book review/report for history. Writing papers for courses seems a central literacy activity for college students, though notetaking and preparing for and taking tests appear to account for more literacy time. A paper of Linh's written for a previous class provides a further window on writing demands in Linh's lower-division educational experience.

Writing from a Previous Class A report done for Linh's introductory biology class in her first quarter as a college student consists of three pages: the first contains two paragraphs on the growth process of a bean plant, and the other two contain labeled drawings of the seed and the seedling plant. On the written part, the instructor has made large checks after sentences that have the requisite information in them. Linh's paragraphs have many of these checks. She receives five points for each paragraph (at one point the comment "excellent!" appears), five points for grammar, and five points each for the two drawings, the full possible twenty points.

Her sentences are generally short and simple with occasional coordination and subordination. Her only errors are in article use, mainly in the absence of an article where one is called for, and a few incorrect choices of articles. However, there are many more correct selections of articles. Of the total possible number of articles, thirty-nine, Linh used 98.5 percent correctly. In the second paragraph, Linh says:

> (1) The simple leaves were developed in the third week of development. (2) Simple leaf is a broad, undivided blade. (3) They were the first true leaves of the plant.

The instructor is not concerned with the stylistic issue of repetition of "developed" and "development" in (1), nor with the break in coherence between sentences (2) and (3), where the pronoun "they" has to look back to sentence (1) for its referent of "the simple leaves." The important thing is that she defined "simple leaf." Linh's report is not sophisticated or inventive; however, it clearly satisfies the task at hand.

The History Report Linh says she spent about three hours writing the draft of her history report. She followed the four question guidelines provided by the instructor and got the material by paging through the book after spending several evenings reading. The instructor's guidelines are not general heuristics but rather are very specific, for example: "How did blacks fare in the military service?" Linh has a paragraph for each of the four points; she adds an introductory paragraph listing them. The first point is in the instructor's exact language, the others she combines and paraphrases. At the end of this first paragraph she has crossed out part of the sentence that encapsulates the main finding: "During the wartime, blacks continued to struggle for equality in which *they achieved very little,*" and replaced it with "*significant gains were achieved,*" reflecting a major shift in her understanding of the content of the book.

Linh's draft shows considerable revising in the process of composing, in at least two phases. Some of her changes come consecutively: she writes a segment ranging from a word to most of a sentence, then crosses it out and continues to write. She also has gone back over this draft and deleted or changed the position of some parts of a main section.

Linh has had a friend read a draft of this report. She notes, "He said it was too general and I need to put details, so I maybe have to rewrite it." She is concerned over the length and sees that adding detail will bring it to the required three pages. The first developmental composition course Linh took stressed providing specific details. Yet, when Linh wrote the early draft of her history paper, her friend had to point out that she needed more details. Having been through a writing course that taught text building with details and examples did not automatically guarantee that she would write a paper for another class with enough detail. However, after receiving the advice, Linh was then able to write effectively in response to that suggestion. Her strategy of seeking advice from a more knowledgeable peer perhaps enables her to draw on past learning in a way that she is not able to alone. Even though the history instructor had emphasized "independent, self-motivated work" on his initial handout, his own facilitative structures engage a zone of proximal development for students like Linh, and Linh takes the initiative to seek collaborative support and assistance when she needs to. Linh says she didn't really have to read the whole book to write the report. She will go through the book again for more details.

Personal Writing

Linh's writing log continues to show her moving apparently comfortably in and out of English and Vietnamese, on the telephone and in notes and letters, gathering and transmitting information, making arrangements, coordinating family and social interests. About some phone calls she makes for her sister she says: "She want to repair contact lens and she want to estimate the price of different doctor, optometrist." Linh recorded the information for her sister.

Linh's log also shows that she left a written phone message for a friend of her sister's and a note to her mother, in Vietnamese, that she was going out for dinner with friends. She writes phone messages in English or Vietnamese depending on what language the speaker is using and who the recipient will be. Reflecting the fairly typical relationship between age of arrival and acquisition of a second language, the older sisters use mainly Vietnamese with friends and family; the younger ones are more likely to use English. Linh also wrote, in Vietnamese, a letter to a friend in Canada, inviting her to visit.

Linh attends a meeting of the Chinese Club and, as treasurer, takes notes for herself. These are in English, noting preparations for the upcoming club picnic:

> Get freshmen to join picnic—list of names, transportation (Yes, No) fee
> ($5.00 paid in advance),

She also notes plans for a carnival and for a workshop later in the quarter. She uses the commercial, quite Americanized spelling of "nite."

These events show Linh's competence across three cultures and her ability to mediate between cultures for her family members. However, she could not negotiate the cultural knowledge demanded in her critical thinking course, where she needed more support to understand the scenarios presented in order to analyze the effectiveness of arguments.

Finishing Up and Looking Ahead

Linh has finished the final draft of her history paper, which satisfies the university's writing requirement for general education courses: the syllabus shows that the paper will be one quarter of the grade, but failure to turn it in results in an *F* for the course.

When Linh's paper is returned, she receives forty-nine of fifty possible points: forty for content, ten for style. At four places in the paper, corresponding in content to the four guiding questions provided by the instructor at the beginning of the quarter, there is a check mark at the end of a sentence with a 10 in the margin; at two of those places the instructor has written "good!" There are a few morphological errors, such as missing the past tense *d* marker; these do not affect the content or comprehension and are not marked. The end comment says "Excellent" and "9 for Style."

Some of the sentences look fairly complex and polished to me. I notice that Linh has not used any quotations; I ask if she copied or put things in her own words. She says she put them in her own words. In "Bakhtin and the Social Reality of Language Acquisition," John Edlund (1988) shows how class texts, both spoken and written, enter students' own production. Linh's writing here seems to echo that of the book she is reviewing, suggesting that she uses "appropriated language before it has been completely assimilated" (60).

The paper is four-and-a-half pages long, handwritten. The introductory paragraph is unchanged from the earlier draft. The other paragraphs have been expanded. The paper appears to be entirely composed of summary of the main points of the book, following the instructor's guiding questions; no particular interpretation or integration with other theories or course materials has been needed.

Final Exams

In Linh's history class, the students have received another set of study topics for the final examination; this time there will be no essay questions, just multiple choice. The math final will be composed of problems such as they have been doing throughout the quarter. Linh knows she can turn to friends for consultation on math problems if she needs it.

Next Quarter's Classes

In the middle of the quarter, students put in their requests for the next quarter's classes. The system is computerized; now, toward the end of the quarter, they learn whether they were placed in the classes they requested. The next quarter will be summer, but the university schedule is year-round and Linh intends to take three four-unit courses. She will try the philosophy/critical thinking course again; she has also registered for sociology and the second developmental writing course, which she must pass before taking freshman composition. Linh liked the first developmental writing course, a team-taught, essay-based, workshop class, and looks forward to taking the next one. Unfortunately, when Linh receives her class schedule for the summer, she learns that she was not enrolled in the developmental writing course she had requested because all the sections were closed at the times she had available. On her brother's advice she has begun to keep a diary in an attempt to maintain her English writing skills.

Nonacademic Writing

Academic writing takes place in nonacademic as well as academic environments, as when a student takes notes on reading or writes a paper at home. On the other hand, sometimes nonacademic writing takes place in what might appear to be restricted academic environments, as evidenced by a series of notes Linh and a friend write in history class. Linh says, "Last time we got bored in the class and I and my friend just wrote some notes." As the lines between academic and nonacademic environments blur, so do those delineating materials: they wrote on the back of a photocopy of Linh's history book review.

In out-of-class writing, Linh writes a note of apology to friends who had wanted to surprise her with lunch for her birthday but couldn't when she arrived later than usual that day. (Two days later they took her out for dinner at a Chinese seafood restaurant.) These friends are Chinese from Cambodia; Linh doesn't write Chinese, and they don't read Vietnamese, so the note is in English. The note shows some nonnative syntax, but it is gracefully constructed and shows considerable communicative competence:

> _____ has just told me that you and _____ did not bring lunch because you intended to take me out and treat me lunch for my birthday, but I did not show up this morning. I am sorry to have you waited for me. At the same time, I appreciated for your thoughtfulness, though I may not show it. Once again, thank you.
>
> Linh

The friends respond: "Your apologize accepted. Talk about it later in the library."

Linh's log shows that she leaves more phone messages for her sisters and writes a note to herself "to remind me to call William regarding the contributing of $20 to child abuse hotline."

Future Goals

In our last meeting, I ask Linh about her education and plans for the future. Her major is finance "because I saw many jobs offer on that field in the classified ads." Linh has no specific answers for my questions about what work she plans to do or about how she wants to live. She says, "I would like to have a high education background and hope that it could help me in looking for a good job in the future."

Implications

This study has provided a close look at the literacy and learning of one student in one term of lower-division (that is, freshman-sophomore) education.
It is thus at the same time thorough and limited. Insofar as her experience is
representative of other students more or less like her—students of color or of
nonmainstream ethnicity, speakers of English as another language or of standard English as another dialect, working-class or lower-middle-class or of
the underclass—some implications can be essayed.

Linh's Abilities

Linh is, by my observation, an intelligent and personable young woman.
English is her third language. Her speech is competent, though she makes
more errors in speaking than in writing, when she has more time to monitor
her production. In my study, she makes more errors in taking notes for critical thinking than for history, where the pressure of keeping up with the
examples drawn from American culture as well as the frequently metalinguistic level of the analysis takes its toll. However, she demonstrates communicative competence: her responses in conversation are nativelike in their
appropriateness and quite understandable. Linh is able to read and use syllabuses, take notes, read texts with varying degrees of success, take tests, and
write assigned papers, all in a language she has learned in early adolescence.
Linh's own responsibility and organization, and her strategies of seeking
peer guidance when needed and of using as much familiarity as she can
establish to help her through new material have served her well. At the same
time, she functions in three languages in her family and social life, often in
complex roles such as translator and mediator for members of her family.
Her nonacademic writing provides evidence of involvement in family and
social life, with friends and extracurricular activities.

Instructional Strategies

First, this study shows the helpful use of something so simple as the blackboard in providing support for new terms as well as for organization of the
class meeting. For students whose first language is not English, material is
made familiar through several modes: reading, seeing terms on the board,
hearing terms in lectures, and using terms in discussion and in writing. Second, study guides and the opportunity to prepare in writing for essay tests
allowed Linh, as she said, to "know" rather than just "memorize" the material. Third, if multiple-choice testing is used, time must be provided for
learners from other language backgrounds to negotiate this very dense,
decontextualized sort of text. Failure should result from not knowing the
material, not for being unable to process the questions quickly.

Curriculum and Institutional Factors

Linh is serious about her studies, though in the academic writing I observed, she is not particularly innovative or given to taking risks. She works hard to do what is asked. This leads to another question: what is being asked?

Linh's writing tasks do not appear to have been very demanding. Her biology report of the previous quarter reflects Freire's (1982) banking principle of education: check marks are placed wherever she has the right information. Her history report requires that she understand the information in the book through independent reading, but she is not asked to do anything more than report it. Her math class appears to consist of abstract problem after problem, and Linh is comfortable with this. She is building on competence she already has and can see her skill and understanding develop incrementally. She is not asked to interact with the material verbally; mainly she solves the problems put to the class by the instructor. In Linh's critical thinking class, quizzes made up of one-word answers comprised 50 percent of the grade. The test she took was multiple choice. The syllabus mentions two reports, weighted together at 10 percent.

These learning activities need not be rejected per se. Disciplinary learning includes gradual ownership of a body of material, through practice of technical skills and through careful reporting. But we might hope that her education will not stop with merely retrieving and returning information. Perhaps later upper-division courses will require more interpretive, integrative writing from her. Yet in fact, since Linh is a finance major, such writing assignments may not occur very often.

In *Academic Literacies*, Chiseri-Strater (1991) might have concluded by suggesting that her two subjects, Anna and Nick, should have learned to learn within the academic system they had enrolled in, but she didn't. She suggested, rather, that they had been shortchanged by being "channeled through coursework without being asked to reflect on, revise, rethink, and personally construct what they [were] learning in one course and connect it to other courses and finally to themselves" (149).

Composition classes offer opportunities to both native and nonnative English-speaking students to explore American cultural themes, to respond, interpret, analyze, criticize, and integrate facts and observations with other knowledge and with their own experience. Of course, the composition class can provide explicit strategies that can be useful in other courses. However, it may also invite students to take risks in exploratory writing, risks that would perhaps not be appropriate in other literacy tasks, for example in Linh's biology report or in traditional essay exams. Further, it can ask students to engage in analytic and integrative thinking and writing that they may not have the opportunity to develop in other arenas. The role of the composition classroom is an important one because it provides time and a safe place and people to collaborate with in these activities. But Linh will enter her second year still trying to get into a required developmental writing course. Some administrators, those who see composition as merely a service course, may argue that such coursework belongs in the high schools or community colleges. However, if speakers of English as another language, those whose language and literacy skills are deemed not to measure up to a standard of college literacy, are to be admitted to universities, then institutions must commit resources that will make it possible for students to take developmental and first-year writing courses early.

But the composition class is only a small part of Linh's university education. Her experience, so far as we have observed it, clearly would benefit from writing across the curriculum programs, with faculty attention to integration of concepts and facts among courses and across disciplines, and with administrative support of faculty development in the use of writing as a means to learn and as a means to integrate learning. The process of fulfilling these goals will build "familiarity" within and across subject matters and will permit students such as Linh to draw on their considerable ability to mediate across languages and cultures.

In the United States, our educational institutions do two things that, considering that they are contradictory, they do remarkably well. Historically we have looked to schools at all levels to provide opportunity to new immigrants, minorities, and the poor for assimilation and upward mobility. If an individual works hard enough, our myth goes, she or he can take advantage of the opportunities our system provides, and indeed many do. However, not included in the myth and unexamined in the popular view of education is the role of educational institutions to sort out the "talented" from the "untalented," with the effect of reproducing the class structure.[6] There isn't room for everybody to be upwardly mobile. We carry out this part of the educational mission through unintentioned differential treatment of students within classes, through tracking—now much more covert but still operating in the public schools—and through the general paradigm of college entrance, whereby students in elite institutions mostly come from elite preparatory institutions or programs, and so on. Once in college, such sorting plays itself out, in the case of new immigrants and nonimmigrant minorities, in patterns of failure and success. Some students, of course, fail because they haven't studied enough. But Linh is not one of those students. She fails in one class because she is not acculturated enough to handle the material that is used to teach the more abstract concepts. She succeeds in classes where the demands are, mainly, to reproduce the concepts and material presented. Where she fails, she is not asked to draw on her own cultural material to substantiate conceptual learning; where she succeeds, she is not asked or guided to develop those strategies that would allow her to "problematize," as Freire (1982) has it, her learning or her experience. Her ability to mediate across cultures, as we saw her do with family and friends, seems not to be invoked at all.

Linh's own goals for her education are, not unreasonably, utilitarian: to get a good job. But we must ask, in the words of an old song, "Is that all there is?" Linh will probably have a fairly good job and economic condition, predictably better than that of her unemployed parents. Her education appears to be on the way to ensuring that. But her education does not seem to include teaching her to ask questions about why she will be living and working in the United States nor why her parents are unemployed here. That is, not only is Linh not being asked to integrate, interpret, and question; she is also not being led to ask *why* she is not being asked to integrate, interpret, and question.

At the very least, on an institution-internal level, this description of one student's experience points out the need for writing across the curriculum. And this means institutional support, faculty development, and encouragement to enable already overworked and underrewarded faculty to incorporate writing in all disciplines. But on another, meta-level, it calls for a critical rethinking of curriculum and the aims of education. Linh's future may hold a better job than she could expect without a college degree, and, at an individual level, that is its own kind of success. Yet she is not being prepared to ask the kinds of questions that might prompt answers that transform her life, the lives of her peers, and perhaps ours as well. In "Critical Literacy and the Postmodern Turn" McLaren and Lankshear (1993) say, "To not ask these questions is to risk being reduced to custodians of sameness and system-stabilizing functions which serve the collective interests and regimes of truth of the prevailing power elite(s)" (381). Academicians may not feel very powerful in terms of the world's work, and those who teach in schools that Linh and her peers attend may not feel particularly elite. Yet a system that defines someone who doesn't learn quickly how to do textbook exercises in Western logical thought as unable to "think critically" is surely a "custodian of sameness" and surely extends the dominance of elitist Western traditions of thought over nonmainstream ways of thinking and being. There are those, of course, who believe that is as it should be.

Two assumptions appear to underlie Linh's education: first, this is as much as Linh and students like her can be asked to do; and second, this is enough. For the former, Linh's abilities to negotiate her education, to interpret academic documents such as syllabuses and assignments, to realize that her ability to succeed on certain tests and her inability to succeed on others depends more on the form of the tests than on her learning, to collaborate with peers or to learn from more experienced students, and to mediate across languages and cultures with her family and friends suggest that she could do far more. As to the latter: it is not enough. We teach students such as Linh with good intentions: we are helping, and it's difficult work; they are often underprepared though motivated to succeed; their language skills are uneven, unfluent. But altruism is a seductive moral stance. With every use of the word *they*, Linh and her peers are reiterated as Other.

As a young woman, Asian American (more specifically, Chinese Vietnamese American), and nonnative speaker of English, Linh is an inhabitant
of the borderlands spoken of by Anzaldua (1987). Her gender, ethnicity, culture, language, and economic status situate her as Other. Her education pre-
pares her to remain so, with the possible modest improvement of her economic situation. One approach might be to provide more writing courses, or
more opportunities for acculturation, or perhaps a raising of standards. These
strategies work to change the individual, to make her or him more acceptable
to the institution. However, the series of immigrations that have characterized the United States from before it was the United States has never left the
country, or the education system, unchanged, and there is no reason to
believe this period in our history will be different in that regard. To the
degree that education is interactive, both the learner and the system must
expect to undergo change. Thus I suggest an approach from a different
direction. Let curriculum, from composition through writing across the curriculum, in testing and in pedagogy, reflect the understanding that literacy—
and critical thinking—are never neutral. Then education of students as disparate in background, language, and experience as the white middle-class
students Chiseri-Strater (1987) described and the working-class, nonnative
English-speaking students of color or different ethnicity such as Linh can
proceed in ways that will, or can, provide, in James Berlin's (1993) words,
"a force for progressive change at all levels of society" (267).

Notes

1. I thank Lee Carroll, Anne Herrington, Michael Holzman, Sandra Mano, and
Mike Rose for helpful discussions during the preparation of this chapter. I also appreciate the thoughtful suggestions from the editors of this volume. This writing is ded-
icated to the memory of James Berlin from whom I have learned so much. I had
expected to send this to him to read; we would all have been richer for his response.

2. For further discussion of institutional constraints, see Heath (1983); Cooper
(1986); and Anderson and Stokes (1984).

3. This research was supported in part by an Affirmative Action Faculty Development grant from California State University, Los Angeles. For reasons of space, the
methodology is not included, but it is available from the author.

4. I deeply regret the absence of Linh's voice in my analysis and interpretation
of her experience. My intention was to collaborate with the students in the second
phase of this study, but because of illness I was unable to continue immediately after
the quarter in which we met, and I subsequently lost contact with her.

5. Linguists would more likely consider this "vague" than "ambiguous." In
ambiguity, there are two (or more) *known* referents, whereas in a case such as this,
"we" does not have recoverable antecedents, they are simply unknown.

6. See Carlson (1993) for a useful discussion of "opportunity" and "talent" as
concepts that serve to reproduce the existing class distribution of education.

13

Facts, Artifacts, Counterfacts, and Differences

Deborah Davies

The Pittsburgh program described by David Bartholomae, Anthony Petrosky, and others in *Facts, Artifacts, and Counterfacts: Theory and Method for a Reading and Writing Course* has been, since the book's 1986 publication, an influential model for teaching basic writing. In the Basic Reading and Writing course described, fifteen students meet with two instructors for six hours a week, reading and responding to seven books related to a single theme (87–89). The program rejects a "skills" curriculum, building instead from the assumption that students "invent the university" by entering into academic discourse (134).[1]

Bartholomae and Petrosky's work empowers all basic writing teachers. According to Susan Wall and Nicholas Coles (1991), situating basic writing students as participants in academic discourse leads to redefinition in which the margin becomes "a vantage point from which the authoritative discourses at the center can be critiqued" (234). However, like Wall and Coles, I question whether the failure to examine the role and status of the literate practices and cultural forms that students bring to their academic experience limits their ability to demonstrate the desired "consciously marginal and critical stance" (234–35).

For the past six years, I have been teaching a basic writing course at Jackson Community College that has significant similarities to the Pittsburgh program. When I first read *Facts, Artifacts and Counterfacts*, I found I could enhance colleagues' respect for my innovations by pointing out those similarities. However, significant differences exist between the two courses; differences that seem more, rather than less, critical after informal classroom research. Given the Pittsburgh program's influence on basic writing instruction, I wish to explore the conceptualizations of invention that inform those differences. I believe that just as women's studies has defined the strategies associated with women's language as different and contextual, rather than deficient, those of us who represent academic expectations for student writing need to investigate our students' rhetorical strategies along with the terms we use to describe them.

Like students in the Pittsburgh program, students in my writing classes analyze aspects of growth and change, read autobiographical material that includes selections by working-class writers, and produce classroom anthologies of their self-selected best work. I designed my course in order to test two perceptions: (1) that basic students benefit from seeing their work in the context of work by other working-class writers, including that of fellow students; and (2) that their ability to write analytically is enhanced by reading passages and writing papers in which affect plays a significant part.

My students are not identical to University of Pittsburgh students. The two groups have a great deal in common, however, including their differences from traditional freshmen. The students I teach are predominantly white, working-class adults and teenagers, although classes at a downtown extension center have more students of color. Some students come from small farms, and many work or have worked in factory jobs. Most are the first members of their families to attend college. Class—what Tillie Olsen (1978) called the greatest unexamined factor—is the marginalizing factor common to most of my students (9). Differences arising from the amalgam of circumstances linked with socioeconomic status are made more complex by race and gender. Marginality initially makes developmental writers vulnerable in any classroom, but that same marginality can become cognitively important if students are encouraged to discuss their differences and commonalities.

Almost all basic writing students have high writing apprehension. One student wrote on the first day of class, "I can't write. My mind goes blank." Then he crossed out his words. This writing apprehension triggered my use of a range of writing samples from outside the classroom. When I first began teaching basic writing, I used a peer workshop in which students read and discussed only one another's work. I soon realized that my students' self-doubts were so strong that when either I or their colleagues identified strengths in a piece of writing, the author dismissed the analysis as patronizing or ill-informed. I began bringing emotionally explicit autobiographical writing excerpts into class in order to allow students to see their work as part of a personally meaningful continuum of unpublished and published work. For five years I gave surveys asking students to evaluate this approach. Response was almost universally favorable.

Such surveys, of course, ignore variables such as student response to the instructor. However, this course was also taught by my former colleague Trish LeNet, who modified it in productive ways and used student-generated anthologies with students who spoke English as a second language. After studying our results, Trish and I concluded that as many or more of our students passed the exit placement exam as had passed before we began this program. In addition, fewer students dropped, and student work was more insightful and complex.

My classroom research, supported by Trish's corroboration, strengthens my conviction that two aspects of the Pittsburgh model's conceptualization of invention are open to question, as is the pattern of instructor response that results from that conceptualization. The first aspect of the Pittsburgh program's conceptualization of invention that must be questioned is a definition of academic discourse that stigmatizes the role of affect in critical thinking. There are fifteen formal writing assignments in the Basic Reading and Writing course—papers for which the goal is "to produce writing that is or can become what we think of as academic discourse—that is, thoughtful, reasoned, coherent prose that reflects a questioning and disciplined mind" (Bartholomae and Petrosky 1986, 91). In order to help students attain this reasoned prose, assignments explicitly direct students to limit the description of highly personal significant events and circumstances:

> Some students ... in a gesture that is indicative of the mutual trust and support that by now has come to characterize the teaching/learning context, *will ignore our suggestion that they not narrate events or circumstances that might be too personal* [emphasis mine], and will volunteer astonishing glimpses of the complexity of their lives ... such glimpses—at times moving, at times tragic, at times unbearably cynical—can jeopardize, in the affective response they cause, the critical stance. (142)

A central assignment asks students to describe major changes involved in adolescence. (Classes of returning adults are assigned themes related to work.) Neither the theme of adolescence nor the theme of working is likely to facilitate exploration of childhood experience, except in the kind of embedded reference that is difficult for inexperienced writers. In fact, students doing this central assignment are told not to go back before the age of fourteen or so, except for background material (71–72). The assignment thus limits ways in which students can identify and analyze commonalities and differences in their early lives.

To further counteract students' tendencies to utilize affect, writers are asked to complete a subsequent assignment designed to make them reflect on "the distance that the act of writing imposes on life" (143). Students are asked to describe the character who appears on the pages they have written, in order to determine whether they can say that they have presented readers with a picture of a complex character, and to contrast their character to those in the books read (143). This attempt to make students reflect on the shifting ways in which meaning is constructed follows hard upon the new and risky process of constructing meaning. And while subsequent drafts and a little emotional distance from a newly written paper can ease a student's transition from the sense of having written her life to having written a version of her life, the proscribed "astonishing glimpses" of students' lives may have signified serious but unrewarded attempts to construct meaning.

Women's studies builds on a different conceptualization of the relationship of affect and invention. *Women's Ways of Knowing* (Belenky, Clinchy,

Goldberger, and Tarule 1986) explores the concept of constructed knowledge, in which women who are aware that "even the most ordinary human being is engaged in the construction of knowledge" learn to weave together "strands of rational and emotive thought" (133–34). Audre Lorde's (1984) work also defends the critical role of affect: "Our feelings and the honest exploration of them become sanctuaries and spawning grounds for the most radical and daring of ideas. They become a safe-house for that difference so necessary to change and the conceptualization of any meaningful action" (37).

We need to ask ourselves whether we really believe that student writers' feelings about their lives, and the honest exploration of those feelings, have no productive role to play in writing classes. Moreover, we must ask whether discouraging such exploration may have negative consequences. Encouraging students to reflect on the "distance that the act of writing imposes on life" makes it sounds as though "distance" is, in itself, an aid to intellectual endeavor. But studies of other disciplines suggest that distance can negatively affect vision.

Jessie Bernard (1987), in her essay "Re-Viewing the Impact of Women's Studies on Sociology," builds on Robert Merton's (1972) analysis of social euphemisms. Merton hypothesizes that the social scientist who creates distance through euphemisms "sometimes comes to act as though the aspects of the reality which are neglected in his analytical apparatus do not even exist." Merton quotes Kenneth Clark: "The tendency to discuss disturbing social issues such as gender discrimination, segregation, and economic exploitation . . . as if these persistent problems did not involve the suffering of actual human beings is so contrary to empirical evidence that it must be interpreted as a protective device" (Bernard 1987, 209). Bernard, pointing out that early sociologists had to struggle to free themselves from an image of sentimental do-goodism, describes the efforts that the University of Chicago's department of sociology expended to prove itself "just as value-free, just as macho, non-emotional and impersonal as the physical and biological sciences" (200). In contrast, Bernard sees women's studies as calling for "the re-introduction of blacked out suffering," and rejecting the erasure of whole areas of reality (210).

By proscribing affect in student writing, those of us in power insist that students use distancing as a protective device. Composition, like sociology, is a discipline that has struggled to gain academic standing; a call for "distance" sounds impersonal, objective, "scientific." However, it is difficult to see how denying student writers opportunities to investigate feelings about the differences that have shaped their lives can, in the long run, produce "reasoned, coherent prose that reflects a questioning and disciplined mind."

In their tendency to see emotion and intellect as dichotomous, Bartholomae and Petrosky reflect the twentieth century's modernist stance. Suzanne Clark's (1991) *Sentimental Modernism* explores ways in which the sanctions of modernism acted and still act to isolate the work of women and other marginalized writers as "sentimental." Clark says modernism involves an implicit politics of style in which "a rationalized order tries to subject the order of emotional connections—sympathy—to its domination and obstructs the formation of social movements by its regulation of emotional appeals . . ." (5). In Clark's view, modernist critics whose influence is still pervasive used "aesthetic antisentimentality to make distinctions, to establish a position of authority against mass culture" (5).

Attempts to limit affect in student writing thus limit ways in which students can explore differences between their lives and representations of the dominant culture. These prohibitions also limit students' ability to investigate ways in which they differ from one another, and commonalities they share. Additionally, limiting affect limits students' chances to achieve agency. When a student shares a personal story, that student may be in the process of converting tragedy to agency. This was true of a student who wrote about having been sent to live, as a child, with a physically abusive relative. She first gained credibility in the eyes of family members when she showed them her anthologized story. It was also true of a student who wrote about having been raped as a child, and who subsequently included her essay in a class anthology, saying her story might help other women.

I cannot imagine reading either essay, and responding by asking the writers to "describe the character who appears on the pages you have written" to help them determine whether they had described a complex character. I am not saying that such an assignment would never be beneficial; rather, for these women, and for other students I have known, it seems like the wrong assignment. Such a subsequent assignment relegates the initial essays to an underclass ghetto, used only as vehicles to "academic discourse," rather than recognizing them for what they are: stories that, in collaborative settings, reclaim areas of reality for academic discourse.

A second critical area in Bartholomae and Petrosky's conceptualization of invention is Bartholomae's characterization of student work as idiosyncratic: "The student has to appropriate (or be appropriated by) a specialized discourse . . . he has to invent the university by assembling and mimicking its language while finding some compromise between idiosyncrasy, a personal history, on the one hand, and the requirements of convention, the history of a discipline, on the other" (Bartholomae 1985, 135).

Karen Burke LeFevre (1987) reminds us that "invention often occurs through the socially learned process of an internal dialogue with an imagined other, and the invention process is enabled by an internal social construct of audience . . ." (2). She also describes more explicitly collaborative (or silencing) situations: "Invention becomes explicitly social when writers involve other people as collaborators, or as reviewers whose comments aid invention, or as 'resonators' who nourish the development of ideas. . . . Invention is powerfully influenced by social collectives . . . which transmit expectations and prohibitions, encouraging certain ideas and discouraging others" (2).

Students' rhetorical strategies are culturally invented in ways that involve internal constructs and external mediation, and as such, they often differ from those of the academic discourse community. One such varying expectation involves situations in which reticence is appropriate. In *Lives on the Boundary*, Mike Rose (1989) suggests that class-related reticence makes emotionally explicit papers difficult for students whose parents have managed a "hard-won assimilation." "You don't want to put that in a paper. That just doesn't belong," one student says. Rose concludes that for some students, some things are "better left unsaid" (178–79).

However, explicitly examining such differing cultural expectations can be beneficial to students and instructors alike. After reading Shirley Brice Heath's *Ways with Words* (1983), which describes children's language development in working-class communities and the "skills, values and knowledge students bring to school" (13), I began discussing conflicting models of politeness with students, showing how one model says, "Speak when you're spoken to; don't say more than you have to, especially to someone in authority," while the academic model says, "Don't be shy. Spit it out and elaborate." When we address such issues, we let our students process them cognitively.

We need to query Bartholomae's characterization of student work as idiosyncratic, recognizing instead that not only is student work culturally influenced, but also that our response to students' work is culturally influenced. Preferred narrative style is another important example of the continuing interplay between rhetorical expectations and factors of class, gender, and ethnicity. While teaching at both the secondary and community college level, I have noticed that many working-class students use topic-associating narratives, although most of the research I have seen connects this form of discourse to ethnicity rather than class.

According to Taylor and Matsuda (1988), topic-centered narratives—the form chosen as "better" by white middle-class children and teachers—exhibit coherence among described events (211). Episodic or topic-associating stories, thought to be used by working-class black children, are identified as "a series of associated segments implicitly linked to a topic, event, or theme, but with no explicit theme or point" (213). Here is an abbreviated example of topic-associating children's language: "I went to the beach Sunday/ and to McDonald's/ and to the park" (215). Courtney Cazden (1988) links this episodic narration to what Geneva Smitherman (1986), in *Talkin and Testifyin*, calls black adult narrative or "concrete narrative . . . whose meandering away from the 'point' takes the listener on episodic journeys," (Smitherman 147–48) and to Gail Martin's (1987) work with Arapaho student narratives and Arapaho narrative style (Martin, 166–67). The clauses in topic-associating stories are often linked by parataxis, defined by Jennifer Coates (1986) as simple juxtaposition (I got up, I went to work.) or connected by coordinating clauses (25). Coates adds that topic-centered stories are more likely to exhibit hypotaxis, the use of subordinating clauses to establish explicit connections

(25). Questioning claims that parataxis is linked to women's language, Coates concludes that linguists agree that "there is nothing intrinsically superior about a construction involving subordinate clauses, but . . . hypotactic constructions are typical of written language, while paratactic constructions are typical of speech" (26).

One of my students described how getting lost when biking as a child brought about his first conscious encounter with racism. When I read the story, his paratactic construction functioned as a successful rhetorical device making me—as much as is possible—relive a common childhood experience through his experience.

> The neighborhood was mostly Catholic people and most of my friends were white then . . . all at once this white guy came out of his house and said, you niggers. Not thinking, I said back, Your mamma, and in minutes a lot of people came out of several different houses calling me and my brother names, throwing sticks and rocks at us chasing us down the street. My foot slipped off the pedal, the gear got stuck and the first thing I did was pray to God. . . .

When I read this story, I was once again the youngest child in my neighborhood, sweating and struggling to propel a heavy, unwieldy bike uphill. Only this time, people were behind me, chasing me, throwing things at me. As I read his paper, I felt the hair on the back of my neck rise. This student gave me the most effective metaphor I've ever had to help me distinguish between growing up in a white working-class neighborhood, and being black and having to move through it. I no longer drive through my old neighborhood with the same sense of nostalgia. Seeing my world through his eyes changed my understanding of my own childhood.

Episodic narrative is a culturally influenced style associated with many silenced groups and devalued in academic writing. However, Coles (1986), in his essay "Democratizing Literature," identifies it as an effective writing strategy used by British workers in autobiographical writing. He refers to Catherine Gallagher's (1978) research, which suggests that working-class autobiographical prose is characterized by the use of "parataxis, understatement, an 'addictive matter-of-factness' (Gallagher, 24) that presents a life without making points about it" (Coles 1986, 676).

Many of my students' most effective pieces of writing are in response to an assignment asking them to write about a memorable experience, possibly but not necessarily from their childhood. A number of writers describe the early loss of a father through death, divorce, or alcoholism, and often effectively use parataxis and understatement. One young white female writer described finding her father dead, with saliva dripping from one corner of his mouth. The paper ended when the writer's grandmother told the dying man, "He could not die. Not yet. Not this way. But he did not listen." The paratactic construction and understatement enhanced the stark emotional impact of the work.

One last example of understatement used as a rhetorical strategy: another student addressed the issue of racism by describing her day as a volunteer playground supervisor. The opening anecdote seems initially irrelevant: a coworker asks the author to speak to a misbehaving child, rather than correcting the child herself. The coworker's prejudice becomes obvious when, at the end of the paper, when she tells the author, "Your kind can be intimidating." Discussing her paper in class, the writer said she chose not to initially identify the opening example as a result of prejudice. She argued that the message was implicit in the story, and that labeling her coworker as prejudiced would change the way people read her experience.

I have concluded that the writer was correct in her assessment that readers would have read her paper differently. Topic-centered papers, with their traditional academic construction, thrust the reader into the stance Peter Elbow (1973) labels as "the doubting game." By remaining in the narrative mode, the writer invites the reader to participate in her experience, playing what Elbow calls "the believing game." Elbow says that the believing game, often identified with solipsism, can be a tool for *breaking out* of solipsism; getting people to move out of their own perceptions and thoughts into someone else's (181–82). Marginalized students become adroit at using narrative writing to solicit belief from the reader. Recognition of that skill can increase students' confidence as they experiment with alternative approaches and writing styles.

Students may not only use a narrative style that differs from our expectations, but they may also use different strategies to construct authority. Bartholomae (1985) says that basic students frequently use the voice of authority associated with a parent or teacher, lecturing readers as though they were children, and concluding such essays with "Lessons on Life" (136–137). This analysis seems to me to be a simplistic reading of a situation in which many students attempt to construct communal meaning using relational values. This issue is related to the stigmatization of affect. Bartholomae does not use the word *sentimental* in this context, but Clark's (1991) analysis of the subjection of sympathy to a rationalized order seems pertinent to the rejection of "inappropriate" advice and homilies. "Lessons on Life" are not necessarily simplistic homilies created by willfully oblivious students. Commonplaces indicate that students are attempting to use Aristotelian rhetoric, by appealing to "the good" they perceive they share—and fear may be all they share—with the academic community. Jay Robinson (1990), in *Conversations on the Written Word,* uses James Boyd White's (1984) term *constitutive rhetoric* to describe students' attempts to constitute character, community, and culture. In fact, Robinson argues, all acts of writing and reading are "nothing more and nothing less than attempts undertaken by human beings to form community with other human beings whose real needs and expectations and understandings are imagined when not known" (101).

Deconstructing commonplaces can also reveal them to be existential: students who have been abused insist we must care for others; students who have had terrible school experiences affirm the value of education. Kirin Narayan (1991) says this "masking of imperfections" can be used to translate numbing bitterness into positive future action (130). Such affirmation can be read as a critique of the sometimes pervasive cynicism noted by Bartholomae and Petrosky. As one of my students said, "I can't afford not to have faith."

The recognition that the rhetorical strategies of developing writers are culturally influenced has critically important implications for instructor response. The response patterns described in *Facts, Artifacts, and Counterfacts,* deriving from the view that student work is idiosyncratic, limit collaboration and isolate writers from one another. When formal writing assignments are discussed by the class, one or two papers are chosen by instructors to be duplicated anonymously and examined by the class as a whole *because they represent problems in development* (Bartholomae and Petrosky 1986, 93). Journal entries, which are designed to encourage the "generation of new ideas [and] the ability to make connections between one book and another or something in a book and the writer's personal experience," are also read by instructors, and are only occasionally chosen for demonstrated strengths and duplicated anonymously for class discussion (92). Students act as discussion leaders while discussing books (157), but there is little evidence that students respond to the content of one another's written work.

Consider the way these response patterns limit collaboration. Each student is asked to write about a recent significant event, one that has "changed the way you are or the way you think about things." Although students are told they can incorporate comments classmates made during discussion of representative papers, the goal of rewriting is "to make your paper a more precise and insightful representation of what you know" after rereading the original paper and noting the instructors' comments (Bartholomae and Petrosky 1986, 57). Students whose papers are not chosen for discussion must rewrite primarily with instructor input.

For feminist instructors, this epitomizes a troubling concept of invention. A student may write something insightful in her journal or in the formal papers, but if the instructor, who is probably from a different background, does not "read" her work empathetically or choose it for discussion, the student must proceed without the resonators that would enable her to continue writing with authority. Since instructors represent what LeFevre (1987) calls the "social collective" of the academy, silence suggests tacit *institutional* prohibitions.

At this point in this chapter, I would like to describe my own attempts to use what Wall and Coles (1991) call an "interactive pedagogy" to empower students. My interest in the social nature of invention began when a class situation forced me to realize that I could not act as a "universal resonator." A class of unusually "marginal" developmental students had inundated me with what I then called "grandparent papers." Floored by the exceptionally saccharine, moralistic writing, I made no attempt to respond to papers, instead telling students to respond to each other at length.

After students had an opportunity to read and respond to each other's papers, revised drafts were less saccharine, more descriptive, and more analytical. In a subsequent assignment asking students to write about growth and change, more than half the class chose to write again about relatives. This time, the papers made obvious what I had initially missed. In writing both assignments, these students were analyzing why they had not lived in "traditional" home situations and what influences had resulted, except in this case, "traditional" was being defined by culture and class. Some papers were tragic, describing death, divorce, illness, or abuse. Others described warm, supportive homes provided by extended family members while a single parent or both parents worked full-time or more. Not only did their writing improve, the students also became more collaborative, experimental, and authoritative. One returning student helped a dyslexic student type. The dyslexic student wrote to his children's school board, urging collaborative education to help students with learning problems. Students wrote to the computer lab, protesting lax help from one tutor. And the woman who wrote about having been raped as a child, having previously told only her husband, included her paper in the class anthology.

My class—which had originally worried me—was constructing meaning without me. I was so impressed with their papers that I started the practice of compiling student essays into a class anthology that I use for two different purposes. The anthology becomes a text for students who write it, but it also becomes a text for students in my class the following term. Using students' work as a text in the subsequent course benefits both writers and new readers. Writers, knowing their work will have a "real" audience in the next term's classes, collaborate, revise, and edit with fervor. And each group of new students, reading the work of previous students who share their backgrounds, can see a range of subjects, styles, and proficiencies.

My experience with that class led me to conclude that I need to learn more about diversity and invention from students' papers and discussions. To do this, I try to create a classroom in which students can identify significant events in their lives without feeling like outsiders, and can write about emotionally important issues in order to facilitate cognitive growth.

The first approach I use to create a collaborative classroom is practicing judicious self-disclosure to validate diversity and challenge students' perception that "real" college students and professionals live perfect lives. Evelyn Torton Beck (1983) has an excellent essay discussing this practice. Her students feel that self-disclosure "humanizes the teacher and makes her more accessible" (289). However, Beck stresses that self-disclosure must not deprive students of their own process (290). For me, self-disclosure begins when students free-write during their first class, and I write, "I spilled my coffee and yelled at my kids today." I sometimes do drafts of assignments with students, describing good memories of growing up in a working-class neighborhood. I am blunt about the difficulty I had returning to school with a sick child. As a result of this last practice, more parents discuss child care problems, and it has become rare for a parent to drop the class.

I also empower a collaborative classroom by using readings that deal with diversity. In these readings, emotions are clearly significant, cognitively important, and sometimes affirming. For example, I have used Alice Walker's (1983) essay "In Search of Our Mother's Gardens" to connect personal writing with literature. I have also used Jim Daniels' poem, "Digger's Birthday," which lists a factory worker's diminishing expectations, but includes his drive home to "the off-key voices/the new shirt, socks, shovel. The love."[2] Students who read about diverse family situations frequently write about nontraditional or extended families. This struggle to come to terms with childhood circumstances may be characteristic of working-class writers. Mary Jo Maynes' (1989) essay "Gender and Narrative Form in French and German Working-Class Autobiographies" notes that a "huge percentage" of working-class autobiographers spent a substantial proportion of their childhood with grandparents or other relatives or in foster homes. She concludes that "the impulse to write autobiography under these circumstances can perhaps be viewed as a product of the distance between the dominant norm and the lived reality" (114).

The distance between the dominant norm and students' lives takes on new significance when students collaborate to construct a critical marginal perspective of that norm. "Dominant," after all, does not always denote circumstances pertaining to the majority. Women's studies has proven that one can be in the majority and not construct dominant norms.

Papers involving early childhood, far from being too emotional or simplistic, can provide students with the kind of collaborative situation that nurtures cognitive growth. For example, when one of my students wrote a paper referring to sleeping, as a child, on "sheet bundle beds," I assumed her choice of words was what Bartholomae (1985) calls "idiosyncratic," and made no comment. But two other students remembered sleeping on mattresses made of a bundle of clothes folded inside sheets or blankets. This discovery led to memories shared by other students: picking cotton, wringing chicken necks, going hungry. At the end of the hour, the writer said, "I thought I was the only one who had memories like this. Now I see it's not just me. There are lots of people in college who remember the things I do."

In complex and interwoven ways, this student's process of inventing had just changed. And what changed was her internal construct of audience, her ability to produce an imagined listening other, her sense of shared language, and her expectation of a resonating audience. I believe she would not have managed to include, or have been comfortable including, sheet bundle beds as "background" in a paper analyzing her adolescent life. Nor would her process of inventing have changed had my comments been her only response. This is not to argue against providing students with the opportunity to read, critique, and write essays that represent the academic community. Students in my classes write both informal and analytical responses to readings selected to help them see expository writing as a process that draws on personal experience. However, I strongly believe that students' writing abilities and analytical abilities can best be demonstrated when writing assignments involve a familiar field of reference. Lack of familiarity with a topic inevitably limits insights.

The effect of familiarity with a field of reference is illustrated by Bartholomae's (1985) critique of sample placement essays. Bartholomae suggests that the more "advanced" essays are those that are set against the "naive" codes of everyday life. "In the advanced essays," he writes, "one can see a writer claiming an 'inside' position of privilege by rejecting the language and commonplaces of a 'naive' discourse." Although he notes the arbitrary nature of the terms *inside* and *naive,* the concept of "informed" discourse versus the "language and commonplaces of a 'naive' discourse" is clearly linked to the rejection of homilies cited earlier.

Yet in the essays used to illustrate the desired difference, each writer seems to be *drawing upon* experience, rather than "writing himself into" a position of privilege. One of the assigned topics is this: "Describe a time when you did something you felt to be creative. Then ... go on to draw some general conclusions about 'creativity'" (Bartholomae 1985, 148). Three student essays about jazz reflect varying amounts of experience (and possibly, class privilege). In the first, the student lists only having been a member of a school jazz ensemble. In the second, the student describes having been a member of a school jazz ensemble and having "through the years ... seen and heard many jazz players, both professional [sic] and amateur." In the third, the student writes, "My mother has often told me of the times, before I went to school, when I would 'conduct' the orchestra on her records" (151–53). Not surprisingly, the essays are ranked in ascending order. Each writer's ability to "write against commonplaces" reflects related life experience. What Noddings and Shore (1994) call "familiar domains" (64) help provide "initial anticipation or intuition" for productive thought (Noddings and Shore, 150). Student ability to "write against commonplaces" can be seen to be socially influenced. When the topic is one with which students are familiar and discussion is possible, they are more likely to write, and be aware that they are writing, against the grain of common assumptions, in the process claiming a "consciously marginal and critical stance."

My students, responding to an interview with a female autoworker in Richard Feldman and Michael Betzold's *End of the Line,* (1988) often work against the "naive" codes of privileged society. The autoworker says:

> One time my son had really bad nosebleeds, and I had to take him to the hospital; but I didn't have insurance, and I wasn't approved for ADC, so they wouldn't treat him. I almost lost my mind, and I vowed I would get a job that would pay medical insurance . . . I made my ninety days by the skin of my teeth. They had me welding on the Bronco Line all day long. It was tough. I got little marks all over my body from the sparks. But I told myself I wasn't going to let the job depress me because I had too many mouths to feed. (66)

Readings that address such dilemmas help students recognize social issues and process them cognitively. Students write about myths about assistance, definitions of "a good worker," declining job expectations, and the changing roles of women. Many women discuss the strains that result from being caretakers without adequate options. They are trying to improve their lives by attending college, but taking classes while being short on time and money exacerbates tensions in their lives. In this assignment, about half of the students write against the grain of societal oversimplification. After discussion, most students who initially take simplistic positions use personal experience for support rather than write homilies. However, simply providing readings is insufficient. Students need a classroom atmosphere that invites experimentation if they are to speak and write against silences.

My students recently demonstrated the power of shared marginalized perspectives in collaborative situations. A white student whose family had moved frequently had had only erratic schooling, but had taught herself to read after she left school. She wrote about an instructor whose sarcasm had driven her out of college. White students sat blank-faced and silent, waiting for my comment. Students of color ignored me and spoke directly to the writer, one saying vehemently, "She had no right to make fun of you because of something you didn't know!" The writer polished her description into a surrealistic denunciation:

> Then I made a fatal mistake. I asked her how to use semi-colons. This triggered a violent metamorphosis in my English professor; her body began to split until the rip reached the base of her neck and stretched up, until the back of her neck was against the fifteen foot classroom ceiling. With mouth open, I looked on in disbelief as her dangling cobra face glared down at me hissing, "Is this my only il . . . lit . . . ter . . . ate?"

"Cobra classes" became a metaphor for destructive learning situations, and the reassuring students took on new authority in the class. On the last day, a student commented, "This is a warm class. Other classes are cold. Separate. But we really got to know each other."

I think that kind of unquantifiable gain is typical of collaborative class-rooms structured to help students consciously experience the social nature of invention. Although I am the only reader of some journal assignments, student-selected journal assignments are shared in groups, as are personal essays, structured response writing, and expository essays. Students some-times respond to one another's work in "circulating journals," a concept introduced to me by Kathleen Geissler. Papers are often shared with the class as a whole, and students are encouraged to respond to the content of each other's portfolios. Electronically networked classrooms facilitate collabora-tion at various stages of the writing process.

If students are to experience the social nature of invention in collabora-tive classrooms, we must structure our classes in order to allow students to teach us and each other, as well as to learn. That means we need to pay close attention to the stories our students tell us, and we need to create situations in which they can hear and value each other's stories. We need to attend to class-related rhetorical strategies, including the role of affect in invention, authorial stance, paratactic discourse, understatement, and writing to consti-tute community.

In "The Ecology of Writing," Marilyn Cooper (1986) writes that textual forms "are at the same time conservative repositories of tradition, and revo-lutionary instruments of new forms of action" (370). As members of the aca-demic community, we want to introduce our students to textual forms that serve as rich repositories of tradition. But we serve neither students' nor our own intellectual growth if we refuse to examine their textual forms, which are also repositories of tradition, and which can also, equally, be revolution-ary instruments.

Notes

1. For detailed descriptions of the Pittsburgh program, see "Teaching and Writ-ing" in Bartholomae and Petrosky (1986) and Bartholomae (1979).

2. For readings in a range of genres, see Coles (1986); Paul Lauter (1982); and Janet Zandy (1995).

14

Women Students' Autobiographical Writing
The Rhetoric of Discovery and Defiance

Joy Ritchie, Manjit Kaur, and Bee Tin Choo Meyer

I learned to make my mind large, as the universe is large, so that
there is room for paradoxes.

Maxine Hong Kingston,
The Woman Warrior

Joy: As a teacher I have had ample evidence that students' autobiographical
writing has an important impact on the way they view themselves as writers
and on the way they come to understand their own lives. Like many writing
teachers, I find that my misgivings about students' autobiographical narratives arise from a number of sources. Autobiographical writing is often
regarded as a mere stepping stone to more sophisticated writing, more about
feelings and experiences than about ideas. It is often considered solipsistic,
egocentric, and, in the current climate, even dangerous, because it may
confirm students' belief in a unified, autonomous selfhood, and thus reen-
force their positions as subjects of prevailing ideology.

The writing of two women, Manjit Kaur and Bee Tin Choo Meyer,
students in an advanced composition class, led me to reconsider such assumptions in our discipline and to question my own views concerning students'
autobiographical writing. Manjit's and Bee Tin's writing highlighted for me
the complexity of autobiographical writing and the difficulty teachers face in
responding to it. Their writing and my response to it have helped me to see that

our traditional understanding of autobiography does not capture the complexity of the conceptual and personal processes involved in the act of writing about one's life, nor does it fully account for the possibilities autobiographical writing holds for students.

My efforts to understand Manjit's and Bee Tin's autobiographical writing led me outside composition theory to recent feminist criticism concerning women's literary autobiography and to postcolonial theory. Here I found perspectives that speak to composition theory and illuminate students' writing, because they challenge me to consider students' personal narratives as a form of noncanonical autobiography and to consider it from the same critical perspective one might use to read women's writing. They also challenge me to consider my cultural perspective as I respond to students' autobiographical writing.

Women's literary autobiography, like students' autobiography, has often been relegated to an inferior status. Seen against the standards of traditional male autobiography, it is often judged to be flawed because of its "nonstandard" form, because it lacks thematic and formal unity, and because it fails to represent a "universal" perspective. Feminist critics have begun to reexamine women's autobiography in light of current theoretical reconsiderations of "the self," the political and gendered nature of language, and the possibilities and problems of representing history and experience. Their rereading of women's writing demonstrates the complexity of writing about one's life, the multidimensional nature of the writing "selves" that may emerge in women's writing, and, most important, the potential subversiveness of autobiographical writing to expose and critique oppressive structures. These perspectives helped me reconsider how Manjit's and Bee Tin's writing might function, like women's literary autobiography, as an opportunity to claim their own voices and to articulate conflicting and fluid identities for themselves in defiance of the limited categories in which their identities as women are often framed.

Like other women, Manjit and Bee Tin also wrestled with the problem of language. How do women find a language and a form in which to represent their experience within the "man-made" tradition of language in an academy? They faced an additional problem of writing in settings that construct them as "nonnative" speakers. They struggled with the sense of fragmentation and contradiction they experienced in their lives, and they explored their culturally assigned categories as students, as women, as Asian women, and as Asian women in this culture that places them in conflicting positions of "native" or "other." Bee Tin and Manjit were caught in a crossfire between Singaporean Chinese or Indian Malaysian and American female identities. Both women identified *with* the world of their mothers and fathers and *against* the identities those cultures prescribe, *with* aspects of American culture and *against* the subjectivity in which American culture constructed them. Facing these conflicts, they attempted to rearticulate their positions as members of the families and communities that give meaning to their lives and to show the historical and political relationships in which their lives have been entwined.

As I talked with Manjit and Bee Tin about their writing, I began to see the extent to which my own cultural assumptions about writing had shaped my responses to their work and how my own conflicting position as a woman in my culture and as a woman in the academy implicated me in the issues about which they were writing. Although I felt they both were exploring territory in their lives that made their writing valuable and important, I worried about my responsibility to help them succeed in the university. I also worried about form, style, and rhetorical considerations and whether this writing would help them find the academic success they hoped to achieve. Finally, I had to reconsider the politics of my stance as a white, Western, university professor. I realized that my attempts to analyze and represent these two women's writing, even from a feminist viewpoint, amounted to an appropriation and recolonization of their lives and experiences. In "French Feminism in an International Frame" Gayatri Spivak (1988) challenges the colonialism of academic feminists who attempt to speak and write about "Third World" women. She argues that academic feminists, instead of speaking *of* them as objects, as "other," as "they," must learn, instead, to listen *to* and learn from them. She further challenges us not to err by reading their lives and texts patronizingly, believing we can "correct" their lives with our "superior theory and enlightened compassion" (135).

As I considered writing *about* Manjit and Bee Tin, I realized that it was more appropriate that they join me in writing this chapter in order to add their voices and perspectives, and in order to let others listen to them and learn from them. As we wrote this chapter, we struggled with the cultural and hierarchical power relationships that make collaboration difficult. At times we each have asked, Whose essay is this? Whose voice is dominant? Is this my voice or a voice Joy or some more distant authority is imposing? What will Manjit, Joy, or Bee Tin think if I say this? Consequently, this has become a chapter about three women learning to negotiate the complexity of the act of writing, of responding to writing, and of writing together in cross-cultural collaboration. This chapter represents only a step in that direction. We are each left feeling compromised in some way with how we represent ourselves or are represented in this text.

My Silence: A Virtue or Taboo?

Bee Tin: I was told that girls should always be quiet and gentle. An obedient child should never talk loudly nor ask too many questions, especially when guests are around lest she be condemned as badly mannered. I should only question at the right time, but when was the right time when half the time was wrong? I didn't ask. I kept my silence. The role I played was a passive one for I retreated from violating any stipulations passed down from generation to generation. Challenging authorities and adults was a taboo. I was confirmed to be a quiet child. My parents had laid down very strict rules.

As a child I quietly obeyed. Other times I was vicious when I rebelled and needed to be disciplined by the cane. This cane often left behind bloody scars and inner injuries that didn't seem to heal. I learned. I seldom went against my parents, and experience further confirmed that my obedience without rebellion was right.

These virtues proved to be different in the American society. Here, people are inculcated with different creative channels of expression. They are encouraged to question, to ask, and to speak up. Be vocal. Be aggressive. No one can infringe or take control of an individual's freedom and choice. People are expressive and demonstrative about what they want and what they think. My silence continued to handicap me in this society. At my first psychology class, I was being introduced. The professor kindly said, "Bee Tin, your culture and your viewpoints are greatly treasured in this class. Feel free to talk and make any comments." For the rest of the semester, I kept quiet. As an adult, I still didn't know when was the right time to talk.

In the highly prized vocal world in America, my silence is a sign of dull wit, insecurity, and insufficient confidence. Silence is a sin the society despises. The demeaning side-glances when one is silent seem to be saying: "It's degrading just to look at you!" These looks, the hostile stares, and the thoughts that followed invade my silence. I question: Do I need to be aggressive to demand what I want? Should I be aggressive just because I am living in an aggressive society? Should I be aggressive because others deem that as superior? But, should I always be passively listening and not respond to anything others say even when it hurts? By keeping silent, will it help at all?

I began writing my "silence" paper because of the lack of awareness of other non-American cultures among the people I encountered in this country. I wanted, I craved, more understanding. I yearned for nonstereotypic ways of looking at us—"the orientals." Despite the fear of exposing the undesired truth, I went ahead writing. I took the risk and pursued the subject with seriousness.

Joy: On the first day of my composition class I asked students to write and then read or tell us a bit about what they had written. When we came to Bee Tin, she read what she had written. I watched her lips move and heard her voice, but it was barely audible, even as everyone became totally still. That was my introduction to Bee Tin. At first I tried to urge her to speak louder, but finally I gave up because it seemed offensive, and the entire class carried on as though they *could* hear her. Although my response and the responses of other students to her writing were positive, we did treat Bee Tin as something of the oddity she describes. We tiptoed around her as we might have if she had had some sort of physical disability or speech problem.

The first exploratory draft Bee Tin wrote was a tidy, impersonal, academic-sounding piece on "battling with cross-cultural issues." She wrote about a Czech student and an African student, and only obliquely about herself. Although she wrote well, my comments on her draft noted that the paper was impersonal and researchlike and that it lacked "voice." I asked, "What is *your* experience?" She was troubled by my comments, uncertain about what I expected. However, her next draft, "My Silence: A Virtue or Taboo?" was a much different paper. It brought together two of the central issues in women's writing—the problem of language and silence and the problem of trying to define one's selfhood amid the conflicting images of self with which women are presented.

At first, I read Bee Tin's paper from my white feminist perspective, thinking of Adrienne Rich and Tillie Olsen. I thought, "Here is a young woman attempting to throw off the oppressive position in which her culture places her in order to find her voice." I encouraged her to write more about her cross-cultural experience, thinking it would help her continue to struggle against limiting definitions of herself. In this respect I indulged in the error Spivak (1988) points out and thus diminished the complexity of her experience. I romanticized her resistance without seeing the conflicts inherent in it. Bee Tin's writing did not merely celebrate joyfully a newly awakened selfhood. Instead, she explored the tensions and contradictions in that selfhood. "Finding a voice" from her perspective was not a universal good. It left her conflicted, caught again in a marginal space between two cultures.

Women's autobiographical writing often emerges from the initial impulse to articulate a selfhood. Bee Tin's writing claimed a voice and a sense of self, but it also asked, Where is the place from which a woman can speak when she must negotiate her gender identities *and* her ethnic or cultural identities at the same time? Bee Tin's writing embodies the conflicts—silent/vocal, aggressive/passive—in which she found herself inscribed. Her essay about silence was, paradoxically, a very vocal act. With it, she thrust her silence and its implications in front of her readers. Instead of allowing me, other students, or herself to maintain unexamined assumptions about the nature of silence or to rest in our stereotypes of Asian students as passive and respectful of authority, her silence, coupled with her willingness to speak about it, challenged our assumptions and our prejudices. "Silence as a refusal to participate in the story does sometimes provide us with a means to gain a hearing. It is voice, a mode of uttering, and a response in its own right," says Trinh Minh-ha in *Woman, Native, Other* (1989, 83). Bee Tin's silence defied the vocal world of the writing class and of American culture. She continued during the semester to concern herself with issues of voice and silence and also to examine how she might represent herself and her life in some authentic manner in the face of categories that define her as "native" and "other."

Bee Tin: My writing was like the construction of a traditional Chinese emperor's palace. The palace was hidden and surrounded by gate after gate, door after door. Each gate leads to another, and yet another. My writing was very much that way. Writing did not stop after each piece was done. With Joy's constant "Tell me more" and "That's very interesting," each piece of my writing led on to another and yet another. Each piece of writing was not a simple entity but an ongoing yet difficult struggle toward the very core of the issues I faced.

I questioned myself each time I read through my writing. I heard myself saying, "Is this really what I want to say? Am I really reliving, rewriting my experiences correctly and truthfully? Will readers understand the content of my writing? Will they be able to interpret my cultural values and existence? Does what I say really mean something to them? Have I written enough? Have I given the reader sufficient contextual information for them to interpret my experiences in the light of my culture?" Hence, in each paper I attempted to pave the reader's road to understanding me and my culture.

Joy: Bee Tin's questions are the questions of many women writers: How does a woman represent her experience in language? Before she had completed a draft of the "silence" essay, she was beginning another that would add further to the picture she was constructing of her culture. Her portfolio was full of multiple drafts and extensions of each essay. It was indeed like the structure of the emperor's palace, one draft paving the way to the next, each saturated with details in order to allow readers to see more clearly and to complicate simplistic images readers might construct of her life in Singapore.

The impersonal, unified writing of her first draft disappeared. She created a series of interlocking, continuous essays that continually refined and revised her depiction of her life. Although Bee Tin suggests that my comments were a constant invitation to write more and to explain herself and her cultural perspective more clearly, when I look back on my comments to her, I realize that my assumptions about form were as traditional as the standards by which critics have often judged women's autobiographical writing. My comments urged Bee Tin to reorganize her essays and to make her position less oblique, more clear and direct. My continued questions—"Who is your audience?" "Where might something like this be published?"—suggested that her writing needed to be tailored to fit a rather narrow range of public or academic forms.

As I continued to read Bee Tin's writing, I began to learn to suspend some of my assumptions about form and completeness. No single essay was a complete entity. There were no grand vistas or encompassing perspectives in Bee Tin's writing. Just as in Chinese palace architecture each gate leads to yet another view, but never a complete one, each essay Bee Tin wrote led to an extension or a revision of some belief, category, or assumption that Westerners hold about Chinese culture. I read Bee Tin's writing as a traveler following the road to find what might lie through the next gate or behind the next wall. From Bee Tin I asked for clarification and for her reflections on where the process was leading her. In turn I attempted to show her where her writing was leading me.

Bee Tin: With Joy's constant "That's powerful" or "That's good, write that down," I continued writing. Feeling anger and perceiving injustice, I wrote the following:

> I was puzzled and confused during my recent trip home. I felt lost. I felt disoriented. The world I grew up in no longer fits me. Is it because I am a woman who is breaking the secret norms? The world that rigorously exacts unbending roles of women attempted to strangle and bridle me into submission. The world is changing; I am also changing. I would be lying if I said I have not been changed by this two years spent in the United States. Friends at home jokingly remarked but with a serious undertone: "You're Westernized. I'm now talking to an American." I hate to hear such an accusation. I don't hate Americans, but I want my identity as a Singaporean Chinese back. I have not lost the grip of my culture. In fact, I might be holding on to my ethnicity more tightly than before. I have changed because I'm no longer bullied into believing that these demure feminine traits must exist in me.

> While I was visiting home I forgot the rules that govern this society. I was asked to help with a graduation party. My friend's sister, Pearl, and I did the dishes. Mind you, only the girls did the washing and cleaning up, with only two other sensitive guys helping us to clear up the mess. I joined the rest of the men later after the dishes were done. My new acquaintances were curious about my overseas life. Talking to them was normal, but it was socially incorrect because they were a group of guys. The older adults, who were playing mahjong in the other room, pierced me with penetrating, disapproving stares. I left the scene with a sense of relief when my friend wanted me to go to the store with him. However, I regretted going with him because when I returned, the disapproving stares became fiercer. I had been wrong to go off with a man at his invitation. It was as if I was imprisoned within all these expectations. Because I wanted to be liberated from all these, I grabbed my first chance to leave. I ran up the stairwell, got my bag, and left. Another big mistake: I left without thanking them and bidding them farewell. Their impression of my wild, unmannerly, and unrestrained "Westernized" behavior was going to remain. But the problem of gender stereotyping is global, not isolated.

Joy: Bee Tin's writing depicts the fragmentation and contradiction in women's experience. Critics of autobiography often suggest that the act of writing is a way of seaming together this sense of discontinuity and fragmentation. However, Susan Stanford Friedman (1988) and Shari Benstock (1988) argue that women's autobiography does something quite the opposite. Because it arises from a much different psychological and aesthetic experience, women's autobiography, like Bee Tin's, often reveals that the image of self a society holds out to women is not a unified whole, but is a fiction, a false construct of the social order that does not take into account the gaps and fissures of the individual's being (Benstock 1988 14, 15, 38).

Bee Tin's writing reveals the conflict among the various images of herself that she is confronting: the image that is mirrored in the glances and judgments of the Westerners around her and in the traditional image of female in which her culture places her, an image that she is questioning; it reveals the image of a Westernized Chinese woman that her family or friends judge her to have taken on; and it reveals the way she also experiences herself. Trinh Minh-ha (1989) says: "*I* is . . . not a unified subject, a fixed identity, or that solid mass covered with layers of superficialities one has gradually to peel off before one can see its true face. *I* is, itself, infinite layers (94).

Bee Tin: I often reflected upon the essence of my writing. Had I successfully communicated to my readers without losing the authentic accent when saying what I wanted to say? Writing, to me, was a difficult condensation of information because of the cultural context I was in. In order not to be misunderstood, I tried to be explicit, but in the course of doing that, had I lost the very accent I wanted to maintain? If I lose the subtleties of my accent, do I lose the essence of my writing?

I've grown as a person and as a writer. Now, I'm tempted to erase the emotionally charged words from my papers. That was how I felt and now, being more mature, should I substitute those for more mature terms? Or am I stealing away the authentic nature of my struggle? Writing in Joy's class encouraged me to constantly, intensely reflect and feel. I think about writing when I'm walking. I think about writing when I'm eating. As I go through door after door, gate after gate, I get a clearer and clearer view of the issues. I wake up trying to make meaning of my struggles. Writing was to me a process of awakening, a process of growth and realization.

It's Not the Way You Think It Is

What gives him the right to do that? Why is it that men do not have to defend themselves? It's time society changed its attitudes and forced men to be responsible.

Who do those people think they are to pass judgment? I want them to understand that some people live lives that might make suicide a reasonable alternative. They need to understand what goes on in the mind of a person thinking about suicide.

Manjit: These are lines from two of the papers I wrote at the beginning of Joy's class. When I first started writing for Joy's class, my life was in a turmoil. There was so much anger then; the resentment flowed. The more I wrote, the more I healed. The anger poured out in my papers and it meant so much to me that someone would be reading it. Just the knowledge of that was sufficient to keep me writing. I felt like I had to tell someone. Joy seemed open to listen to what I had to say.

I was brought up in a very rigid, strict, religious, and male-dominated family that followed every rule, regulation, and restriction in the traditional Sikh culture in Kuala Lumpur. My life since birth was very structured. Until I went to school, I was at home with my mother, picking up little details about being a woman that might be useful to me in the future. Once I graduated from high school, my parents would release themselves of this "burden" and pass me over to my husband who, in turn, would take care of me while I played the dutiful role of a housewife and mother until I died.

Before I came to the United States, I was restless and eager to leave the hellhole I was brought up in. I became claustrophobic in my own home; the walls were closing in on me and if I didn't get out soon, I felt, I was going to be buried alive. I told my best friend that when and if I did get out, I wasn't ever going to come back. In fact, I wasn't even going to miss anybody, especially my mother.

Joy: If Bee Tin's writing whispered respectfully, Manjit's shouted its anger at her parents, her culture, at Westerners and their culture. Instead of the tidy, impersonal writing I often receive from students at the beginning of the semester, Manjit's writing was immediately vocal, angry, personal, and emotionally charged. It was full of outrage and shocking in its honesty. My response to Manjit's writing raised several difficulties. I valued her writing because it coincided with my understanding of the purposes that university writing classes can achieve—to help decenter students and help them begin to critique their own racial/ethnic, gendered, and social class positions as they encounter perspectives different from their own. She did not allow her readers to be smug or satisfied with North American attitudes toward and treatment of women and minorities.

I also wanted to encourage Manjit's writing because she wrote with conviction about subjects that concerned her, subjects that also concerned me. She seemed already to have a feminist's awareness of the politics of gender (although I don't think she would have called herself a feminist at the time). I hoped that through writing Manjit could make visible to herself and others the inequities of her life. The autobiographical writing of minority and "third-world" women like Manjit has gained considerable attention as part of the struggle of oppressed and silenced people. But, as Spivak (1988) reminds us, Westerners like me have often looked at this writing with their own political and philosophical agendas, either romanticizing the political resistance that seems evident in the writing or reading patronizingly and avoiding the real, material problems both in the texts and in the lives those writers lead.

On the other hand, I believed my relationship to Manjit was that of teacher, not therapist. I could not provide solutions to the problems she faced. I realized that Manjit's anger came from the complexities of her own unique experience, which I could not hope to understand. But I also recognized that writing might help Manjit address her own problems. When she wrote about the sexual harassment she experienced at her job, I saw writing as an important first step to reporting it. My encouragement to "keep writing" came from my belief that by articulating her experience she might begin to untangle the complexities of that experience for herself. I now have a much better sense of how complicated that process is. As Manjit wrote, everything did not automatically become all right. She kept uncovering more questions and conflicts in her life. It was a continuous process of articulating that which was emerging, shifting, and fluid.

Manjit: My first paper was about people whom I called "god-players." I wrote about the racism I was experiencing in my job as a janitor in one of the university's residence halls. Although I came from the upper middle class of my culture, I had to earn money to pay tuition. But I was angry at the treatment I received from other women students who only saw me as a woman cleaning up their restrooms and hallways. In writing this paper I exposed an underside of the image of the well-groomed American college woman by exposing their selfishness, childishness, and filthiness as well as their arrogance and racism.

My next paper was sparked by the response of women students in a women's literature class to a film about a girl who was sexually assaulted. Many of the women in the class blamed the girl for being stupid and for not seeing and resisting the situation she was getting into. "Run . . . come on run, you silly girl," yelled Marcie at a character in a film we were watching for our Women's Literature class. Marcie yelled, "Look at that. She's actually going with that jerk. How dumb can a girl be?"

I sat there motionless, not saying a word. My eyes were glued to the television, but my mind was far away. I remembered that at one time I, too, did exactly the same thing Connie did. Does that make me dumb? Does that make me stupid? I wondered if women will always have to fight to protect themselves. Will society continue to blame the victim? I felt shocked in that women's literature class. In my culture, women are often blamed, but I expected something different here. It was shocking to hear these American women say what a male in Asian society would say: "She asked for it." I thought something was wrong. Maybe I was more sensitive because I was there once. But I felt like saying to those students, "Wake up! I want you to learn something." I didn't say it in that class, but I could say it in my writing.

I also wrote to protest the attitudes toward suicide I see in this culture. The essay described a person who is thinking about committing suicide. The narrator's voice describes how the person assembles the pills, contemplates whether or not there are enough of them, mixes the orange juice and vodka. Juxtaposed with those concrete details are quotes from MTV and Lisa

Stansfield. The conflicting inner voices push the narrator forward toward suicide and hold her back. In a final segment of the paper, I recall the story of Vinny, my high school friend:

> As it is typical in our culture for parents to dominate their children, it was not a shock to see my friends being pressured into doing things against their wishes. As soon as we graduated from high school, our futures were very much laid out for us. Those who had the opportunity to proceed with college were allowed to do so as I was, temporarily postponing the fate that awaited them, but those who didn't go to college had to succumb to the plans of their parents. Most of my friends weren't as lucky as I was and were thrown into marriages without their consent. Their life-time mates were selected and approved for them by their parents and relatives. Before they could wink their eyes, they were "sold" to the chosen one and his immediate family.
>
> Vinny was no exception; she could not elude the fate awaiting her, no matter how hard she tried. Naturally she was unhappy. Who wouldn't be, when the person you are expected to spend the rest of your life with is as well-known to you as the stranger who lives three blocks down the road? Even though she was married into his family, she was never accepted as one of them. This treatment added to her misery.
>
> In a frustrated moment, she gulped down as much kerosene as she could before her mother stopped her. Vinny wanted to escape so badly that it was worth giving up her life, but nobody was willing to set her free. Vinny thought attempting suicide was the best solution to solving all her problems. But there were no sympathetic, loving, understanding faces awaiting her when she got out of the hospital. What was awaiting her was a divorce suit and very angry faces. Her husband had filed for a divorce for he thought she was an ungrateful wife. Her in-laws were furious and encouraged the divorce. They felt that she had tarnished their name. When a girl tries to commit suicide, society naturally assumes that she is abused by the family she lives with. She turned to her natural family, only to be shunned by them, too.

Joy: Each of Manjit's papers challenged some set of American values or attitudes, and they did so from the vantage point of her experience in Malaysian culture, without privileging that culture. She took up one injustice, one conflict after another, and experimented with and attempted to invent forms that communicated the variety of cultural perspectives from which she was attempting to understand issues such as racism, sexual abuse, and suicide.

Her papers on suicide and abuse seemed to echo Gayatri Spivak's (1988) admonition to white Western feminists. Manjit seemed to say to us, "Just because you hold certain attitudes concerning suicide or sexual abuse, don't think those values are universally applicable to all women." Her writing challenged the homogenizing representations of women's experience generated by her culture and by mine: It said, "No you're wrong. That's not the way it is; you may think you know who I am, but you don't." I connected this to Julia Kristeva's (1980) notion that women must continue a "negative practice" to undermine the categories in which women have been placed, so that they may say, "that's not it" and "that's still not it" to such categories (139). At the same time, however, Manjit was writing a critique of this culture. She allowed me and her fellow students to see how sexism and racism functioned in our culture. Seen through the eyes of a woman experiencing the "triple bind" of being a woman, a native, and an "other," it was even more compelling.

Like many women's literary autobiographies, Manjit's writing allowed her to define and examine her own experience, but it also had a hortatory, even polemical tone intended to challenge and change the attitudes of people about her. Her writing was clearly intended for an audience beyond the teacher. But I was also reading her writing as a teacher, and I worried about rhetorical problems in her writing. Her style was melodramatic, passionate, and sometimes accusatory, and she and I both worried that readers would be alienated rather than enlightened. And, indeed, some of them were unprepared for Manjit's indictments of U.S. culture.

It was tempting to place her writing in a special category as "foreign-student" writing. I wasn't sure what to expect of her or whether I ought to be pleased that she was writing as well as she was for a "nonnative" speaker of English, a patronizing response that she has taught me to avoid. To some degree, my responses and those of other students were motivated by our sense that she was an exotic person from a world we could only imagine. She was the "other," that which we are not.

By traditional standards, her writing was fragmented and unfocused. Manjit often began with a vignette or scene in which she used dialogue to set the stage for what she wanted to say. Then she might shift to another scene or episode. The paper about suicide resembled a montage, cutting from the narrator's living room, to MTV, to Malaysia. Often the narrative was circular, returning at the end to the point where it had begun. Two or three of her papers employed sudden shifts in voice like those found in the paper concerning suicide. Manjit's writing raised what Deborah Cameron (1990) suggests is another central issue in women's writing—the question of rationality and irrationality (11). She raised the subject tangibly as she wrote about depression, suicide, and anger, and she raised it in the "irrational" forms she invented for her writing.

An excerpt from one of my responses to a revised draft shows my ambiguity toward her writing. I encouraged Manjit to clarify the sequence of events, to make them more linear and unified. I said further: "Sometimes you slip into very melodramatic or exaggerated language. It sounds more like the language of romance novels or soap operas. For me as a reader, that's distracting."

Manjit: I used Joy's class to get out my frustrations. I must have burdened Joy with my writing. Looking back at my papers, I can feel that anger, hear the hatred. But I now hate these papers. They sound so dismal and pathetic. I complain about everything from society to my family. All I do is condemn somebody or something. The voice is definitely there; one can almost picture the writer and hear her. My writing makes dramatic changes on the readers. They are what I call eye-openers; they make the reader think. I like the effect that has, the thought and feelings they provoke, but after a couple of them, readers must get tired.

Joy: Manjit says that she burdened me when she wrote so angrily and passionately. She says that she worried that I might have felt I had to encourage her in order not to make her more upset or depressed. Her writing did demand my empathy and support. But it also evoked more than that. In one of our conversations Manjit described my response to her writing as a "hunger for information." My comments continually asked her for more "context," more details, to allow me to better understand her culture and the circumstances that provoked her writing. As a reader, I became more of an anthropologist or ethnographer than a writing teacher, recognizing all the potential to become colonizer in assuming that stance, also.

I also began to think of other models that might help me understand Manjit's writing. I thought about similar shifts in perspective I had to make when I read Leslie Marmon Silko's *Ceremony* or Maxine Hong Kingston. In *The Woman Warrior* (1977), Kingston yells at her story-telling mother, "I don't want to listen to any more of your stories; they have no logic. They scramble me up" (235). I thought of the changing perspectives and voices in Toni Morrison's writing, in which the narrator's voice often mutates and shifts, and in which Morrison refuses the reader a unified, linear, or even rational place from which to read. I began to see that Manjit's writing was not fragmented or disjointed, but multivoiced, straining against a Western unified perspective and the resulting identities imposed on women.

Trinh Minh-ha (1989) points out that only Western rhetoric reduces writing to "clear expression, often equated with correct expression" (16). The language of Taoism and Zen, for example, is full of circularity and paradox that seem nonsensical to Westerners. Writing, she says, must not be reduced to a clear unambiguous message. Trinh Minh-ha argues that when they write, women express their thoughts and passions, but they also act to "radically question the world through the questioning of how-to-write" (16, 17). Manjit's writing certainly questioned the world.

Manjit: My mother tried to give me the best of two worlds. She wanted me to be like other girls, yet she wanted me to be above them with an education. So I was sent to a missionary school. Very soon English became my first language and what little I had learned of my mother tongue, Punjabi, slowly deteriorated. I wonder why my mother chose to have me learn

English first, instead of Punjabi. My grandmother insisted that I be taught Punjabi. My cousins were learning Punjabi, so why should I be made the odd one out? I question myself: "Why can't I speak Punjabi as fluently as I can English?" I cannot say that I was never taught Punjabi. My mother tried, but instead she learned to speak English from me. Unfortunately, no one taught her how to write or read in English. Now that I am far away from my mother, I am frustrated at not being able to communicate with her. I know English and she doesn't. She knows Punjabi and I don't. I can't write to my mother in Punjabi, and she can't write in English. I am angry at her for doing this to me. Didn't she see what the consequences would be? Didn't she ever think what it would be like for me, not being able to communicate with my own mother? I keep trying to point my finger at somebody, but there really isn't anybody to blame. I don't think my mother ever anticipated my leaving her. Who would think of sending their child, especially a daughter, miles away from home to pursue an education? Sometimes I felt she disliked the fact that she had to send me away. She wanted me to be educated, literate, but part of her resented sending me away, for school was the place that would modernize me, drag me away from her values, tear me from my traditional culture. But those changes didn't happen in the way she might have imagined.

My writing and the women's literature classes I have taken have played a major role in influencing me. They have helped me define my views and promote the change in me. I know I've changed since I came here, but I also had some of these impulses before I came. At home there was no outlet. Here I can say what I want, when I want, without having to worry about traditions. Writing to the student newspaper about a sexist joke at the International Student Dinner, for example, took a few days to gather my courage. But I had to do it. I'm more willing to step forward and fight now, not just shout at the top of my voice, but make a firm statement. This is my parents' influence, too. I was always told if I wanted to make "noise," it had to be for a worthy cause.

Still sometimes I feel that each time I put my thoughts down on paper I'm betraying someone or something. It's either my family or culture or childhood. Now that I've been able to deal with my anger and hurt, come to terms with it, I realize that I don't like that way of writing anymore. I want to write, but I want the wonderful stories to come out. I want to write about childhood memories, cultural festivals, beliefs and superstitions in my culture. I realize that I have so much to tell. Like Amy Tan, I want to write about my mother, her life, her beliefs, and her attitudes. I no longer want to make excuses for my mother; I want to be proud of her. I don't want to be ashamed of who I am, where I come from, the way I was brought up, my color, my accent. I want to be accepted as myself, and to do that I need to write about and appreciate myself and my culture.

A question remains about my ability to do this. To me, English is my first language, yet many people don't see it that way. Most Americans

assume I don't know English and sympathize with me when I tell them I am
an English major. In my Renaissance literature class they say, "This must be
really hard for you," ignoring that it is also really hard for them. My Asian
friends shun me when I disclose my major. I don't blame their reactions
though. I, too, once looked up at friends who could speak "good" English.
They were superior. They had something that I didn't, and now all of a sudden, I am the superior one among my Asian friends. I learned English. I tried
hard to succeed in school, for I was always told that if I didn't know English,
I would end up nowhere. Back then, as Bharati Mukherjee (1989) says in
Jasmine, "To want English was to want more than you had been given at
birth, it was to want the world" (68). And now that I have English, I have
lost my world.

Bee Tin: My writing has changed a great deal. As I climb the academic
ladder in my graduate program, I feel dehydrated. Some of the blood is being
drained out of my writing. I'm aware that I've lost some of that strong voice
in my writing. I've taken on a much softer voice in my academic writing.

I also think about this language I'm fluent in that is not called my own.
I want more people to understand the power of the English language that has
permeated other societies. English is not just a white, Western language. It
has taken root and has uprooted our firmer roots. I cannot let this matter rest
when I think about my parents' situation. My parents are fluent in Malay,
Hokkien, Cantonese, Teochew, and Mandarin, and they understand some
Tamil and Hainan. Their linguistic knowledge has gone beyond mine. But in
our Westernized society today, they are handicapped. They are looked upon
as working-class, blue collar. They lack a passport in the present society
because they don't speak English. The residential estate where I live in Singapore has a well-developed security control. Security guards patrol with
their walkie-talkies twenty-four hours a day. Because my dad does not speak
English, some security guards have looked upon him with suspicion. When
one of the cars in the parking lot was scratched, they accused him of being
responsible. If you walk into a store and start to speak fluent English, you
can be sure of better service than those who do not. English has become a
language you can use to impress, suppress, and oppress.

I think in order for education to succeed as a multicultural endeavor,
teachers need to understand that there is more than one right way. Alex
Moore (1990) says in "Khasru's English Lesson": "The study of the arts in
a multicultural curriculum necessitates a conscious break in our ethnocentric
tendency to interpret and value art forms from the baseline of our cultural
forms. It implies a need to be open-minded and willing to confront our own
in-built attitudes and prejudices" (25).

Manjit: I have been lucky compared to some of my other Asian friends.
A professor has never said to me, "You will have to work twice as hard

because you are a 'nonnative' speaker." Nor have I been told on the first day of class that the class is going to be difficult for me. I wish people would refrain from doing that after noticing our skin color or accent. Those do not indicate the power we have over English. I feel like asking, "Do you know enough of my background to assume that I will not be able to communicate or write effectively in your class? Do you know that we gave up our language to learn yours because ours was deemed unprofitable? Then how can you place me in a 'nonnative' category when all my life I have struggled with and conquered the English language?" I wish people would look into us, beyond our color, beyond our accent, and learn to understand and appreciate us. I wish professors and teachers would look into our papers and search for our contexts and appreciate who each of us is and what we are writing instead of being clouded by their general ideas of language and culture.

Joy: Manjit and Bee Tin have made me reconsider the nature and functions of students' autobiographical writing. Their writing shows that students' autobiographies do not need to leave them fixed in sentimental or reductionist views of selfhood. Autobiographical writing can reveal more clearly the political and ideological context in which they live and write. Their experience suggests that autobiographical writing can lead to continual re-visioning, because it allows contradictions to surface and become available for reexamination. Writing in the space of those contradictions also may enable students to defy the categories that might otherwise silence or erase their experience. This defiant writing has become a point of departure for Bee Tin and Manjit to understand themselves and the political nature of social roles, education, gender, race, and language.

Manjit and Bee Tin challenge me also to reexamine my response to students' writing. They challenge me to become an ethnographer in all my writing classes, although not an ethnographer who merely composes a detailed description and interpretation of the "exotic" culture she has studied, and thus recolonizes her "subjects." Current ethnographic theory argues that the study of "others" ought to become an opportunity to make the "familiar strange," to draw attention to and question the observer's values and perspectives as well as those of the observed. It may help teachers to make strange and call into question the familiar assumptions from which we read student writing.

As a teacher-ethnographer, I cannot pretend to fully understand my students, inscribe them in my tidy theories, or generalize my experience to theirs. I must listen to them, attempt to understand *their* vision of their life. Then I must listen again to how I am naming them, to my definitions and categories. My best and most useful response to Manjit and Bee Tin seems to have been simple—to invite them to keep writing. It questioned them with a genuine "hunger" for information and clarification; it allowed them to find and pursue their own subjects like an obsession, and, however problematic, to find what was inchoate. Finally, the ethnographer's rather than the colonizer's stance continually asks students to interpret their writing and examine their assumptions. It asks, "What does this experience mean to you?" "What has shaped your understanding of it?" "What are you trying to achieve?" It insists that they reflect on this process and consider what they were learning from it.

Like Manjit and Bee Tin, all of my students need such responses to help them see their writing as an interpersonal, rhetorical *action* rather than merely as an academic activity. Manjit's writing demonstrates the increasing effectiveness a writer can achieve as she "goes public" with writing in a forum beyond the classroom. Manjit, in particular, has seen the response her writing has received at conferences and in local public forums. She has learned to choose and reevaluate the language in which she writes in order to speak to a genuine audience, to enter actual ongoing conversations rather than merely mimicking academic conventions and conversations. The teacher-as-ethnographer's response seems far less dangerous, finally, than one that demands conformity and timidity of form and style. How can we expect students to become critically literate, when we confine them to a language that in some cases has constructed and maintained their silence? Like Bee Tin and Manjit, all of my students need responses that support their bold attempts to write defiantly and to question the world.

Works Cited

Adler, Edna. 1969. "Deafness: Research and Professional Training Programs on Deafness Sponsored by the Department of Health, Education, and Welfare." *Journal of Rehabilitation of the Deaf* 1: 1–52.

Anderson, Alonzo B., and Shelley J. Stokes. 1984. "Social and Institutional Influences on the Development of Writing." In Goelman, Oberg, and Smith, 24–37.

Anzaldua, Gloria. 1987. *Borderlands: The New Mestiza.* San Francisco: Spinsters/ Aunt Lute.

————. 1983. "Speaking in Tongues: A Letter to 3rd World Women Writers." In *This Bridge Called My Back: Writings of Radical Women of Color,* eds. Cherrie Moraga and Gloria Anzaldua, 165–173. New York: Kitchen Table, Women of Color.

Aronson, Anne. 1988. "Breaking Silence in the Discourse Community." Paper presented at Conference on College Composition and Communication, St. Louis.

Asante, Molefi K., and William Gudykunst, eds. 1989. *Handbook of International and Intercultural Communication.* Newbury Park, CA: Sage.

Ashworth, Mary. 1991. "Internationalism and Our 'Strenuous Family.'" *TESOL Quarterly* 25.2: 231–243.

Atwell, Nancy. 1987. *In the Middle: Writing, Reading, and Learning with Adolescents.* Portsmouth, NH: Boynton/Cook.

Auerbach, Elsa Roberts. 1993. "Reexamining English Only in the ESL Classroom." *TESOL Quarterly* 27.1: 9–32.

Baker, Charlotte, and Robin Battison, eds. 1980. *Sign Language and the Deaf Community: Essays in Honor of William C. Stokoe.* Washington, DC: National Association of the Deaf.

Baldwin, James. 1988. "A Talk to Teachers." In Simonson and Walker, 3–12.

Barrera, Rosalinda B. 1992. "The Cultural Gap in Literature-Based Literacy Instruction." *Education and Urban Society* 24.2: 227–243.

Bartholomae, David. 1979. "Teaching Basic Writing: An Alternative to Basic Skills." *Journal of Basic Writing* 212: 85–109.

————. 1985. "Inventing the University." In *When a Writer Can't Write,* ed. Mike Rose, 134–165. New York: Guilford.

Bartholomae, David, and Anthony Petrosky. 1986. *Facts, Artifacts, and Counterfacts: Theory and Methods for a Reading and Writing Course.* Portsmouth, NH: Boynton/Cook.

Beach, Richard, and Lillian S. Bridwell, eds. 1984. *New Directions in Composition Research*. New York: Guilford.

Beck, Evelyn Torton. 1983. "Self-Disclosure and Commitment to Social Change." In *Learning Our Way: Essays in Feminist Education,* eds. Charlotte Bunch and Sandra Pollack, 185–291. Trumanberg, NY: Crossing.

Becker, Alton L. 1992. "Silence Across Languages: An Essay." In *Text and Context: Cross-Disciplinary Perspectives on Language Study,* eds. Claire Kramsch and Sally McConnell-Ginet, 115–123. Lexington, MA: Heath.

Belanoff, Pat. 1991. "The Myths of Assessment." *Journal of Basic Writing* 10.1: 54–66.

Belenky, Mary Field, Blythe McVicker Clinchy, Nancy Rule Goldberger, and Jill Mattuck Tarule. 1986. *Women's Ways of Knowing: The Development of Self, Mind, and Voice*. New York: Basic.

Bellugi, Ursula. 1980. "How Signs Express Complex Meanings." In Baker and Battison, 53–73.

Benstock, Shari. 1988. "Authorizing the Autobiographical." In *The Private Self: Theory and Practice of Women's Autobiographical Writings,* ed. Shari Benstock, 10–33. Chapel Hill: University of North Carolina Press.

Berg, Allison, Jean Kowaleski, Caroline LeGuin, Ellen Weinauer, and Eric A. Wolfe. 1990. "Breaking the Silence: Sexual Preference in the Composition Classroom." *Feminist Teacher* 4.2/3: 29–32.

Berger, Peter L., and Thomas Luckmann. 1966. *The Social Construction of Reality: A Treatise in the Sociology of Knowledge*. New York: Doubleday.

Berlin, James. 1987. *Rhetoric and Reality: Writing Instruction in American Colleges, 1900–1985*. Carbondale: Southern Illinois University Press.

———. 1993. "Literacy, Pedagogy, and English Studies: Postmodern Connections." In Lankshear and McLaren, 247–269.

Berlin, James, and Michael J. Vivion, eds. 1992. *Cultural Studies in the English Classroom*. Portsmouth, NH: Boynton/Cook.

Bernard, Jessie. 1987. "Re-Viewing the Impact of Women's Studies on Sociology." In *The Impact of Feminist Research in the Academy,* ed. Christie Farnham, 194–216. Bloomington: Indiana University Press.

Bizzell, Patricia. 1990. "Beyond Anti-Foundationalism to Rhetorical Authority: Problems in Defining 'Cultural Literacy.'" *College English* 52.6: 661–675.

———. 1991. "Politics in the Writing Classroom." Paper presented at WPA/ADE Conference, Skidmore College, Saratoga Springs, New York.

Bleich, David. 1987. *Guidelines for the Final Essay. L161—Studying One's Own Language*. Bloomington: Indiana University, Department of English.

———. 1988. *The Double Perspective*. New York: Oxford University Press.

Bond, Michael. H., ed. 1986. *The Psychology of the Chinese People*. New York: Oxford University Press.

Bourdieu, Pierre. 1984. *Distinction: A Social Critique of the Judgment of Taste*. Cambridge, MA: Harvard University Press.

Bridwell-Bowles, Lillian. 1992. "Discourse and Diversity: Experimental Writing within the Academy." *College Composition and Communication* 43.3: 349–68.

Brill, Richard G., ed. 1984. *International Congresses on Education of the Deaf: An Analytical History, 1878–1980.* Washington, DC: Gallaudet College Press.

Britton, James, et al. 1975. *The Development of Writing Abilities (11–18).* London: Macmillan.

Brodkey, Linda. 1989. "On the Subjects of Class and Gender in 'The Literacy Letters.'" *College English* 51.2: 125–141.

Bulkin, Elly, Minnie Bruce Pratt, and Barbara Smith. 1984. *Yours in Struggle: Three Feminist Perspectives on Anti-Semitism and Racism.* Ithaca: Firebrand.

Burke, Kenneth. 1969. *A Grammar of Motives.* Berkeley: University of California Press.

Calkins, Lucy McCormick. 1986. *The Art of Teaching Writing.* Portsmouth, NH: Heinemann.

Cameron, Deborah, ed. 1990. *The Feminist Critique of Language: A Reader.* New York: Routledge.

Camp, Roberta. 1992. "Portfolio Reflection in Middle and Secondary School Classrooms." In *Portfolios in the Writing Classroom: An Introduction,* ed. Kathleen Blake Yancey, 61–79. Urbana, IL: National Council of Teachers of English.

———. 1993. "The Place of Portfolios in Our Changing Views of Writing Assessment." In *Construction Versus Choice in Cognitive Measurement: Issues in Constructed Response, Performance Testing, and Portfolio Assessment,* ed. Randy Bennett, 183–212. Hillsdale, NJ: Erlbaum.

Carlson, Dennis. 1993. "Literacy and Urban School Reform: Beyond Vulgar Pragmatism." In Lankshear and McLaren, 217–245.

Cazden, Courtney B. 1988. *Classroom Discourse: The Language of Teaching and Learning.* Portsmouth, NH: Boynton/Cook.

Cde Baca, Betty, Dave D'Evelyn, Richard Kelly, Ernie Lopez, Isabel Lopez, and Audrey R. Alvarado. 1990. *Toward a New Beginning.* (December). Denver: LARASA.

Chapman, Constance A. 1991. "Writing and Oral Communication: A Study of Three African-American Families in the United States Sunbelt." Ed.D. diss., Columbia University.

Charrow, Veda R. 1974. *Deaf English: An Investigation of the Written English Competence of Deaf Adolescents.* Ph.D. diss., Stanford University.

Chase, Geoffrey. 1988. "Accommodation, Resistance and the Politics of Student Writing." *College Composition and Communication* 39.1: 13–22.

Chiang, Yuet-Sim D. 1992. "The Process-Oriented Writing Workshop and 'Nonnative' Speakers of English: A Teacher-Researcher Study." Ph.D. diss., University of Nebraska, Lincoln.

Chiang, Yuet-Sim D., and Mary Schmida. 1996. *Inside Out: English Literacy, Language Identity, and Native Language Loss Among Asian Americans of Non-*

English Language Background. NCTE grant-in-Aid Research Report. Urbana, IL: National Council of Teachers of English.

Chiseri-Strater, Elizabeth. 1991. *Academic Literacies: The Public and Private Discourse of University Students.* Portsmouth, NH: Boynton/Cook.

The Chronicle of Higher Education. 1991. "English as a Second Language" [position announcement]. (20 February,) B20.

Clark, Suzanne. 1991. *Sentimental Modernism: Women Writers and the Revolution of the Word.* Bloomington: Indiana University Press.

Cliff, Michelle. 1988. "A Journey into Speech." In Simonson and Walker, 57–62.

Coates, Jennifer. 1986. *Women, Men, and Language: A Sociolinguistic Account of Sex Differences in Language.* New York: Longman.

Cochran-Smith, Marilyn, and Susan L. Lytle, eds. 1993. *Inside/Outside: Teacher Research and Knowledge.* New York: Teachers College Press.

Cohen, Leah Hager. 1994. *Train Go Sorry: Inside a Deaf World.* Boston: Houghton Mifflin.

Coles, Nicholas. 1986. "Democratizing Literature: Issues in Teaching Working-Class Literature." *College English* 48.7: 664–80.

Collins, Patricia Hill. 1986. "Learning From the Outsider Within: The Sociological Significance of Black Feminist Thought." *Social Problems* 33.6: 14–32.

Columbo, Gary, Robert Cullen, and Bonnie Lisle, eds. 1982. *Re-reading America.* New York: St. Martins.

Conciatore, Jacqueline. 1990. "Nation's Report Card Shows Little Progress: Black Students Close Gap." *Black Issues in Higher Education* 6.22: 30–31.

Connors, Patricia. 1982. "Some Attitudes of Older Students of Composition." *College Composition and Communication* 33.3: 263–266.

Cook-Gumperz, Jenny, ed. 1986. *The Social Construction of Literacy.* London: Cambridge University Press.

Cooper, Marilyn M. 1986. "The Ecology of Writing." *College English* 48.3: 364–75.

Cooper, Marilyn M., and Michael Holzman. 1989. *Writing as Social Action.* Portsmouth, NH: Boynton/Cook.

Daniels, Jim. 1989. *Digger's Territory.* East Hampton, MA: Adastra.

Darling-Hammond, Linda, Jacqueline Ancess, and Beverly Falk. 1995. *Authentic Assessment in Action: Studies of Schools and Students at Work.* New York: Teachers College Press.

Delpit, Lisa. 1995. *Other People's Children: Cultural Conflict in the Classroom.* New York: Norton.

Deneire, Marc Gerard. 1993. "Democratizing English as an International Language." *World Englishes* 12: 169–178.

DiPardo, Anne. 1993. *A Kind of Passport: A Basic Writing Adjunct Program and the Challenge of Student Diversity.* Urbana, IL: National Council of Teachers of English.

Dolnick, Edward. 1993. "Deafness as Culture." *Atlantic Monthly* 272.3: 37–51.

Donaldson, Margaret. 1978. *Children's Minds*. New York: Norton.

Dyson, Anne Haas. 1990. "Research Currents: Diversity, Social Responsibility and the Story of Literacy Development." *Language Arts* 67.2: 192–205.

Edlund, John R. 1988. "Bakhtin and the Social Reality of Language Acquisition." *The Writing Instructor* 7: 56–67.

Elbow, Peter. 1973. *Writing Without Teachers*. London: Oxford University Press.

———. 1981. *Writing with Power: Techniques for Mastering the Writing Process*. New York: Oxford University Press.

———. 1990. *What Is English?* New York: MLA.

———. 1991. "Reflections on Academic Discourse: How It Relates to Freshmen and Colleagues." *College English* 53.2: 135–155.

Farr, Marcia, and Harvey Daniels. 1986. *Language Diversity and Writing Instruction*. Urbana: ERIC/National Council of Teachers of English.

Feldman, Richard, and Michael Betzold, eds. 1988. *End of the Line: Autoworkers and the American Dream*. New York: Weidenfeld and Nicholson.

Ferdman, Bernado M. 1990. "Literacy and Cultural Identity." *Harvard Educational Review* 60.2: 181–204.

Fisher, Walter R. 1987. *Human Communication as Narration: Toward a Philosophy of Reason, Value, and Action*. Columbia: University of South Carolina Press.

Fiske, John. 1991. "For Cultural Interpretation." Unpublished paper. Madison: University of Wisconsin.

Fleischer, Cathy. 1992. "Forming an Interactive Literacy in the Writing Classroom." In Berlin and Vivion, 182–199.

Foley, V. D. 1975. "Family Therapy with Black, Disadvantaged Families: Some Observations on Roles, Communication and Technique." *Journal of Marriage and Family* 1: 29–38.

Fox, Helen. 1994. *Listening to the World: Cultural Issues in Academic Writing*. Urbana, IL: National Council of Teachers of English.

Fox, Thomas. 1990. *The Social Uses of Writing: Politics and Pedagogy*. Norwood, NJ: Ablex.

Freeman, E. B., J. Samuelson, and T. Sanders. 1986. "Writing Instruction: New Insights from Ethnographic Research." *Journal of Research and Development in Education* 19.2: 10–15.

Freire, Paulo. 1982. *Pedagogy of the Oppressed*. Trans. Myra Bergman Ramos. New York: Continuum.

Friedman, Susan Stanford. 1988. "Women's Autobiographical Selves, Theory and Practice." In *The Private Self: Theory and Practice of Women's Autobiographical Writings*, ed. Shari Benstock, 34–62. Chapel Hill: University of North Carolina Press.

Frye, Marilyn. 1990. Plenary Address. National Women's Studies Conference, Akron, Ohio.

Furth, Hans G. 1973. *Deafness and Learning: A Pychosocial Approach*. Belmont, CA: Wadsworth.

Gallagher, Catherine. 1978. "Workers." *University Publishing* 5:1+.

Gallaudet, Edward Miner. 1988. *History of the College for the Deaf, 1857-1907.* Lance J. Fischer, and David L. deLorenzo, eds. Washington, DC: Gallaudet University Press.

Gannett, Cinthia. 1981. *Gender and the Journal.* Albany, NY: SUNY Press.

Gannon, Jack R. 1989. *The Week the World Heard Gallaudet.* Washington, DC: Gallaudet University Press.

———. 1981. *Deaf Heritage: A Narrative History of Deaf America.* Silver Spring, MD: National Association of the Deaf.

Gates, Henry Louis, Jr. 1990. "Opening Academia Without Closing It Down: A Bad Case of Academic Autism." *New York Times* IV, 5:1 (9 December).

Geertz, Clifford. 1986. "The Uses of Diversity." *Michigan Quarterly Review* 24.1: 105–23.

Gilyard, Keith. 1991. *Voices of the Self.* Detroit: Wayne State University Press.

Giroux, Henry. 1983. *Theory and Resistance in Education: A Pedagogy for the Opposition.* South Hadley, MA: Bergin & Garvey.

———. 1988a. *Schooling and the Struggle for Public Life: Critical Pedagogy in the Modern Age.* Minneapolis: University of Minnesota Press.

———. 1988b. *Teachers as Intellectuals.* South Hadley, MA: Bergin & Garvey.

Goelman, Hillel, Antoinette Oberg, and Frank Smith, eds. 1984. *Awakening to Literacy.* Portsmouth, NH: Heinemann.

Goetz, Judith Preissle, and Margaret D. LeCompte. 1984. *Ethnography and Qualitative Design in Educational Research.* Orlando: Academic.

Goodlad, J. I. 1987. "Schools and Universities Can—and Must—Work Together." *Principal* 67.1: 9–15.

Graves, Donald H. 1983. *Writing: Teachers and Children at Work.* Portsmouth, NH: Heinemann.

Greenwood, Claudia. 1990. " 'It's Scary at First': Reentry Women in College Composition Classes." *Teaching English in the Two Year College* 17: 133–142.

Hairston, Maxine. 1992. "Diversity, Ideology, and Teaching Writing." *College Composition and Communication* 43.2: 179–193.

Hall, Edward T. 1976. *Beyond Culture.* Garden City, NY: Anchor.

Hall, Stephanie. 1989. "Train-Gone-Sorry: The Etiquette of Social Conversations in American Sign Language." In Wilcox, 89–102.

Hammersley, Martyn, and Paul Atkinson. 1983. *Ethnography: Principles in Practice.* London: Tavistock.

Haraway, Donna J. 1991. *Simians, Cyborgs, and Women: The Reinvention of Nature.* New York: Routledge.

Harding, Sandra, ed. 1987. *Feminism and Methodology: Social Science Issues.* Bloomington: Indiana University Press.

———. 1991a. "Who Knows?: Identities and Feminist Epistemology." In Hartman and Messer-Davidow, 100–115.

————. 1991b. *Whose Science? Whose Knowledge?* Ithaca: Cornell University Press.

Harste, Jerome C., Virginia A. Woodward, and Carolyn L. Burke. 1984. *Language Stories and Literacy Lessons.* Portsmouth, NH: Heinemann.

Hartman, Joan E., and Ellen Messer-Davidow, eds. 1991. *(En)gendering Knowledge: Feminism in Academe.* Knoxville: Tennessee University Press.

Heath, Shirley Brice. 1981. "Toward an Ethnohistory of Writing in American Education." In Whiteman, 25–45.

————. 1982. "Questioning at Home and at School: A Comparative Study." In *Doing the Ethnography of Schooling: Educational Anthropology in Action,* ed. George Spindler, 102–131. New York: Holt.

————. 1983. *Ways with Words: Language, Life, and Work in Communities and Classrooms.* Cambridge: Cambridge University Press.

Hero, Rodney. 1990. "Self-identification and Political Attitudes of Spanish-Surnamed Coloradans." Unpublished paper presented at the *Excellence in Diversity and Diversity in Excellence Symposium: Multicultural Perspectives in Higher Education.* Denver, Colorado.

Herzberg, Bruce. 1991. "Composition and the Politics of the Curriculum." In *The Politics of Writing Instruction: Postsecondary*, eds. Richard Bullock and John Trimbur, 97–117. Portsmouth, NH: Boynton/Cook.

Hoffman, Eva. 1989. *Lost in Translation: A Life in a New Language*. New York: Dutton.

hooks, bell. 1984. *Feminist Theory: From Margin to Center*. Boston: South End.

————. 1989. *Talking Back: Thinking Feminist, Thinking Black.* Boston: South End.

Horton, Myles, and Paulo Freire. 1990. *We Make the Road by Walking: Conversations About Education and Social Change.* Philadelphia: Temple University Press.

Hull, Glynda, Mike Rose, Kay Losey Fraser, and Marisa Castellano. 1991. "Remediation as Social Construct: Perspectives from an Analysis of Classroom Discourse." *College Composition and Communication* 42.2: 299–329.

Hurston, Zora Neale. 1990. *Their Eyes Were Watching God.* New York: Harper.

Johnson, Robert E., Scott K. Liddell, and Carol J. Erting. 1989. *Unlocking the Curriculum: Principles for Achieving Access in Deaf Education.* Gallaudet Research Institute Working Paper, 89–3.

Josey, Alex. 1968. *Lee Kuan Yew*. Singapore: Times.

Kachru, Braj B. 1986. *The Alchemy of English: The Spread, Functions and Models of Non-native Englishes*. Oxford: Pergamon.

Kachru, Braj B., Wimal Dissanayake, Douglas A. Kibbee, Numa Markee, Jane Nicholls, Tamara M. Valentine, and Robert Phillipson. 1993. "Review Symposium: Symposium on *Linguistic Imperialism.*" *World Englishes* 12: 335–373.

Kachru, Yamuna. 1988. "Cognitive and Cultural Styles in Second Language Acquisition." *Annual Review of Applied Linguistics*. New York: Cambridge University Press.

Kannapell, Barbara. 1980. "Personal Awareness and Advocacy in the Deaf Community." In Baker and Battison, 105–116.

————. 1989. "Inside the Deaf Community." In Wilcox, 21–28.

Kaplan, Robert B. 1986. "An Introduction to the Study of Written Texts: The 'Discourse Compact.'" *Annual Review of Applied Linguistics*. Rowley, MA: Newbury.

Keller, Evelyn Fox. 1982. "Feminism and Science." In *Feminist Theory: A Critique of Ideology,* eds. Nannerl O. Keohane, Michelle Z. Rosaldo, and Barbara C. Gelpi, 113–126. Chicago: University of Chicago Press.

Kelly, Leonard P. 1988. "Relative Automaticity without Mastery: The Grammatical Decision Making of Deaf Students." *Written Communication* 5.3: 325–51.

Kingston, Maxine Hong. 1977. *The Woman Warrior: Memoirs of a Girlhood Among Ghosts*. New York: Random.

————. 1980. "How Are You? I Am Fine, Thank You. And You?" In *The State of the Language*, eds. Leonard Michaels and Christopher Ricks, 152–157. Los Angeles: University of California Press.

Kristeva, Julia. 1980. "Woman Can Never Be Defined." Trans. Marilyn A. August. In *New French Feminisms,* eds. E. Marks and I. De Courtivron, 137–141. Amherst: University of Massachusetts Press.

Labov, William. 1972. *Language in the Inner City: Studies in the Black Vernacular English*. Philadelphia: University of Pennsylvania Press.

————. 1973. In *Varieties of Present-Day English,* eds. Richard J. Bailey and Jay L. Robinson, 319–354. New York: Macmillan

Lane, Harlan. 1992. *The Mask of Benevolence: Disabling the Deaf Community*. New York: Knopf.

Lankshear, Colin, and Peter L. McLaren, eds. 1993. *Critical Literacy: Politics, Praxis, and the Postmodern*. Albany: SUNY Press.

Larsen-Freeman, Diane. 1991. "Second Language Acquisition Research: Staking Out the Territory." *TESOL Quarterly* 25.2: 315–350.

Lauter, Paul. 1982. "Working-Class Women's Literature." In *Women in Print I,* eds. Joan E. Hartman and Ellen Messer-Davidow 109–134. New York: MLA.

Lave, Jean, and Etienne Wenger. 1991. *Situated Learning: Legitimate Peripheral Participation*. Cambridge: Cambridge University Press.

LeFevre, Karen Burke. 1987. *Invention as a Social Act*. Carbondale: Southern Illinois University Press.

Lensmire, Timothy J. 1994. *When Children Write: Critical Re-Visions of the Writing Workshop*. New York: Teachers College Press.

Lim, Shirley Geok-Lin. 1991. "The Scarlet Brewer and the Voice of the Colonized." MLA Convention, San Francisco.

Lorde, Audre. 1980. *The Cancer Journals*. New York: Spinsters, Ink.

————. 1984. "Poetry is Not a Luxury." *Sister Outsider*. Trumansburg, NY: Crossing.

Lou, Mimi WheiPing. 1988. "The History of Language Use in the Education of the Deaf in the United States." In *Language Learning and Deafness*, ed. Michael Strong, 75–98. Cambridge: Cambridge University Press.

Lu, Min Zhan. 1987. "From Silence to Words: Writing as Struggle." *College English* 49.4: 437–448.

————. 1991. "Redefining the Legacy of Mina Shaughnessy: A Critique of the Politics of Linguistic Innocence." *Journal of Basic Writing* 10.1: 26–40.

Lucas, Ceil, ed. 1990. *Sign Language Research: Theoretical Issues*. Washington, DC: Gallaudet University Press.

McClelland, Ben. 1991. "Cultural Studies and Teaching." Paper presented at Exploring Cultural Studies in the Teaching of Writing and History, University of Missouri–Kansas City.

McCrum, Robert, William Cran, and Robert MacNeil. 1986. *The Story of English*. New York: Viking Penguin.

McKay, Sandra Lee, and Sarah Warshauer Freedman. 1990. "Language Minority Education in Great Britain: A Challenge to Current U.S. Policy." *TESOL Quarterly* 24.3: 385–405.

McKay, Sandra Lee, and Gail Weinstein-Shr. 1993. "English Literacy in the U.S.: National Policies, Personal Consequences." *TESOL Quarterly* 27.3: 399–419.

MacKinnon, Catherine. 1988. "Desire and Power: A Feminist Perspective." In *Marxism and the Interpretation of Culture*, eds. Cary Nelson and Lawrence Grossberg, 105–121. Urbana: University of Illinois Press.

McLaren, Peter L., and Colin Lankshear. 1993. "Critical Literacy and the Postmodern Turn." In Lankshear and McLaren, 379–419.

Malinowitz, Harriet. 1995. *Textual Orientations: Lesbian and Gay Students and the Making of Discourse Communities*. Portsmouth, NH: Boynton/Cook.

Markova, A. K. 1979. *The Teaching and Mastery of Language*. White Plains, NY: Sharpe.

Martin, Gail. 1987. "A Letter to Bread Loaf." In *Reclaiming the Classroom: Teacher Research as an Agency for Change*, eds. Dixie Goswami and Peter R. Stillman, 166–167. Portsmouth, NH: Boynton/Cook.

Matalene, Carolyn. 1985. "Contrastive Rhetoric: An American Writing Teacher in China." *College English* 47.8: 789–808.

Mayberry, Rachel, and Rhonda Wodlinger-Cohen. 1987. "After the Revolution: Educational Practice and the Deaf Child's Communication Skills." In *They Grow in Silence: Understanding Deaf Children and Adults*, eds. Eugene D. Mindel and Vernon McCay, 149–86. Boston: College-Hill.

Maynes, Mary Jo. 1989. "Gender and Narrative Form in French and German Working-Class Autobiographies." In *Interpreting Women's Lives*, ed. Personal Narratives Group, 103–128. Bloomington: Indiana University Press.

Merton, Robert K. 1972. "Insiders and Outsiders: A Chapter in the Sociology of Knowledge." *American Journal of Sociology* 78: 9–47.

Mill, John Stuart. 1960. *Autobiography of John Stuart Mill.* New York: Columbia University Press.

Miller, Susan. 1991. *Textual Carnivals: The Politics of Composition.* Carbondale: Southern Illinois University Press.

Minh-ha, Trinh T. 1989. *Woman, Native, Other: Writing Postcoloniality and Feminism.* Bloomington: Indiana University Press.

Mitchell, Jacquelyn. 1982. "Reflections of a Black Social Scientist: Some Struggles, Some Doubts, Some Hopes." *Harvard Educational Review* 52.1: 27–44.

Moffett, James. 1983. *Teaching the Universe of Discourse.* Portsmouth, NH: Boynton/Cook.

Moore, Alex. 1990. "Khasru's English Lesson: Ethnocentricity and Response to Student Writing." *The Quarterly for the National Writing Project and the Center for the Study of Writing* 12.1: 1–3.

Moores, Donald F. 1987a. "The Cycle Changes: Elementary and Secondary Education in the 1990s." *Gallaudet Today* 18.1: 12–17.

———. 1987b. *Educating the Deaf: Psychology, Principles and Practices.* 3d ed. Boston: Houghton Mifflin.

———. 1990. "Research in Educational Aspects of Deafness." In Moores and Meadow-Orlans, eds. 11–24.

Moores, Donald F., and Kathryn P. Meadow-Orlans. 1990. "Introduction." In Moores and Meadow-Orlans, eds. 1–10.

———. eds. 1990. *Educational and Developmental Aspects of Deafness.* Washington, DC: Gallaudet University Press.

Moss, Pamela A. 1992. "Shifting Conceptions of Validity in Educational Measurement: Implications for Performance Assessment." *Review of Educational Research* 62.3: 229–258.

———. 1994. "Can There Be Validity Without Reliability?" *Educational Researcher* 23.2 : 5–12.

Moss, Pamela A., Jamie Sue Beck, Catherine Ebbs, Barbara Matson, James Muchmore, Dorothy Steele, Caroline Taylor, and Roberta Herter. 1992. "Portfolios, Accountability, and an Interpretive Approach to Validity." *Educational Measurement: Issues and Practice* 11.3: 12–21.

Moss, Pamela A., and Roberta J. Herter. 1993. "Assessment, Accountability, and Authority in Urban Schools." *The Long Term View* 1.4: 68–75.

Mphahlele, Es'kia. 1993. "Educating the Imagination." *College English* 55.2: 179–186.

Mukherjee, Bharati. 1989. *Jasmine.* New York: Grove.

Mura, David. 1991. *Turning Japanese: Memoirs of a Sansei.* New York: Atlantic Monthly.

Murray, Donald M. 1982. *Learning by Teaching: Selected Articles on Writing and Teaching.* Portsmouth, NH: Boynton/Cook.

Myklebust, Helmer R. 1960. *The Psychology of Deafness: Sensory Deprivation, Learning and Adjustment.* New York: Grune and Stratton.

Narayan, Kirin. 1991. "According to Their Feelings." In *Stories Lives Tell: Narrative and Dialogue in Education,* eds. Carol Witherell and Nel Noddings, 113–135. New York: Teachers College Press.

Ndebele, N. 1987. "The English Language and Social Change in South Africa." *The English Academy Review* 4: 1–16.

Neisser, Arden. 1983. *The Other Side of Silence: Sign Language and the Deaf Community in America.* New York: Knopf.

Neverow-Turk, Vara. 1991. "Researching the Minimum Wage: A Moral Economy for the Classroom." *College Composition and Communication* 42.4: 477–483.

Ngugi wa Thiong'o. 1986. *Decolonising the Mind: The Politics of Language in African Literature.* Portsmouth, NH: Heinemann.

Noddings, Nel, and Paul J. Shore. 1984. *Awakening the Inner Eye: Intuition in Education.* New York: Teachers College Press.

North, Stephen M. 1987. *The Making of Knowledge in Composition.* Portsmouth, NH: Boynton/Cook.

Ogbu, John U. 1985. "Research Currents: Cultural-Ecological Influence on Minority School Learning." *Language Arts* 62.8: 860–869.

Ogbu, John U., and M. E. Matute-Bianchi. 1986. "Understanding Sociocultural Factors: Knowledge, Identity, and School Adjustment." In *Beyond Language: Social and Cultural Factors in Schooling Language Minority Students,* 73–142. Los Angeles: California State University, Evaluation, Dissemination and Assessment Center.

Olsen, Tillie. 1978. "Silences—Its Varieties." *Silences.* New York: Delacorte.

Ong, Walter J. 1982. *Orality and Literacy: The Technologizing of the Word.* New York: Methuen.

———. 1975. "The Writer's Audience is Always a Fiction." *PMLA* 90: 9–12.

Owomoyela, Oyekan. 1992. "Language, Identity, and Social Construction in African Literatures." *Research in African Literatures* 23.1: 83–94.

Padden, Carol A. 1990. *Deaf Children and Literacy: Literacy Lessons.* Geneva, Switzerland: International Bureau of Education.

Paley, Vivian Gussin. 1979. *White Teacher.* Cambridge, MA: Harvard Universtiy Press.

———. 1981. *Wally's Stories: Conversations in the Kindergarten.* Cambridge, MA: Harvard University Press.

Peirce, Bronwyn Norton. 1989. "Toward a Pedagogy of Possibility in the Teaching of English Internationally: People's English in South Africa." *TESOL Quarterly* 23.3: 401–420.

Pennycook, Alastair. 1989. "The Concept of Method, Interested Knowledge, and the Politics of Language Teaching." *TESOL Quarterly* 23.4: 589–618.

Perl, Sondra. 1983. "Understanding Composing." In *The Writer's Mind: Writing as a Mode of Thinking*, eds. Janice N. Hays, Phyllis A. Roth, Jon R. Ramsey, and Robert D. Foulke, 43–51. Urbana, IL: National Council of Teachers of English.

Perrone, Vito. 1994. "How to Engage Students in Learning." *Educational Leadership* 51.5: 11–13.

Pheterson, Gail. 1986. "Alliances Between Women: Overcoming Internalized Oppression and Internalized Domination." *Signs* 12: 146–160.

Philips, Susan U. 1972. "Participant Structures and Communicative Competence: Warm Springs Children in Community and Classroom." In *Functions of Language in the Classroom*, eds. Courtney Cazden, Vera P. John, and Dell Hymes, 370–394. New York: Teachers College Press.

———. 1982. *The Invisible Culture: Communication in Classroom and Community on the Warm Springs Indian Reservation*. New York: Longman.

Phillipson, Robert. 1992. *Linguistic Imperialism*. Oxford: Oxford University Press.

Pomerenke, Paula, and JoAnna Mink. 1987. "The Needs of Adult Learners in Composition." *Teaching English in the Two Year College* 14: 205–210.

Pride, John B. 1983. "Linguistic Competence and the Expression of Cultural Identity." In *Varieties of English in Southeast Asia*, ed. R. B. Noss, 50–91. Singapore: SEAMEO Regional Language Centre.

Projection of Education Statistics to 2005. 1995. Washington DC: U.S. Department of Education.

Quirk, Randolph. 1968. *Essays on the English Language*. Bloomington: Indiana University Press.

Raimes, Ann. 1987. "Language Proficiency, Writing Ability, and Composing Strategies: A Study of ESL College Student Writers." *Language Learning* 37.3: 439–467.

———. 1990. *How English Works: A Grammar Handbook with Readings*. New York: St. Martin.

———. 1991. "Out of the Woods: Emerging Traditions in the Teaching of Writing." *TESOL Quarterly* 25.3: 407–430.

Ray, Ruth. 1993. *The Practice of Theory: Teacher Research in Composition*. Urbana, IL: National Council of Teachers of English.

Reagan, Timothy. 1985. "The Deaf as a Linguistic Minority: Educational Considerations." *Harvard Educational Review* 55.3: 265–77.

———. 1986. "American Sign Language and Contemporary Deaf Studies in the United States." *Language Problems and Language Planning* 19: 282–89.

———. 1988a. "Multiculturalism and the Deaf: An Educational Manifesto." *Journal of Research and Development in Education* 22.1: 1–6.

———. 1988b. "The Oral-Manual Debate in Deaf Education: Language Policies in Conflict." *Journal of the Midwest History of Education Society* 16: 19–33.

————. 1989. "Nineteenth-Century Conceptions of Deafness: Implications for Contemporary Educational Practice." *Educational Theory* 39.1: 39–46.

————. 1990. "Cultural Considerations in the Education of Deaf Children." In Moores and Meadow-Orlans, eds. 73–84.

Rich, Adrienne. 1986. *Blood, Bread and Poetry: Selected Prose 1979–1985*. New York: Norton.

Robinson, Jay. 1990. "Literacy and Conversation: Notes Toward a Constitutive Rhetoric." In Robinson, ed. 93–113.

————. ed. 1990. *Conversations on the Written Word*. Portsmouth, NH: Boynton/Cook.

Rodriguez, Richard. 1982. *Hunger of Memory: The Education of Richard Rodriguez*. New York: Bantam.

Rose, Mike. 1984. *Writer's Block: The Cognitive Dimension*. Carbondale, IL: Southern Illinois University Press.

————. 1989. *Lives on the Boundary*. New York: Penguin.

Sacks, Oliver. 1989. *Seeing Voices: A Journey into the World of the Deaf*. Berkeley: University of California Press.

Saussure, Ferdinand de. 1974. *Course in General Linguistics*. Trans. W. Baskin. Glasgow: Collins.

Schieffelin, Bambi B., and Marilyn Cochran-Smith. 1984. "Learning to Read Culturally: Literacy Before Schooling." In Goelman, Oberg, and Smith, 3–23.

Schuster, Marilyn R., and Susan R. Van Dyne. 1985. "Syllabus Redesign Guidelines." In *Women's Place in the Academy: Transforming the Liberal Arts Curriculum*, eds. Marilyn R. Schuster and Susan R. Van Dyne, 279–290. Totawa, NJ: Rowman and Allanheld.

Scollon, Ron, and Suzanne B. K. Scollon. 1981. *Narrative, Literacy, and Face in Interethnic Communication*. Norwood, NJ: Ablex.

Shaughnessy, M. 1977. *Errors and Expectations: A Guide for the Teacher of Basic Writing*. New York: Oxford University Press.

Shen, Fan. 1989. "The Classroom and the Wider Culture: Identity as a Key to Learning English Composition." Staffroom Interchange. *College Composition and Communication* 40.4: 459–466.

Shweder, Richard. A. 1991. *Thinking Through Cultures*. Cambridge, MA: Harvard University Press.

Silko, Leslie Marmon. 1986. *Ceremony*. New York: Penguin.

Simonson, Rick, and Scott Walker, eds. 1988. *Multi-Cultural Literacy: Opening the American Mind*. St. Paul: Graywolf.

Sledd, James. 1969. "Bi-dialectalism: The Linguistics of White Supremacy." *English Journal* 58.9: 1307–1315, 1329.

————. 1988. "Product in Process: From Ambiguities of Standard English to Issues that Divide Us." *College English* 50.2: 168–176.

Smith, Dorothy. 1979. "A Sociology for Women." In *The Prism of Sex*, eds. Julia A. Sherman and Evelyn Torton Beck, 135–187. Madison: University of Wisconsin Press.

Smith, Larry E. 1983. *Readings in English as an International Language*. Oxford: Pergamon.

Smitherman, Geneva. 1986. *Talkin and Testifyin: The Language of Black America*. Detroit: Wayne State University Press.

Sommer, Robert. 1989. *Teaching Writing to Adults*. San Francisco: Jossey-Bass.

Spivak, Gayatri Chakravorty. 1988. "French Feminism in an International Frame." *In Other Worlds, Essays in Cultural Politics*, 134–153. New York: Routledge.

Stafford, William. 1978. "A Way of Writing." *Writing the Australian Crawl: Views on the Writer's Vocation*. Ann Arbor: University of Michigan Press.

Stam, Robert. 1987. *Subversive Pleasures: Bakhtin, Cultural Criticism and Film*. Baltimore: Johns Hopkins University Press.

Stock, Patricia L., and Jay L. Robinson. 1990. "Literacy as Conversation: Classroom Talk as Text Building." In Robinson, ed. 163–238.

Stokoe, William C. 1960. *Sign Language Structure*. Silver Spring, MD: Linstok.

Stokoe, William C., Dorothy Casterline, and Carl G. Croneberg. 1976. *A Dictionary of American Sign Language on Linguistic Principles*. Rev. ed. Silver Spring, MD: Linstok.

Strevens, Peter. 1980. *Teaching English as an International Language*. Oxford: Pergamon.

———. 1982. "World English and the World's English—Or, Whose Language Is It Anyway?" *Journal of the Royal Society of Arts* 130: 418–428.

Stuckey, J. Elspeth. 1991. *The Violence of Literacy*. Portsmouth, NH: Boynton/Cook.

"Students' Right to Their Own Language." 1974. *College Composition and Communication*. Special Issue. 24 (Fall).

Szwed, John F. 1981. "The Ethnography of Literacy." In Whiteman, 13–23.

Tarvin, William, and Ali Yahya Al-Arishi. 1991. "Rethinking Communicative Language Teaching: Reflection and the EFL Classroom." *TESOL Quarterly* 25: 9–27.

Taylor, Orlando L., and Maryon M. Matsuda. 1988. "Storytelling and Classroom Discrimination." In *Discourse and Discrimination,* eds. Geneva Smitherman-Donaldson and Teun A. van Dijk, 206–220. Detroit: Wayne State University Press.

Ting-Toomey, Stella, and Felipe Korzenny, eds. 1991. *Cross-Cultural Interpersonal Communication*. Newbury Park, CA: Sage.

Tollefson, James W. 1989. *Alien Winds: The Reeducation of America's IndoChinese Refugees*. New York: Praeger.

Tompkins, Jane. 1987. "Me and My Shadow." *New Literary History* 19.1: 169–178.

Treesberg, Judith. 1991. "The Death of a 'Strong Deaf.'" *The Nation* 252 (11 February): 154–158.

Triandis, Harry C., Robert Bontempo, and Marcelo J. Villareal. 1988. "Individualism and Collectivism: Cross-cultural Perspectives on Self-ingroup Relationships." *Journal of Personality and Social Psychology* 54.2: 323–338.

Trybus, Raymond. 1980. "Sign Language, Power, and Mental Health." In Baker and Battison, 201–17.

Tuman, Myron C. 1988. "Class, Codes, and Composition: Basil Bernstein and the Critique of Pedagogy." *College Composition and Communication* 39.1: 42–51.

VanCleve, John V., ed. 1987. *Gallaudet Encyclopedia of Deaf People and Deafness.* New York: McGraw-Hill.

VanCleve, John V., and Barry A. Crouch. 1989. *A Place of Their Own: Creating the Deaf Community in America.* Washington, DC: Gallaudet University Press.

Vann, Roberta J., and Roberta G. Abraham. 1990. "Strategies of Unsuccessful Language Learners." *TESOL Quarterly* 24.2: 177–198.

Vygotsky, Lev S. 1986. *Thought and Language.* Trans. Alex Kozulin. Cambridge, MA: MIT Press.

Walker, Alice. 1983. *In Search of Our Mother's Gardens.* New York: Harcourt.

Wall, Susan, and Nicholas Coles. 1991. "Reading Basic Writing: Alternatives to a Pedagogy of Accommodation." In *The Politics of Writing Instruction: Postsecondary,* eds. Richard Bullock and John Trimbur, 227–246. Portsmouth, NH: Boynton/Cook.

Weeks, Jeffrey. 1987. "Questions of Identity." In *The Cultural Construction of Sexuality,* ed. Pat Caplan, 31–51: London: Tavistock.

Weiler, Kathleen. 1988. *Women Teaching for Change: Gender, Class, and Power.* Critical Studies in Education Series. South Hadley, MA: Bergin & Garvey.

White, James Boyd. 1984. *When Words Lose Their Meaning: Constitutions and Reconstitutions of Language, Character, and Community.* Chicago: University of Chicago Press.

Whiteman, Marcia Farr, ed. 1981. *Variation in Writing: Functional and Cultural Differences,* vol. 1 of *Writing: The Nature, Development, and Teaching of Written Communication.* Hillsdale, NJ: Erlbaum.

Wilcox, Sherman, ed. 1989. *American Deaf Culture*: *An Anthology.* Silver Spring, MD: Linstok.

Williams, Patricia J. 1991. *The Alchemy of Race and Rights.* Cambridge, MA: Harvard University Press.

Winefield, Richard. 1987. *Never the Twain Shall Meet: Bell, Gallaudet, and the Communications Debate.* Washington, DC: Gallaudet University Press.

Woodward, James. 1976. "Black Southern Signing." *Language in Society* 5: 211–218.

———. 1980. "Sociolinguistic Research on American Sign Language: An Historical Perspective." In Baker and Battison, 117–33.

———. 1982. *How You Gonna Get to Heaven If You Can't Talk to Jesus? On Depathologizing Deafness.* Silver Spring, MD: T.J.

Zandy, Janet. 1995. *Liberating Memory: Our Work and Our Working-Class Consciousness.* New Brunswick, NJ: Rutgers University Press.

Zeichner, Kenneth M. 1983. "Alternative Paradigms in Teacher Education." *Journal of Teacher Education* 34.3: 3–9.

Contributors

Anne Aronson is an assistant professor in the Writing Department at Metropolitan State University, St. Paul, Minnesota, where she teaches composition, professional writing, and women's studies. Her research interests include feminist approaches to composition, basic writing, adult development, and the material conditions of composing.

Brenda Jo Brueggemann, an assistant professor at Ohio State University, has published other essays on deafness and literacy issues in *Rhetoric Review, College English, Disability Students Quarterly,* and *Ethics and Representation in Qualitative Studies of Literacy,* edited by Gesa Kirsch and Peter Mortensen (NCTE, 1996). She is currently at work on a book manuscript, *Lend Me Your Ear: Rhetorical Constructions of Deafness.*

Constance Chapman, a Fulbright Scholar who spent 1996–1997 lecturing and conducting research in Ghana, West Africa, is an assistant professor of composition in the Department of Learning Support Programs at Georgia State University. She is also the school relations coordinator of the Peachtree Urban Writing Project. Her previous work has appeared in the *Georgia Journal of Reading and Research* and *Teaching in Developmental Education.*

Yuet-Sim Darrell Chiang teaches courses in reading and composition, and composition theory and practice at the University of California–Berkeley. Her research focuses on the impact of English literacy on the linguistic and cultural identities of language minorities, and the processes with which these (sometimes contradictory) identities are articulated both by students and by composition theorists and practitioners. You can direct your comments to her at chiang@uclink4.berkeley.edu.

Deborah Davies is an associate professor in the Language and Literature Department at Jackson Community College, Jackson, Michigan. She has a bachelor of arts degree and graduate credits from the University of Michigan, and a master of arts degree in creative writing from Michigan State University, where she is currently a doctoral student in the English Education program.

Emily Decker is currently the associate director of the Washington Center for Improving Undergraduate Education, a public service center of The Evergreen State College. Previously, she served as associate director of assessment at the English Composition Board at the University of Michigan, where she helped design and implement a portfolio-based writing assessment for incoming students and taught undergraduate writing courses.

Sally Barr Ebest (formerly Reagan) is an associate professor of English and the director of Composition at the University of Missouri–St. Louis. She has presented papers and published articles on the reading-writing connection, reader response theory, collaborative learning, and graduate education. Her publications include *Writing With: New Directions in Collaborative Teaching, Learning, and Research* (SUNY Press) and *Writing From A to Z* (Mayfield). Her essay in this collection is taken from research involved in developing a book-length manuscript entitled *Changing the Way We Teach: Preparing the Next Generation of Professors.*

Helen Fox is a lecturer at the University of Michigan, where she teaches composition, international grassroots development, and community-based learning courses that help students make sense of multicultural and social justice issues in the United States. Her book, *Listening to the World: Cultural Issues in Academic Writing,* was published by the National Council of Teachers of English in 1994.

Kathleen Geissler is associate professor of English at Michigan State University and associate director of the Center for Integrative Studies in Arts and Humanities, where she directs a writing-intensive general education course. She has taught writing and women's studies, composition theory and pedagogy, history of rhetoric, and theories of literacy and reading. She is coeditor of *Doing Feminisms: Teaching and Research in the Academy* and cocurator of a multimedia CD-ROM, *Immigration and Migration.*

Roberta J. Herter teaches English at Henry Ford High School in Detroit, where she codirects a school/university collaboration. Her research interests include writing assessment, critical theory, and the sociocultural aspects of literacy.

Manjit Kaur completed an M.A. degree in English at the University of Nebraska–Lincoln. She has taught writing and literature courses at Peru State College in Nebraska and is a reader for the literature journal *Prairie Schooner.*

Ted Lardner teaches writing and creative writing at Cleveland State University. His work has appeared in *English Journal, The Writing Instructor, Readerly/Writerly Texts,* and *Diversity,* as well as *Caliban, Zone 3, Colorado Review,* and other journals. He is associate professor of English and codirector of the Poetry Center.

Bee Tin Choo Meyer has an M.A. in educational psychology and recently has been employed at the Nebraska Department of Social Services.

Renee Moreno is completing a Ph.D. at the University of Michigan. Her research interests include education, composition, Latino/a studies, and women's studies. Her current research examines storytelling in the lives of Latinos.

Her next project will be a history of radical schooling in the Southwest and will examine the role of radical schools in the lives of Latinos.

Pamela J. Olano is a scholar in residence at the Newcomb Center for Research on Women at Tulane University in New Orleans, Louisiana. She is currently working on a book entitled *Southern Decadence: The Last Hundred Years of Gay Life in New Orleans.*

Joy Ritchie is associate professor of English and Women's Studies at the University of Nebraska–Lincoln. She is coordinator of composition and teaches courses in composition, women's literature, feminist theory, and literacy studies.

Shirley K. Rose is associate professor of English and director of composition at Purdue University. Her publications include articles in *College English, College Composition and Communication, Rhetoric Review, Journal of Teaching Writing,* and *Writing Program Administration.* Her current scholarly and research interests include gender and composition, citation studies, and writing program administration.

Alice Roy is professor of English and Linguistics at California State University, Los Angeles, former composition coordinator, and currently director of the M.A. Option in Composition, Rhetoric, and Language. Her articles on language and literacy have appeared in *Text, Semiotica, College English, College Composition and Communication, Writing Program Administration, The Writing Instructor, Journal of Teaching Writing,* and others. She is coeditor of *Perspectives on Plagiarism and Intellectual Property in a Postmodern World* (SUNY Press, 1998).

DATE DUE

APR 2 1 2010		
RECD MAY 1 1 2009		